LEGALIZED PROSTITUTION
IN GERMANY

LEGALIZED PROSTITUTION IN GERMANY

Inside the New Mega Brothels

Annegret D. Staiger

INDIANA UNIVERSITY PRESS

This book is a publication of

Indiana University Press
Office of Scholarly Publishing
Herman B Wells Library 350
1320 East 10th Street
Bloomington, Indiana 47405 USA

iupress.org

Manufactured in the United States of America

First printing 2022

Library of Congress Cataloging-in-Publication Data

Names: Staiger, Annegret Daniela, author.
Title: Legalized prostitution in Germany : inside the new mega brothels /
Annegret Staiger.
Description: Bloomington, Indiana : Indiana University Press, [2022] |
Includes bibliographical references and index.
Identifiers: LCCN 2021022639 (print) | LCCN 2021022640 (ebook) |
ISBN 9780253058966 (hardback) | ISBN 9780253058935 (paperback) |
ISBN 9780253058942 (ebook)
Subjects: LCSH: Prostitution—Germany. | Prostitution—Law and
legislation—Germany | Prostitutes—Social conditions—Germany.
Classification: LCC HQ198 .S73 2022 (print) | LCC HQ198 (ebook) |
DDC 306.740943—dc23
LC record available at https://lccn.loc.gov/2021022639
LC ebook record available at https://lccn.loc.gov/2021022640

An earlier version of chapter 5 appeared as "Perceptions about Pimps in an
Upscale Mega Brothel in Germany," in *Third Party Sex Work
and Pimps in the Age of Anti-Trafficking*, ed. Amber Horning
and Anthony Marcus (Cham, CH: Springer), 151–176.

CONTENTS

ACKNOWLEDGMENTS

WRITING THIS BOOK HAS BEEN A LONG JOURNEY from its inception to its end. Numerous people helped me overcome challenges along the way.

First and foremost, I want to acknowledge all the women and men who let me in on their lives to the extent that they felt comfortable, not knowing how naive my questions would be or how unpleasant an association with me may prove. Whether as entrepreneurs, freelancers / sex workers, or clients, making themselves available to a researcher and her questions is a leap of faith, considering that this industry is still subject to considerable stigma. I am greatly indebted to them for the trust they had in me and am aware of the pain that some of my questions caused. Their generosity is a gift that I feel a strong obligation to return, which I hope to do through sharing their stories, insights, and experiences as honestly as I can, by situating them in the broader context and with the nuances that give them meaning. Most of all, perhaps, I feel the obligation of raising the moral questions that this work examines—questions of unreasonable service demands, of labor unfairness and shoddy management practices, and of the social isolation that particularly women entrepreneurs are saddled with, but also of unexpected vulnerabilities and dependencies. To ensure the confidentiality of research participants, all the names I mention in the following are pseudonyms, but I believe the people I thank here will easily recognize themselves in the book.

I feel particularly indebted to Martin. Without him and his contacts in the industry, I don't know what I would have been able to accomplish. Gaining his trust was crucial to move this project to the next stage. His sense of honesty and integrity and his commitment to doing the right thing helped to create a spirit of community and support on the client forum he ran, which has revealed to me the vulnerabilities of being a client and the challenges that men face when they become paying sex clients. This, of course, does not excuse or belittle any of the abusive comments that forum members made nor acts they committed. Tragically, the violence sex clients can unleash is a serious risk for sex workers and did not escape me. I am also indebted to Alexander, an author in his own right whose generosity toward sex workers is legend to those who know him. Alexander, like Martin, has shown in so many ways that being a client or an entrepreneur is no indication of your moral character. I feel deep gratitude for Alexander and Martin's help and friendship.

Among the staff at the Flamingo, the sauna club brothel where I made the bulk of my observations in the field, I am particularly grateful to Brigitte. She was a madam with whom I felt an instant kinship, and she helped me to feel greatly accepted at the club and balanced along the way. I hope for us to meet again. A particular thank-you also to Natasha, Katharina, Lavinia, and Alena, the four women portrayed in detail in chapter 4. They are all from entirely different backgrounds, and through our interactions, they gave me personal and sustained insight into what it is like to live and work at the Flamingo. Thanks also to the many others who opened up to me while working at the Flamingo, including the staff, for their extraordinary acceptance. Even if the familiality the club cultivated had an oppressive quality, many of the staff were genuinely warm and caring and treated me like one of them, although I am also aware that my presence eventually became a liability for some.

Many officials in Neuburg contributed to this project, including the social workers in the Human Services Department, the staff of the Health Department and the Zoning Office, and particularly the police departments of Neuburg and its neighbor cities. All of them were very generous with their time and had patience with my questions. I am particularly thankful to the social workers who invited me to the Night Owl, thus giving me the opportunity to get to know the women sex workers who constitute the public face of Neuburg's red light district. The present as well as the past police chiefs for the unit of prostitution were extraordinarily helpful with information. This applies also to the police captain, who took me on patrols and shared with me his personal views on and challenges of doing this work. I am grateful for their openness to reveal to me the painful details of their work and the challenges it can entail for their own mental health.

At Clarkson, I am particularly grateful to Claudia Hoffman, an anthropologist at heart and a professor of film and literature in our multidisciplinary department. Claudia read many drafts of this book and tirelessly helped me to see its merit and significance. Then there are the colleagues and friends from our Impossible Projects working group who read and commented on several drafts of chapters and even the photographs—in particular Lisa Propst, Sara Jane Kastner, Joanie Lipson Freed, and Jennifer Knack. Others at Clarkson commented on drafts in various stages, including Chris Morrison and JoAnn Rogers after they read an early version of "Portrait of the Girls." Our then student Hennessy Garcia, presently a full-time activist for Black Lives Matter, read the entire book in its raw form and gave me invaluable feedback.

A special thank-you is also due to the late Dan Bradburd, my former anthropology colleague at Clarkson. Dan was an exemplary supporter and mentor, a department chair who fought for me to get funding to begin an entirely new research project in Germany after tenure, and who fought for me when I was initially denied a sabbatical because my research project was deemed too dangerous. Dan, an expert in economic anthropology, was early on intrigued by my writing on the gift in sex for sale and has greatly encouraged me to pursue this theoretical treasure trove.

Faculty and students at Babes Bolyai University in Cluj, Romania, where I was fortunate to spend two semesters as a Fulbright Scholar, have helped me along in this journey. In particular, Professor Maria Roth and Eva Laszlo provided invaluable assistance in understanding sex work and sex trafficking from a Romanian perspective. A particular thank-you also to Sorana Constantinescu, a former student who since has earned a PhD in sociology and is an accomplished researcher in her own right, for the many discussions about gender relations in Romania and the US. This list of acknowledgments would not be complete without Susan Dewey, who has been a great inspiration and support. Since we met ten years ago at the AAA on a panel on prostitution, we have remained in contact and developed a collaboration from which I have benefited multiple times. I must also thank Christian Zlolniski at the University of Texas at Arlington, a dear friend since graduate school, who has offered supportive critique of every chapter and emotional support when I needed it.

My partner, Humy, has been a forever active listener who, during our daily Skype sessions, has been a sounding board and a critical ear and given me multiple fresh insights from a nonspecialist perspective. Special thanks also to my son Meshach, who put up with me being gone months at a time, particularly during the summer and winter breaks between 2008 and 2011.

Last but not least, I want to thank my family in Germany: Angela and her daughter, Deborah, and Eva and Paul and their children, who accompanied me on the emotional ups and downs that were part of entering the field. They included me in their lives as the aunt from America coming home, they challenged me on my views about gender, and they provided me with the cultural foil through which to interpret my immersion into the field and my reimmersion into my former home.

I hope this book strikes a chord with people who read it and that it provides insight into a world that remains inaccessible and hidden to many. When I was doing fieldwork, I was often furious about the statements people made, about the acts I witnessed, or about the injustices I discovered. For the most part, I have chosen to hold back my judgments in this ethnography to convey to the reader a more immediate experience of what being in the field is like without the benefit of a moral assessment, so readers can judge for themselves. Of course, being the author of a text and an ethnographer, I am perfectly aware that my descriptions are ultimately always highly subjective.

LEGALIZED PROSTITUTION
IN GERMANY

INTRODUCTION

Getting In

*I*T WAS MY THIRD VISIT TO THE FLAMINGO, *one of the fancy new sauna club brothels and an ideal setting to study the flashy new prostitution culture that had arisen since the legalization of prostitution in 2002. Hoping to build a trusting relationship with the PR manager over a series of interviews, I had been struggling to find excuses to request follow-up meetings with him. Rudy, the PR manager, was obviously itching to show me the club and how it was run, but he was also adamant that doing research there would be out of the question. When I pressed him, he said, "The girls here will scratch out your eyes. They will fight you. For you to hang out at the club is just not an option." Being asked for an interview by a professor—from New York, of all places—was not something that happened to him every day; maybe it was flattering, but apparently, it was also a potential risk. "The girls do not want to be watched and studied by someone who is not from the milieu," Rudy said. "They might be afraid that you are the wife of a client. The women here can be vicious." I had heard that women who were not sex workers themselves were not welcome in some commercial sex venues in Germany, such as on the Reeperbahn, the famous red light district of Hamburg. To the women at the club, however, to whom I told this story later, Rudy's comments did not make a whole lot of sense.*

His hesitation to let me do ethnographic research at the club was in sharp contrast to a visit a few weeks earlier from a news reporter, who was given full access to the club. The article he wrote about the Flamingo and its clients was rather critical. Nevertheless, it had worked for the bottom line of the club, because it had raised its visibility in the media and had caused a notable uptick in clients. "Any news is good news. Even bad news is good advertisement for us and will get our name out there and [bring in] more visitors," Rudy explained. This argument could have worked for allowing me to do research there as well. However, at that moment, I decided not to press the issue because the premise of ethnographic research is to protect the confidentiality of all participants, and thus anything I would publish about the club would not even mention its real name.

Sitting in his spacious office, with pictures of his family on the wall and an oversize monitor behind an equally oversize desk, I was looking out of the window onto adjacent commercial properties and open fields. I sensed that something was different today. On my previous visits, Rudy had always staged a special welcome, from picking me up from the train station in an impressive Humvee to presenting me with a lavish buffet and a first glimpse of the inside of the club. Not today, though. As I would soon find out, Rudy was consumed by an accusation of sex trafficking against the club.

Halfway through our conversation, he abruptly suggested we go and meet Hans, the owner of the club, in the girls' lounge.[1] Hans was already there when we arrived. His muscular body was squeezed into an elegant suit that almost burst at the seams, his deep tan emphasized by the shiny gold necklace he was wearing. I remembered the comment of a social worker who had described Hans as having the typical "milieu type" look. Hans was seething about the trafficking charge against the club, and Rudy acted as if he wanted to outperform his boss in his own demonstration of outrage. Neither one of them minced their words in their contempt for the sex worker who had brought the charges against them.

Sensing an opening, I asked Hans, "You let a male reporter come in here and stick his nose into every aspect of the club, and you were okay with that. Why don't you let me, an anthropologist trained to study people, do the same and provide a story from a woman's point of view?"

Hans looked at me with an expression that suggested he was contemplating whether this could make sense. "Maybe we should do that," he said. Seizing the opportunity, I instinctively reached out my hand in a gesture to seal the deal. As he shook my hand, it did not escape me that the trafficking accusation had obviously played into my hand, and I felt a sense of unease, wondering whether my presence would lend legitimacy to the Flamingo.

Field notes, June 2009

The Flamingo, a large and upscale FKK sauna club, was one of the new luxurious establishments that offered a combination of sauna, night club, and brothel, where clients could leisurely mingle with sex workers for extended periods of time. Sauna club brothels emerged in 2002 and have multiplied rapidly since then. The acronym *FKK*, meaning "free body culture" (*Freikörperkultur*),[2] appropriated the name of the eponymous nudist movement of the early twentieth century and its wholehearted embrace of the naked body and all things natural; similarly, the new FKK sauna club brothels echoed the nation's cultural attitudes toward sexuality—attitudes that are considerably more relaxed than in the United States. For example, unlike in the US, there is no debate in Germany about whether sex education in schools should exist and how it should be taught; there is no vocal culture of conservative Christians advocating for premarital chastity and against abortion; and sex shops are fixtures even in small cities and busy downtown areas, with Beate Uhse's erotic shops having been an established household name since the 1960s (Crouthamel 2014).[3] Moreover, nudity is not only mandatory in saunas but also not uncommon at the beach and sometimes even in public swimming pools. Unlike in the United States, where the age of consent is, depending on the state, between sixteen and eighteen, the age of consent in Germany is fourteen.[4] And the terms *slut* and *whore*—used in the United States as powerful insults against women on the basis of their purported sexual behavior—are not used as frequently and do not have the same punch in Germany. Unlike the United States, where prostitution is legal in only a few counties in Nevada, Germany legalized prostitution through the Prostitution Act of 2002.[5] Germany also has a much more developed welfare system than the United States, offering universal health care, generous unemployment insurance, free college education, and vocational education that is the envy of many countries. With such a tight social safety net in place, sex work as a means for economic survival would appear to be much less likely.

How does prostitution operate in such a society? Would the 2002 legalization provide sex workers with safe and fair working conditions, spare them the stigma associated with their profession, and protect their clients from being labeled as deviants or misfits? Could Germany be a showcase for a society where sex can be pursued not only free from the fetters of reproduction and long-term commitment but also free from legal persecution? What could scholars, policy makers, activists, and students learn from the German example?

Shaking hands with Hans Hartmann, the owner of the Flamingo, opened up this new world as a research site to me. Despite the fact that Germany was purportedly an open society in regard to sexuality, I had found that gaining access to this industry had been exceedingly difficult. It took me six months of fieldwork before I was able to find brothel owners who allowed me to visit them at their establishments. However, I was still merely an occasional visitor hoping to get my foot in the door one way or the other. These visits had not been exactly spontaneous; I had had to arrange them well in advance. During those visits, I could talk to owners and managers but rarely had the opportunity to talk to sex workers or clients. I had managed to find clients willing to talk to me, but only outside the actual sex work environment. With Hans's permission to do research at the Flamingo, this all suddenly changed. I now could observe firsthand what was going on inside a brothel rather than sticking to scheduled visits with owners or managers.

The contradiction between an image of Germany's progressive attitude to sex and sexual commerce and the difficulty of getting access to this industry was reflected in other realms as well. As difficult as it was to get into the brothels, so it was to find men who admitted that they frequented them, at least among my friends and acquaintances. From the perspective of those inside the milieu, distance to *Soliden* (respectable folks) was an unwritten law.

The contradictions between the apparent normality of commercial sex and my actual difficulties to access commercial sex venues—at least to me, as a woman researcher—were matched by the contradictions insiders held about the industry. Thus, some women brothel owners—usually also working as madams—who made a comfortable living from this industry condemned prostitution in the harshest tone, while a number of sex workers took it on themselves to convince me how pleasurable this work was for them and how it afforded them sexual self-confidence and financial autonomy, even emotional or sexual satisfaction. Such ambivalence was perhaps the most profound for the clients in the Flamingo, who would become a critical part of this study. For some, the club experience was heaven on earth and a door to a never-dreamed-of world of sexual fulfillment, but for others, it was the source of tremendous guilt and a feeling of dependency that put them at odds with society at large. The red light milieu offered them an experience that, for all its apparent accessibility, remained a world unto itself and, beyond the context of the brothel, incompatible with their own.

Studying Legalized Prostitution

Sex worker rights activists and scholars doing research on legalized prostitution (Bernstein 2007; Brents, Jackson, and Hausbeck 2010; Brents and Hausbeck 2007; Kelly 2008; Weitzer 2012, 2017) regarded Germany's

Prostitution Act of 2002 as a promising policy and Germany itself as a progressive society for allowing its citizens to engage in buying and selling sexual services without fear of legal repercussions, as a society that no longer squandered precious resources on a victimless crime, and as a model that could offer best-practice advice on how to arrive at a more humane regime of prostitution governance that guaranteed fair labor conditions but also personal autonomy and sexual freedom. However, critics of the legalization, both scholars and activists, charged that it had made Germany a destination country for traffickers and a place where prostitution was rampant and sex trafficking widespread. These critics argued or suspected that what appeared to be sexual tolerance and enlightenment masked or even condoned a de facto flourishing of coercion and sexual repression. Outspoken critic of legalization Sheila Jeffreys argued that such laws effectively turned the state into a pimp (2009).

Studies of legal prostitution are exceedingly rare within the burgeoning ethnographic research on sexual commerce. In his book *Legalizing Prostitution*, Ronald Weitzer (2012) compared legal prostitution policies in three different European countries and was hopeful about what he found: "When prostitution is legal and regulated by the authorities, much of the regulation is designed to control third parties who run brothels and other indoor businesses, forcing them to improve working conditions, and more generally, empowering workers vis-a-vis managers and owners" (2012, 25). Like Weitzer, who provided evidence-based recommendations to the international policy debates on prostitution (2012), Barbara Brents and her colleagues, sociologists at the University of Nevada, have been studying legal brothels in Nevada, focusing on labor, state policies, and broader economic trends (Brents, Jackson, and Hausbeck 2010; Brents and Hausbeck 2007; Brents and Jackson 2013). Meanwhile, the anthropologist Patti Kelly examined legalized prostitution in Chiapas, Mexico, and showed how state-regulated prostitution functioned within the context of the neoliberal state.

This book contributes to this small number of studies on legal prostitution. It explores how sex workers make a life and a living, how men act when they are sex clients, and how brothels are organizing sexual experiences for sale. This study also examines the cultural ramifications of sexual commerce in the larger society. It describes how sex for sale and sexuality are represented in public space and media, how new business models create new prostitution cultures, and how various actors interact with and relate to each other. The intimate connections among different actors of this industry are central to this story. As this book shows, a critical tool for developing and maintaining these intimate connections were gift exchanges between different participants. Even though prostitution is an institution that for many represents the quintessence of commodified intimacy and the wrongs of mixing sex with market exchange,[6] I argue that complex relationships of trust and affection emerge within and through these relationships and form a web of shared vulnerabilities that structures the culture of commercial sex.

Exploring the brothel industry in one metropolitan region and in one upscale sauna club, the book provides an image of the industry hardly compatible with news of the rise of low-cost brothels and rampant sex trafficking circulating in the media at the time and shared across the political spectrum, from the radical feminist Alice Schwarzer to the conservative Boulevard Press *Bild*, and from mainstream newspapers like *Die Welt* to left-leaning weeklies like *Der Spiegel*. However, neither does this book show the brave new world of a liberated and emancipated sexual commerce that some scholars had hoped for (Bernstein 2007).

A Brave New World of Prostitution in Postindustrial Societies?

A number of scholars have argued that sex work is linked to precarity; selling sex becomes one of few means of survival or an opportunity to move out of poverty, a central theme in prostitution studies of the Global South. For example, both Denise Brennan's (2001, 2004, 2014) and Mark Padilla's (2007) studies of sex workers in the Dominican Republic—whether women in the former or heterosexual men in the latter—show how developing and maintaining romantic relationships with clients are some of the only means that economically marginalized Dominicans have to survive, although many of these relationships are doomed to fail. Tiantian Zheng's (2009) and Kimberley Hoang's (2015) ethnographies of karaoke bars in Vietnam and China, respectively, showed the considerable economic mobility and respect hostesses—who are primarily from rural areas—can attain through their sexual and erotic labor. Meanwhile, scholars of the more prosperous Global North have shown the economic opportunities that sex work offers to predominantly lower-class women. Susan Dewey's work with striptease dancers in New York (Dewey 2011) and with street-involved women with substance issues engaging in survival sex (Dewey and St. Germain 2016) shows two very different scenarios of economic opportunity that sex work offers, although not without also revealing the often considerable risks these women have to take to make a living through sexual labor. That erotic labor in the Global North can also be quite lucrative is shown in Takeyama's (2016) ethnography on male hosts and their female clients in karaoke clubs in Japan; in Bernstein's comparative study of women providing girlfriend sex in San Francisco, Göteborg, and Amsterdam (2007); or in the study of Barbara Brents and her colleagues (Brents and Hausbeck 2007) for the legal brothels of Nevada.

Taking on the issue of sex work as a means of economic survival, Bernstein (2007) asked, Why does it thrive even in advanced social democracies such as the Netherlands, Belgium, and Germany—countries that have welfare provisions to protect women from having to engage in survival sex? Similarly, one can ask why men continue to buy sexual services even though dating platforms such as Tinder and changing sexual mores have made the pursuit of sexual encounters—even outside the commercial venue—more accessible than ever.

Since the 1990s, sociologists have discussed the rise of commodified intimacy and argued for a trend toward more fluid sexual relationships (Bauman 2014; Giddens 1992; Illouz 2017) as the hallmark of contemporary postindustrial societies. Bernstein (2007), in particular, has used this theoretical foundation to develop a framework about a new sexual ethics. Rather than placing sexuality in the service of reproduction and committed relationships, Bernstein argues that contemporary postindustrial societies—such as Sweden, the Netherlands, and the United States, where she conducted ethnographic research of sex work—follow the idea of a "recreational sexual ethic" (2007, 6), where commodified sexuality and intimacy offer an opportunity to experience sexual relationships without the fetters of formal or committed relationships. "In postindustrial cities throughout North America and Western Europe . . . a brave new world [has sprung up] of commercially available intimate encounters that are subjectively normalized for sex workers and clients alike" (Bernstein 2007, 7).

Central to Bernstein and others' ethnographies of prostitution and the sex industry is the concept of sexual labor and its embeddedness in the market as the main framework through which to explore prostitution. Thus, Denise Brennan (2001, 2003, 2004) has shown how Dominican sex workers are making a life by engaging in relationships with European tourists, while Rhacel Parreñas (2011) used the concept of emotional labor to explain the work of Filipina women in Japan's karaoke bars. In the United States, Barb Brents and her colleagues explored the concept of emotional labor in Las Vegas's brothels (Brents and Hausbeck 2007; Brents and Jackson 2013). Looking at the role of the economy more broadly, Akiko Takeyama (2016), in her analysis of male host clubs in Japan, showed how their rise was closely aligned with Japan's economic crises and its bubble economy, while Kimberley Kay Hoang (2015), who studied karaoke clubs and their role in the Vietnamese finance sector, illustrated the fundamental role that commercial sex venues played in securing and maintaining international financing.

What such labor and market-based analyses of prostitution have in common is that they are firmly situating the sexual transaction within the context of a market exchange. Crudely expressed in a phrase attributed to Charlie Sheen—"I don't pay prostitutes to come. I pay them to leave" (Cryer 2015)—the concept of a market exchange operates on the idea that transactions based on money leave no outstanding debt. The sociologist Georg Simmel (1907) argued more than a hundred years ago that the exchange of money for a service or goods relieves the transactional partners of any form of future commitments, with no register of compromised morality, with no obligations to engage further, and without emotional attachments to the transaction partners (cited in Bernstein 2007). Relieved of the emotional baggage of romantic relationships, commodified sexuality thus can offer a more ethical form of sexuality, as nobody must be convinced of a love that might end promptly with the fulfillment of sexual desires (Prasad 1999).

And yet, emotional attachments between sex workers and clients are by no means rare. Ethnographies of prostitution from around the world have provided numerous examples of how relationships that started in commercial sexual transactions often morph into long-term affective commitments, sometimes even marriage (Padilla 2007; Parreñas 2011; Mitchell 2015; Takeyama 2016) and transnational families. This shows it is not only sex workers who are seeking attachments but also their customers. Feelings of attachment, emotional gratitude, expectations of relationships, and moral obligations to repay, however, are the hallmark of a different mode of exchange: not of the market but of the gift. As Marcel Mauss ([1925], 1990) showed almost a century ago, gift exchanges are a protracted, open-ended form of exchange wherein partners in the transaction become tied to each other through a dynamic imbalance between giver and receiver. As gifts are a means to enter a relationship, they are not returned immediately but require the initial recipient to endure the moral debt of an unreturned favor before a return gift can be given. Once the original recipient becomes the new gift giver, the new recipient—and original gift giver—now has to endure moral indebtedness and moral inferiority. The goals of gift exchanges are not the objects or gifts themselves but the relationships that form between gift givers and gift recipients over time.

Such gift exchanges and the open-ended relationships they produce are key characteristics in the culture of prostitution I describe here, particularly in the prolonged interactions I witnessed at the Flamingo. There, some men were indeed in search of "care objects" rather than sex objects and often cultivated relationships with favorites to whom they showed loyalty and sometimes even faithfulness. That meant, however, that instead of engaging in a labor of *bounded authenticity* (Bernstein 2007, 6), where service and commitment were finite, sex workers at the Flamingo engaged in a labor of *boundless intimacy* where service and social interaction were open-ended. Extended relationships based on gifts and saturated with affective ties were not limited to a sex worker and client dyad, however, but also occurred in relationships rarely explored within commercial intimacy: between clients and the club, between employees and their boss, and even among clients themselves. Instead of showing the Flamingo as an institution offering the moral freedom of no-strings-attached sex, then, this study shows how it provided a space for relationships with strings attached, a haven that was offering bonds of affection and a place of belonging.

Labor, Governance Regimes, and Beyond

At the heart of the debate about prostitution—and commodified intimacy more generally—is whether it is compatible with sexual justice and gender equality, and whether prostitution without exploitation is possible. Radical feminists and abolitionists fall on one side of this divide and sex work activists and their advocates on the other. Their positions correspond roughly to the dominant governance systems: criminalization, legalization, and decriminalization. Criminalization advocates argue that the existence of prostitution itself is a sign of gender and sexual domination and there-fore demand that the state criminalizes sellers and buyers as well as third parties. Abolitionism is a milder form of criminalization represented in the so-called Nordic model of prostitution that criminalizes the buyer but not the seller of sex. Abolitionist scholars and criminalization advocates con-sider legalization and decriminalization to be a state-endorsed system of women's exploitation (Farley 2004, 2006; Hughes 2002; Jeffreys 2009). In contrast, sex work activists and sex-positive researchers favor legalization, a governance system in which the state regulates sex workers and the venues in which they work. Scholars and activists advocating for decriminalization (Agustín 2008; Agustín 2007; Amnesty International 2015; Brents and Hausbeck 2001; Hydra e.V. 2015; Kempadoo, Sanghera, and Pattanaik 2012; TAMPEP 2009a; Weitzer 2012) demand a governance system where prostitution is decriminalized to ensure sex workers enjoy the same labor rights and recognition as other laborers.

Studying legal prostitution in a prosperous welfare state where women's rights are recognized and protected, where people generally have a positive relationship to sexuality, and where the vast majority of sex work takes place indoors (TAMPEP 2009a) offers ideal conditions to find out whether the promises associated with legalization have materialized: Can it offer safe working conditions? Are sex workers autonomous and free from dependency on brothel owners, traffickers, or other third parties? Has it eliminated the stigma associated with this work and restrictions on sex workers' social lives? Has sex work become a job like any other, with the same labor protections and welfare benefits provided by other jobs? And finally, does it offer the kind of sexual liberation, the "brave new world of commercially available intimate encounters that are subjectively normalized for sex workers and clients alike," that Bernstein (2007, 7) envisioned?

A focus on this "brave new world" of legalized sexual commerce demands an equal focus on clients—actors who are often maligned as deviant or socially deficient and study subjects that only recently have received scholarly attention (Grenz 2005; Jones and Hannem 2018; Milrod and Weitzer 2012; Sanders 2008). What kinds of relationships do these men seek, what kinds of connections do they entertain with sexual service providers, and what is their relationship to the brothel owners and other third parties and the socializing environment that legal prostitution makes possible? Does the stigma of the deviant john apply to them, and if so, how do they deal with it and with their role as sexual consumers in a society that also subscribes to norms of gender equality? Finally, in an era where some men bemoan the erosion of masculine privileges, does legalized prostitution embolden them? Does a society in which male sexual gratification is merely a matter of economic resources give men the means to consolidate their dominant role in the gender order? Does it function as a means of masculine reaffirmation?

This ethnography of legal prostitution and the cultural context in which it is embedded does not provide simple answers or solutions. Combining a macro perspective of the red light industry in a thriving metropolitan region with the micro perspective of one particular FKK sauna club, the Flamingo, this study illustrates the world of striking new prostitution regimes, with confident women who labor independently and clients who understand themselves as members of a moral community that gives them a sense of belonging. But it also shows the rise of dubious labor regimes, of questionable alliances, and of new forms of coercion. By recognizing the affective relationships entailed in this industry, it offers a new framework to recognize the varieties of exchanges and relations in commercial sex. Offering a theoretical framework that goes beyond concepts of labor and the market economy, the dimensions in which prostitution has been customarily theorized, this book explores the modality of the gift and its associated dimensions of affect and connectedness. This helps to reframe questions about prostitution and about sexual labor, about intimacy and relationships. Thus, *Legalized Prostitution in Germany* explores the confluence of several sets of often juxtaposed realms: of the public face of labor and the private face of intimacy, of the need for belonging and the fear of banishment, and of the emotional relationships between actors that are embedded within entangled economies of the market and the gift and a web of shared vulnerabilities where everyone is marginalized in one way or the other, whether as sex worker, client, madam, pimp, migrant, employee, brothel owner, or some combination of those things—a web that, for better or for worse, keeps everyone suspended within it.

The Prostitution Act of 2002

Even before 2002, prostitution in Germany was not considered a crime, although it saw various degrees of state regulation. A brief progressive period in the late 1920s soon gave way to the repressive state control of prostitution under the Nazis (Hunecke 2011; Roos 2002, 2017). After the end of World War II and the nation's division, the two states enacted different regimes: prostitution became illegal in East Germany and remained legal in West Germany.

The concept of immorality (*Sittenwidrigkeit*) remained central to state-regulated prostitution before 2002. Because sex work was considered immoral, workers could not sue clients for failure to pay for services, and they could not enter formal employment relationships and therefore were not eligible for employment-related benefits such as unemployment insurance, retirement, and health insurance. Furthermore, health checkups for sex workers—dreaded because of their invasive nature and as a means of state control—were mandatory, and some cities required registration with the police. Brothel owners were in a similar legal limbo, always hovering around the charge of procurer and thus subject to be closed down at a moment's notice. Thus, while prostitution was de jure legal, de facto it was an industry subjected to multiple forms of surveillance and lack of legal protections, a situation that was particularly troubling for sex workers (Hunecke 2011; Roos 2002, 2017).

Sex worker rights organizations such as Hydra e. V., Berlin in the 1970s and the Green Party together with the Social Democrats in the 1990s demanded an end to the definition of prostitution as an immoral trade and a recognition of the rights of sex workers to become eligible for the same labor protections and social benefits as those who engaged in other types of work.[7]

In 2000, the Supreme Court decided that public opinion no longer regarded prostitution as immoral. This set the path for the Act Regulating the Legal Situation of Prostitutes (Prostitution Act) of 2002 to pass, with the goal of allowing sex work to become a legally recognized form of labor. The new law allowed workers to sue clients for nonpayment, but clients could not sue sex workers for their services. Sex workers were now able to enter formal employment relations and gain labor protection in line with other professions, thus bringing them on a more equal footing with other forms of labor (Kavemann and Rabe 2009; Kavemann 2008; Kavemann et al. 2007a), while the dreaded mandatory health checkups (*Bockscheine*), which sex workers viewed as invasive, humiliating, and a means to harass and intimidate them, were officially abolished.

Another pillar for the legalization of prostitution was the constitutional right of citizens to sexual self-determination. This not only applies to sexual preferences but also includes one's decision to engage in prostitution. As Kavemann wrote (2008) in a report to the federal government, "In a state which is neutral as [sic] regards *weltanschauung* [worldview], as reflected in the German Basic Law, the law must respect a person's voluntary, autonomous decision to engage in prostitution as long as it does not violate any rights of others. Engaging in prostitution on one's own authority does not automatically violate a prostitute's human dignity. Since free

Figure 0.1 Election poster of the Green Party (*Bündnis 90/Die Grünen*) demanding social security benefits for sex workers. "Never without it. Equal rights—also for prostitutes."

self-determination is an expression of human dignity, individuals first and foremost decide for themselves what 'dignity' means for them" (Kavemann 2008, 11). The Prostitution Act of 2002 also limits what an employer or brothel owner can demand a sex worker to do. This limited power of directive (*eingeschränktes Weisungsrecht*) means an employer or brothel operator cannot command a sex worker to accept particular clients or to perform specific practices (Kavemann 2008).

Doing away with the legal charge of immorality and recognizing sex workers' autonomous decision to enter prostitution led to the elimination of the legal ambiguity of brothel owners and thus gave them an incentive to abide by the laws, although this has been rather controversial.[8] Before the passage of the Prostitution Act, brothel owners could be charged with pimping or trafficking if they offered good working conditions for sex workers. This meant that they faced the constant threat of their businesses being shut down. *Good working conditions* here could mean as little as offering condoms, clean and modern rooms and facilities, or enjoyable dining opportunities. The logic was that creating a pleasant work environment would give sex workers an incentive to remain in prostitution, a legal but undesirable and immoral economic activity. Without this constant threat of being charged with procuring, pimping, or similar charges, brothels could now offer sex workers better and more competitive working conditions (Renzikowski 2007, 2009, 2012) and, as lawmakers hoped, had an incentive to collaborate with police and authorities by remaining vigilant about extortion, pimping, theft, or tax evasion, all crimes considered widespread in the red light industry (*Milieudelikte*).

For brothel owners and operators, the advantages of the new prostitution law were arguably substantial. As the financial manager of the Flamingo explained to me, now that they were no longer subjected to the caprice of law enforcement, brothels had become a much safer investment. This might help explain the emergence and rapid spread of the large and luxurious FKK sauna club brothels such as the Flamingo since 2002. With their extravagant facilities, aggressive advertisement, large number of sex workers, and often staggering size, they soon became the flashiest and most visible manifestations of a new red light industry and, with it, a new prostitution culture.

Legalization and Its Discontent

While some prostitution scholars looked at Germany as an example of a best-practice case for a progressive legislation to emancipate sex workers (Weitzer 2012), Germany's Prostitution Act stirred debates at home and abroad. Other European countries that had liberal prostitution laws in the past started to implement more restrictive policies. Thus, Sweden introduced the Nordic model in 1999, with Norway following suit in 2008 and Iceland in 2009. In the Nordic model, sex work itself is not illegal, but purchasing sexual services is, as are any kind of third parties involved in profiting from sexual labor. The Netherlands, which had legalized prostitution in

1999, put in new restrictions on Amsterdam's red light district (Outshoorn 2012). While the Nordic model enjoys popularity with many supporters, particularly feminists, critics have argued that it is far less successful than generally claimed and that is has forced a large number of sex workers underground to find clients.

Some of the effects of the German Prostitution Act of 2002 were described by Kavemann and her colleagues in a series of detailed studies for the federal government (Kavemann et al. 2007; Kavemann 2008; Kavemann and Rabe 2009). She found that freelancing rather than formal employment remained the most prominent type of labor arrangement, not only because few brothel operators offered formal employment but also because most women preferred to work anonymously. That meant health insurance, pension contributions, long-term care, unemployment insurance, and other benefits the law intended to make accessible to sex workers remained the sole financial obligation of the worker. For those who engaged in sex work only sporadically, health insurance was usually obtained through other forms of employment, welfare arrangements, or a spouse. For labor migrants, however, who worked in Germany only intermittently and who planned to eventually return home, paying into an expensive private health insurance and retirement account in Germany was not financially viable. The law, then, had comparatively little impact on the social benefits for workers, and a majority of international migrants had no health insurance.[9] To what extent sex workers knew of the law is also questionable. None of the women I met in the course of this research seemed to be aware of its existence. What they had noticed, however, was the income tax they now were forced to pay, usually collected by the prostitution venues where they worked.[10]

Legalization of prostitution, as I will show, was an uneven process on other accounts as well. While the Prostitution Act of 2002 in theory could be described as decriminalization rather than legalization because it eliminated state control such as mandatory health checkups, abolished laws that criminalized brothels, and normalized the labor of sex workers by making them eligible for labor benefits, it was de facto often overruled by city and state bylaws. Thus, each of Germany's sixteen states decides on some key aspects of prostitution while municipalities decide on others. This interplay between federal law and state and local regulations produces a perplexing legal tapestry of what at first sight looks like a uniform governance system of prostitution (Kontos 2009; Pates 2012). The case of Neuburg, as I shall show, provides a particularly striking example of such a de facto regulation of the sex industry.[11]

The Brothel of Europe and Sex Work Migration

By the time I began this research in 2008, the debate about legalized prostitution in Germany was in full swing. One reason for the public outcry was the fear that the new law was quickly turning Germany into a haven for sex traffickers. Another concern was a growing unease about an emerging image of commercial sex as an article of mass consumption and as a commodity for which one could drive a hard bargain, suggested through club names such as *Geizclub* (Miser Club) and flat-rate sex clubs.[12] News shows regularly featured reports about sex trafficking and the rise of organized crime networks in prostitution. On the political stage, Chancellor Angela Merkel of the conservative Christian Democrats pledged to reform the Prostitution Act. Ursula von der Leyen, then minister for Family Affairs (BMFSFJ),[13] publicly disagreed with the law and its tenets in 2007, stating, "Prostitution is not a job like any other—leaving prostitution is the goal" (BMFSFJ 2007). At the level of the European Parliament, British MP Mary Honeyball spearheaded a campaign for the Nordic model, an initiative that was passed by the European Parliament in 2014, although with no binding obligations for EU states to adopt it as policy.[14]

The debate about prostitution remained a mainstay in the media for years. Private TV channels such as SAT2 offered a constant fare of edutainment about the new brothel landscape in Germany, while the government-sponsored TV stations regularly offered talk shows that invited experts to speak about the rights and wrongs of prostitution.[15] Feminist organizations such as Terre des Femmes and the antitrafficking umbrella organization KOK[16] expressed their concerns about the law and the apparently growing number of women being trafficked, as did publicity-savvy organizations such as FEMEN, who staged numerous protests against the new sauna clubs. Alice Schwarzer, editor of *Emma*, an influential feminist news magazine, criticized the new era of mega brothels that the legalization of prostitution had ushered in (Schwarzer 2008), as did the influential leftist news magazine *Der Spiegel*. A phrase used widely in the media was "Germany— the Brothel of Europe."[17]

While this phrase was coined by Frantz Fanon and his critique of the Caribbean sex tourism serving its ex-colonizers, it alluded to the fact that since the late 1990s, the proportion of international migrants among sex workers had grown dramatically. Although statistics are hard to come by, for the time period for which data exists, the proportion of international sex-work migrants in Germany grew from 52 percent in 1999 to 60 percent in 2005 (Kontos and Shinozaki 2007) and from 60 percent in 2006 to 65 percent in 2008 (TAMPEP 2009a). In Neuburg, this trend was even more pronounced, as the number of international sex work migrants grew from 40 percent in 2000 to more than 90 percent in 2015.[18]

The fastest growing segment among these labor migrants consisted of women from the new member states of the European Union in East and Central Europe, who now had the right to work anywhere within the European Union. Between 2008 and 2011, the most intense part of this ethnographic fieldwork, women from Romania and Bulgaria made up the single largest nationality among sex workers. They followed earlier waves of sex-work migrants from Eastern Europe that coincided with their home countries' entry into the European Union, such as Czech Republic, Poland, and Hungary. With the European Union granting citizens of its member states free mobility within the EU, these labor migrants did enjoy legal status and labor permits that were significantly harder to come by for others.

That so many women from the poorer parts of Europe would travel to Germany to engage in sex work, however, was not an altogether haphazard development; it was also due to an EU regulation imposed upon most of the countries entering after 2004. This so-called 2-3-2 rule—which included Romania and Bulgaria—stated that for a limited number of years following EU membership, de facto until 2013, citizens from these countries could work in Germany only as freelancers, not as employees with social benefits, and live there only as long as they were able to support themselves (Staiger 2009). Considering these stipulations, prostitution offered one of few opportunities for work that did not require language skills or formal degree certificates and was lucrative enough to maintain the required minimum earnings. This regulation, based on the protection of Germany's domestic workers, was one of the key factors that led to the sharp increase of women from Eastern Europe in the sex industry (Staiger 2009).

The Prostitute Protection Law of 2017

After the long and sustained controversy in the media about the Prostitution Act and the trafficking it had allegedly caused, and despite the fact that the Federal Criminal Police Office (Bundeskriminalamt) showed a steady decrease in sex trafficking cases and their victims (Bundeskriminalamt 2009, 2013, 2017) and fierce protests from sex worker rights organizations, the Parliament (*Bundestag*) passed an amendment to the law in 2016, called the Prostitute Protection Law (*Prostitutionsschutzgesetz*), which went into effect January 1, 2017. The new law introduced a number of regulations. As of 2017, a few years after the active fieldwork component of my research had ended, condom use became mandatory for all types of sexual intercourse, including oral sex, and entrepreneurs who want to open prostitution businesses are now subject to criminal background checks. While these new regulations are sensible, other aspects of the law are more problematic. For example, sex workers are required to register with officials in the city in which they work and undergo mandatory counseling with hastily trained social workers. Ostensibly a means to detect victims of trafficking, registration has been heavily criticized by sex worker rights organizations because its efficacy in identifying abuse is highly questionable and because it forces sex workers to reveal their identities.[19] In some respects, then, the new law constitutes a return to state regulation (*Reglementierung*) as it existed almost a hundred years earlier, before the Prevention of the Venereal Disease Act in 1927 ushered in a more liberal prostitution regime (Roos 2002, 2017; Hunecke 2011). The new Prostitute Protection Law thus seems to be based more on political arguments, moral assessments of prostitution, and a vocal antitrafficking campaign than on evidence-based research. It is my hope that this book will give policy makers, public health and legal scholars, outreach workers, and activists a tool to better assess key dynamics in this industry.

Studying Prostitution in Neuburg

Neuburg is in many ways an ordinary city. It does not have the metropolitan feel of trendy Berlin or the international reputation associated with Hamburg and its famous red light district, the Reeperbahn. Neuburg also lacks the seedy image of Frankfurt and its train station area (Bahnhofsviertel), a red light district disproportionately represented in the few studies about prostitution in Germany that do exist (Kreuzer 1989; Ruhne 2006; Weitzer 2012). In contrast, Neuburg is relatively inconspicuous: like many sister cities of similar size across Germany, it has army bases and trade conventions and has a generally high standard of living. As such, it offers a view into a site of prostitution that is neither particularly glamorous nor especially traumatic.

The metropolitan region of Neuburg and its neighboring cities form a relatively densely urbanized region consisting of five million people, with Neuburg the cultural and administrative center. It is home to a thriving industry of some very large and many midsize companies and a growing service sector that today makes up 80 percent of employment in the region. It is also one of the more prosperous regions in Germany and in Europe overall, with good employment opportunities.

Neuburg, more so than its smaller neighbors, is a culturally diverse city, including descendants of immigrants from Southern Europe who came during the postwar boom years as guest workers; immigrants from former socialist countries of Eastern Europe, particularly during the Yugoslav Wars in the 1990s; and from Russia. Since the expansion of the European Union in the first decade of the millennium, a large number of immigrants were citizens from the new member states.

Boasting salaries among the highest in Western Europe and a relatively stable economy, Germany remains an attractive destination for labor migrants. In 2010, one of four residents in Neuburg had a migration background. One expression of this cultural diversity that struck me when I first started fieldwork there was the variety of clothes and head coverings I saw Muslim women wearing on my daily commute—from middle-aged and older women wearing long blue coats and simple head scarves tied under the chin, forming a characteristic A-frame silhouette, to young women wearing stylish hijabs that framed their faces elegantly and dressed in formfitting dresses with tight-fitting jeans underneath. In fact, it was not uncommon to see a young woman wearing a hijab accompanied by a friend with no head scarf at all. Such head coverings were but one particularly visible manifestation of this kaleidoscope of cultures, ethnicities, and nationalities in Neuburg.

The surrounding cities, many of them still rather rural areas when I lived there in the '70s and '80s, had grown to midsize towns or merged with others, forming what urban geographers call conurbations. These neighboring cities retained quainter appearances than Neuburg, with a less cosmopolitan feel. One of the luxuries I came to appreciate when I was doing fieldwork in Neuburg was the convenience of an extensive public transportation system that was fast, modern, and affordable and allowed me to experience the city cheek by jowl.

Prostitution Venues: Apartment Brothels, Eros Centers, and FKK Sauna Clubs

Laws that regulate sexual commerce locally vary by state and local governance, as do the kind of establishments where sexual commerce takes place. Cities such as Hamburg and Nuremberg, for example, are known for window prostitution while Fürth, Nuremberg's smaller sister city, prohibits it. Cologne and Bonn feature sex boxes (*Verrichtungsboxen*) (Stern.de 2005) or drive-in locations (Gasser 2010) similar to the *tippelzones* in Amsterdam as a means to control street prostitution. Other cities like Augsburg and Stuttgart allow prostitution in trailers (*Wohnmobile*) parked in less populated areas around the city. All these venues come with their own advantages and disadvantages. For example, while working in trailers or on the street is often considered the riskiest form of sex work because it occurs in relative isolation, it offers independence from managers and owners. Window prostitution, considered by many to be particularly objectifying, offers workers a degree of communality with fellow workers. Meanwhile sauna club brothels, though they are among the most luxurious brothel establishments, are more stressful for some sex workers than less upscale establishments, which afford greater autonomy over one's work.

In this book, I will concentrate on three types of brothel venues that are among the most common forms in Neuburg and other cities: apartment prostitution, Laufhäuser and eros centers, and, finally, FKK sauna clubs. Each of these types represents a particular ambience and a specific niche in the prostitution culture, with sex workers and clients often staying faithful to one particular type. Apartment prostitution (*Terminwohnungen*) offers the smallest venues: apartments, often in inconspicuous buildings throughout the city, are typically run by a woman who also acts as a manager; three to seven sex workers work and often live there too; and a madam (*Hausdame*) who takes care of the day-to-day running of the brothel. They are among the most expensive establishments.

Laufhäuser and their more recent counterparts, eros centers, are at the opposite end of such apartment brothels. Laufhäuser and eros centers are the lowest-priced indoor brothels, offering no frills and no space for socializing between clients and workers. They typically have twenty to over one hundred women working there and are often repurposed hotels where sex workers rent rooms by the day or the week; clients freely walk through the corridors in search of a service provider of their liking.

Sauna club brothels, the largest brothel establishments, can have one hundred sex workers or more. They are at the opposite end of eros centers in regard to luxury, with sophisticated spa and sauna facilities as well as a bar and a large lounge area where sex workers and clients can spend time socializing in an atmosphere that is both spa and club.

Most women work in a particular establishment for a few days to a few weeks before moving on to another location, though they often return. This kind of circular migration is due to the industry's constant demand for changing service providers but also to sex workers' desire to remain anonymous. The combination of living and working spaces, common to all three establishments, helps migrant workers from abroad and women from other towns, as they don't need to expend additional effort to find temporary housing. However, it can also become an arrangement that subjects sex workers to usury and keeps them spatially and socially isolated.

Methodology

My fieldwork in Germany took place between 2008 and 2015 over three sites. In the first stage, which lasted about five months in the first half of 2008, I concentrated on Neuburg, a large regional center, and its historic red light district (RLD); in the second stage, which lasted another four months between the winter of 2008 and the summer of 2009, I conducted interviews with eleven different brothel owners in Neuburg and surrounding cities; in the third phase, between 2009 and 2010, I conducted another five months of participant observation at the Flamingo. In the years between 2010 and 2015, I conducted selected follow up interviews and had an opportunity to spend more time doing ethnographic observation at a different sauna club.

The fact that this field research took place not in a new and unfamiliar place but rather in my native country and even my hometown, both of which I had left decades earlier, provided unexpected challenges and required a constant process of readjustment and remembering. As Dan Bradburd (1998, 168) wrote, "Ethnography is precisely concerned with *not* being detached from the subjectivity of the speaker and the experiencer." That subjectivity was intensified and complicated through the memories that came alive when I revisited the place of my childhood and adolescence.

"Don't walk around like a whore," my father would say whenever my older sister had decided to wear a skirt that was a few inches too far above her knee, or when we had experimented with the mini lipsticks our aunt had snuck to us on her visits. It was different at my maternal grandmother's house, where *Praline*, a sexy girlie magazine—a cross between *Hustler* and the *National Enquirer*—was laid out on the living room table, enjoying the light of day without any sense of shame, and the subject of great curiosity on my visits.

Going back to Germany to do ethnographic fieldwork about what I assumed would be the land of sexual liberation brought back some of these long-forgotten memories of my childhood and their contradictory messages. My father's concern about his teenage daughter's hemline in the 1970s, when miniskirts were the generally approved fashion, was a bit extreme. And soft-porn magazines like *Praline* were freely accessible in any newspaper store or might even be laid out at a doctor's office without raising a lot of eyebrows.

My long absence from Neuburg and my subsequent lack of familiarity with the place required a constant stitching together of what I remembered with what I saw. I often wondered whether my memory was reliable or whether I had changed. Much of what I saw on my first leg of fieldwork—described in chapter 1—seemed utterly perplexing to me. On other occasions, I suddenly realized how contradictory the representation of sexuality had been during my formative years.

Another unexpected challenge was the difficulty of entering the prostitution scene. I considered myself a seasoned ethnographer, but gaining access to the red light milieu (*Rotlichtmilieu*), as my informants called it, turned out to be trying. Although the Prostitution Act had been passed seven years earlier at the time of my first fieldwork visit and nearly a decade earlier at the second round of fieldwork, and although it was a constant presence on German television, I had problems finding any insider willing to talk to me. Brothel operators I contacted by phone or email were extremely guarded toward outsiders. Franz, an owner of a long-established brothel explained, "We usually do not talk to respectable folk [*Solide*]." As a woman who was not a sex worker, I was eyed with bewilderment in striptease clubs or hostess bars in the red light district, where I was usually the only female visitor. Attempts to visit the historic Laufhaus—a three-story building extending the entire length of a locked-off street—ended in a standoff with a very tall, fierce-looking middle-aged woman in a white lab coat who intercepted me and sent me on my way. This "walk-through house"—the literal translation for Laufhaus—was off-limits to me, she explained as she glanced at my modest skirt and blouse and my Birkenstock sandals.

Germany's Prostitution Act had seemed to signal an enlightened approach to sex, so my difficulty in making contact took me by surprise and made me wonder why there was such gender segregation within the industry. If legalizing prostitution were based on an enlightened and emancipated notion of sexuality and sexual commerce, then why would I, as a woman, not have the same freedom as men to purchase sex and access brothels? It seemed to me that in Neuburg's red light industry, where businesses catered to strictly heterosexual tastes, women had access only as service providers, madams, or business owners, not as clients or visitors. In contrast, men were able to move in and out of sex industry venues with ease, whether they were clients or working in the industry.

Faced with the difficulty of gaining access, I contacted people and organizations on the periphery of the industry, including law enforcement, social services, and health departments as well as client forums, sex shops, and newspaper editors. Unlike many other cities, Neuburg did not have a sex worker rights organization or self-help group of its own, such as Hydra in Berlin or Kassandra in Nuremberg, which are supported, at least in part, through municipal or state funding. Instead, Neuburg had a special unit within its Social Services Department dedicated specifically to sex workers and their needs. Long before the Prostitute Protection Law of 2017 made counseling services a mandatory program, the Prostitution Unit offered information about housing and health care services, about addiction recovery and social security, and about childcare services and exit programs. The unit engaged in outreach social work as well as in-house counseling support. One of their outreach institutions was the Night Owl, a small communal café located in the heart of Neuburg's RLD, which catered primarily to older and destitute sex workers. Visiting the Night Owl twice a week over the first few months helped me get to know some of the regulars there, many of them women in their fifties and older who had been working in the district for many years, sometimes for decades.

After numerous futile attempts to make contact with brothel owners, I eventually gained the trust of the administrator of a local online platform for sex clients. The admin was well-connected and trusted by entrepreneurs, as the site also placed ads for local brothels and invited sex workers and managers to participate in discussions. It was a crucial hub for all things related to sexual commerce.

I had stumbled upon the client forum after my many unsuccessful cold calls to brothel owners and found it to be an invaluable source of information. After lurking on the forum, as members call it when nonregistered visitors read their contributions, I met with the administrator and, after mutual sympathies, discovered he was as interested in my research as I was in his experiences and views. Having run the client forum for almost a decade, he had acquired lots of customers among the local brothel venues and personally advocated for me with many of his advertisement clients. With his support, I was finally able to gain access to eleven brothel owners who agreed to open-ended and, in several cases, repeat interviews. The owners and managers I interviewed comprised a rough sample of the different establishments in the RLD: from traditional brothels in the red light district to apartment brothels in the city at large, and from eros centers to sauna clubs in Neuburg's periphery and the surrounding cities. I also became a formal member of the client forum and participated in several of their semiannual meetings, during which I met a variety of sexual service providers and clients from different establishments.

Eventually I also gained the trust of the owners of two glamorous new sauna clubs: first FKK Club Flamingo between 2009 and 2010 for a total of five months, and then, briefly in 2014, Club Ecstasy. In this third stage of my fieldwork, I conducted participant observation, interacting regularly with a large number of staff, sex workers, and clients in the context of the club.

Research at the sauna clubs was the most intense, exciting, and eye-opening part of my fieldwork. As I dressed like one of the madams, in more or less formal clothes, and was close to them in age, clients often came up to me and complimented me on how well the club was run, how beautiful the women were, and how happy they were that such a club existed. Apparently, many clients initially assumed I was a madam or part of the management before I could explain to them that I was a researcher. Among the staff and girls, as everyone referred to the sex workers, word gradually spread that I was there to do research.

On my visits to the Flamingo, which lasted between several hours and several days, I would typically meet new clients and catch up with those I had already talked to, and I developed a rapport with quite a few of the many regulars. Regular visits to the sauna clubs over a two-year period provided me with a long-term perspective of the experiences of sex workers, clients, and staff, many of whom remained loyal to the Flamingo, and gave me insight into the club as a social site and into people's relationships with each other. A short-term follow-up study of Club Ecstasy confirmed many of my observations at the Flamingo.

Chapter Overview

The book explores the subject of legal prostitution by first situating it within the broader context of Neuburg and its red light district before moving into the intimate space of the FKK Sauna Club Flamingo. Thus, I begin in chapter 1, "Sex in the Public Sphere," by taking the reader on a walk through Neuburg and its abundant representations of sexuality in public: in outdoor advertisement, political slogans, and public announcements. This exploration of visual inscriptions in the urban space also reflects the process of reimmersing myself in the place of my upbringing and my native culture. The bumps in readjustment and the struggle of coming to terms with this visual barrage of sexualized imagery bring into relief not only different representational practices but also, I argue, different sexual imaginaries reflected and created in this urban landscape and bring to light the broader societal fabric in which legalized prostitution is embedded.

Chapter 2, "The Decline of a Red Light District," documents the changes in Neuburg's historic red light district before and after the legalization of prostitution. Listening to sex workers' stories of a district in decline, I describe how sexual commerce has been increasingly regulated and crowded out by non-sex-related businesses. Before the Prostitution Act of 2002—and unaffected by it once it was established—local city government and police had subjected the district to a growing surveillance regime, making it an increasingly less attractive site for sexual commerce. Meanwhile, a new geography of sexual commerce emerged in prostitution venues in the urban periphery. This chapter then shows how local governance structures and legislation override the federal law regarding prostitution. This is critical to understanding the de facto organization of prostitution and its uneven implementation.

Chapter 3, "The New Red Light Geography and Changing Regimes of Prostitution," examines the three most common new prostitution venues outside the traditional red light district: small apartment prostitution, large eros centers, and fancy sauna club mega brothels. These three venues occupy different niches in the industry in regard to location, management, client culture, and labor regimes. I show how especially the new sauna club mega brothels have devised a client culture and labor regime that allow owners to increasingly capitalize on the unpaid labor of sex workers. Clients are now offered unprecedented opportunities for socializing with sex workers, selling a "girlfriend experience" that facilitates the formation of extended and affectionate bonds. For sex workers, however, this arrangement entails a new layer of exploitation. Rather than offering a form of emancipated sexual labor through *bounded authenticity*, I argue that these luxury club mega brothels demand a sexual labor of *boundless intimacy* wherein sex work is increasingly open-ended in both time and emotional investment.

The rest of the book moves the focus from the macro perspective of the organization of the sex industry in Neuburg and its surroundings to the micro perspective of the Flamingo, the new sauna club brothel. With an in-depth ethnography of this new type of establishment, I begin in chapter 4, "Work and Life at the Flamingo—Portraits of the Girls," with the stories of four women working at the club. Given the hesitation of many of my research participants to talk directly about their work, I use a narrative style that revolves around our interactions at the club and fragments of their lives they chose to reveal. From the middle-aged German woman who calls herself a "milieu junkie" to the young woman from Bulgaria who supports her extended family back home, their stories show a perplexing familiarity with exploitative partners as well as a degree of control over such relationships, a refusal to portray themselves as victims, and a fierce sense of independence and self-reliance.

Chapter 5, "Zuhälter on the Brothel Floor and Labor Discipline," takes up the question of Zuhälter—sometimes called *third parties*, a term with fewer negative connotations—at the club, and how various actors talk about them. Whereas sex workers, clients, and even madams complained about the abundance of Zuhälter among the clients, management denied such a claim. Zuhälter themselves remained elusive or unwilling to participate in interviews. The scenario that emerged, however, was that club management tolerated—if not encouraged—the presence of Zuhälter because they were able to exact a form of labor discipline from sex workers in a way management was legally not able to do. This raises the question of the extent to which even an upscale legal brothel needs to depend on exploitative third parties for their labor management.

Chapter 6, "The Gift in Sex for Sale: Prestige, Belonging, and Coercion," traces the affective relationships that emerge between sex workers and clients, clients and management, and management and employees. Prostitution has been studied primarily in the context of labor and market exchange, where transactions are finite, leaving the client with no outstanding obligations after the purchase. Yet, I argue, the brothel also is the site of gift exchanges, where relationships develop over time and intimate emotional attachments are formed: from clients who fall in love with sex workers to clients seeking to acquire prestige vis-à-vis other clients, and to employees for whom the club has become a family. I show here how the relationships that are fostered over gift exchange, however, are not always amicable but also create emotional entanglements and ambivalent relationships, from connectedness to indebtedness, from "girlfriend sex" to infatuation, or from generosity to manipulation and coercion, thus also highlighting the ambiguities entailed in the affective world of prostitution.

Chapter 7, "Sex Clients—at the Club, on the Forum, and at the Pub," focuses on the clients and traces their social relationships and intimate bonds in three different settings: as sex clients at the club, as online forum members, and finally as buddies who regularly meet at a pub. Relationships between clients are rarely the systematic focus of studies of prostitution. While the club is where the action is, a critical space for clients is the client forum, where clients engage online and sometimes in person. The forum provides not only spaces to relive their experiences or get titillated but also a place for compassion and community, where clients share intimate details without the fear of stigma and condemnation. If gifts and the relationships they engendered were critical to relationships inside the Flamingo, the gifts clients exchanged through sharing stories were critical to creating and maintaining their community. However, the closer they came to this community, the higher their risk of alienation with society at large. For some, then, this sense of attachment created spirals of entanglement and dependency from which they found it difficult to extricate themselves. This shows the importance of understanding the role of the gift economy in prostitution and its role in tying together its various actors.

In the conclusion, I return to the broader question of legalized prostitution in Germany and how the new brothel venues have rewritten the relationships between brothel owners, clients, and sex workers and their relationships with society at large. In this new legalized prostitution regime, where sex workers perform "girlfriend sex" but work harder than ever, where clients socialize with each other but also feel increasingly alienated from society at large, and where owners use Zuhälter to discipline workers whom they call "guests," the brothel nevertheless thrives on generating a sense of belonging for its participants. This ethnography, then, throws a light not only on the new forms of labor that have arisen in the legalized prostitution but also on the varieties of intimate relationships facilitated in legalized prostitution and the ambiguous location sexual commerce occupies in contemporary Germany.

Notes

1. "Girls" (*Mädels* or *Mädchen*) is the term sex workers commonly use for themselves, as do their clients and staff. While it may sound belittling and infantilizing, it has connotations of respect, attractiveness, desirability, and youthfulness. Even mature sex workers in their forties or fifties use the term to refer to themselves. I have therefore decided to use this emic term throughout the book. For further explanation on how this term is used, see chapter 4.

2. *Freikörperkultur* was a back-to-nature movement celebrating the body and nudity that emerged in the late nineteenth century and was particularly prominent in Germany. In the early twenty-first century, it has to some extent become mainstreamed in the form of nudist beaches, saunas, and sometimes public swimming pools. Calling sauna club brothels *FKK clubs*, which is now widely accepted, is a euphemism and clearly coopts the original meaning of FKK.

3. Having dominated the market since 1962, the Beate Uhse shops filed for bankruptcy unexpectedly in 2017 (*Handelsblatt Today*, 2017) and was replaced by a new online erotica empire Orion, which is a primarily online retailer.

4. The law is based on the concept of sexual self-determination and age of consent. Sexual self-determination is the right of an individual to be able to engage in sexual behavior. The age of consent (*Mündigkeit*) is fourteen. Below this, a person is not considered mature enough to make decisions about sexual acts. However, anyone over the age of twenty-one engaging in sex acts with someone between the ages of fourteen and sixteen can be prosecuted. See Articles 176 and 181 of the German Criminal Code (*Strafgesetzbuch*), accessible at https://www.gesetze-im-internet.de/stgb/__176.html.

5. The Prostitution Act is formally called the Law to Regulate the Legal Relationships of Prostitutes (Prostitutionsgesetz—ProstG). It was passed in 2001 and went into effect January 1, 2002. It is hereafter referred to as Prostitution Act of 2002.

6. Viviana Zelizer (2005) called this the "hostile worlds" approach (20ff).

7. As Ina Hunecke (2011) has shown, the issue of prostitution was not part of the post–World War II feminist movement until the mid-1970s, when a group of sex workers and others founded Hydra, a sex worker rights organization, in Berlin (https://www.hydra-berlin.de/en/). Opposed to the social work approach, which they considered inseparable from control and coercion, and guided by efforts to control venereal diseases, Hydra advocated for autonomy and sex-worker-based training. Similar organizations were formed in other cities, such as Madonna in Bochum in 1981 (https://www.madonna-ev.de) and Doña Carmen in Frankfurt in 1991 (http://www.donacarmen.de). Juxtaposed to these sex-worker-led organizations are faith-based organizations such as SOLWODI (https://www.solwodi.de/) and civic organizations such as KOK (https://www.kok-gegen-menschenhandel.de) that tend to focus on victim identification and the political goal of abolitionism (Hunecke 2011). The legalization of prostitution, as it would be widely called, was a culmination of the efforts of sex worker rights organizations, the political left, and a change in public attitudes. Sex worker rights organizations criticized the prostitution law of 2002 for not addressing the situation of irregular migrants, who were in a situation of particular vulnerability. The Prostitution Protection Law of 2017, with its increased focus on surveillance, also passed despite concerted efforts by sex worker rights organizations.

8. Joachim Renzikowski (2009) writes, "*Die mit der Streichung von Paragraph 180a Absatz 1 Nr 2 STGB verbundene Entkriminalisierung der Förderung der Protitution gehört zu*

den umstrittensten Teilen des Prostitutionsgesetzes. Ihre Revsision wird seitdem immer wieder von verschiedenen Gesetzesintiativen gefordert." (Author's translation: "The decriminalization connected to the deletion of Article 180a, Section 1 and 2 of the Criminal Code is one of the most controversial aspects of the Prostitution Law. Its revision has been demanded repeatedly in different legal reform initiatives.") (133).

9. See the latest report of Steffan, Körner, and Netzelmann (2019) about the assessment of services that health departments offer to sex workers. According to this study, 65 percent of foreign sex workers who contacted health departments did not have any form of health insurance.

10. Neuburg followed the so-called *Düsseldorfer Verfahren*, where sex workers are assessed a pretax in the amount of up to €30, to be paid every day of work, independent of actual earnings. This tax was often collected by the brothel operator. Sex workers could have it adjusted to actual earnings when filing their annual income tax return. Sex worker organizations such as the BSD considered it an unlawful taxing of prostitutes (Rechtslupe 2016).

11. *Neuburg* is a pseudonym to protect the confidentiality of people, organizations, and businesses.

12. See, for example, *Badische Zeitung* 2009; Stern.de 2009.

13. BMFSFJ is the acronym of the Federal Ministry for Family, Seniors, Women, and Youth (Bundesministerium für Familie, Senioren, Frauen und Jugend).

14. This resolution of the European Parliament has only symbolic meaning, as it is up to each European Union member state to develop its own governance regime of prostitution (European Parliament 2014).

15. For state-sponsored news stations, see, for example, the ARD Talkshow *Menschen bei Maischberger* or the WDR talkshow *Hart Aber Fair*.

16. The organization KOK (*Koordinationskreis gegen Menschenhandel*) describes itself as "a German NGO network and coordination office against trafficking in human beings. Currently, KOK consists of 38 member organizations across Germany. This is a unique network as it represents a broad variety of different groups, including faith-based organizations and sex workers' rights groups" (quoted from the website https://www.kok-gegen-menschenhandel.de/en/home).

17. The phrase has been used in Germany at least since 2003 and appears in numerous newspaper and magazine articles. See, for example, *Der Spiegel* 2013; Kiewel et al. 2012; mk online 2016; and Reinsch 2015.

18. According to statistics collected by the Neuburg Police Department.

19. Interview with the director of Kassandra e.V., Nuremberg, summer 2018.

1

SEX IN THE PUBLIC SPHERE

"THE PUBLIC CHARACTER OF THE JOINTLY INHABITED INTERIOR of our lifeworld is both inside and outside at once" (Habermas 2004, 3). Doing ethnographic research in Neuburg was a return home. I had left Germany in the late 1980s when I was in my midtwenties, so it was little surprise that things looked different from what I remembered. Moreover, Neuburg was not just any German city but the city of my childhood and early adulthood. My local dialect marked me instantly as a native to the people I met, even if my vocabulary occasionally included words nobody had used in the last twenty years, and my unfamiliarity with the new public transportation system was met with consternation by locals who insisted that it had always been that way. Although intimately familiar with the culture and the place, I often found myself perplexed by the abundant erotic imagery in public spaces: the blatantly sexualized portrayal of women in media, the pervasive use of sexual double entendres in public speech,[1] and the nonchalance of advertisement for sexual commerce in the cityscape. Compared to the United States, Germany had always seemed a more liberal and permissive society, at least in regard to drinking alcohol, speeding on the autobahn, and sex. Nevertheless, I was unprepared for the brave new world of erotic invitations I encountered on billboards, in advertisements, and in public slogans, and I was surprised that they were tailored almost exclusively to heterosexual men. Had I turned into a prude, or had Germany turned backward into a dark age of unbridled sexism, gender inequality, and heterosexual male gaze?

As I tried to gain entry to Neuburg's world of commercial sex for my ethnographic project, I had plenty of time to contemplate this sexual imagery and wonder how it was different from that in the United States. Could this visual landscape reveal something about why prostitution was so much more palatable to Germans than to Americans—a country where clients are customarily presented as perverts, considered social misfits, and referred to as deviants, and where sex workers are made either the subject of a pervasive rescue industry or the object of public shaming or both? Was there a relationship between how sexuality was presented in society and how prostitution was regulated by the government, with sex work treated as "a job like any other," the slogan used by sex worker activists? More broadly, how was sexuality imagined in a society that decided to legalize prostitution at a moment when many of its neighbors—such as Sweden, Norway, and Iceland—were undertaking steps to restrict it?

By taking the reader with me on a walk through the streets of Neuburg, this chapter explores representations of sexuality in outdoor spaces—its content, audience, and implied meanings—from the perspective of a pedestrian, or what Certeau (1984) has called "a flâneur."[2] Looking at what the German philosopher and sociologist Jürgen Habermas has called "jointly inhabited" public space (2004, 3), as I am recording my own reacquaintance with Germany and discovery of its exterior and interior sexual worlds in outdoor advertisement and public speech, I hope to familiarize the reader with this different imagery: the visible and invisible repertoires of sexual representations and their implied sexual scripts.

Sexuality in Public Spaces

As Habermas (1996) reminds us, public discourse and contestation and the spaces in which they take place are central to democracy: viewpoints are disseminated and challenged, and positions are negotiated. A crucial aspect of public space is the claim to civility and legitimacy (Habermas 1996). Public space is linked to the democratic space of the public sphere, in which people come together and engage in various forms of interaction. Public space and the freedom of members of the public to come together in this space and voice their opinions—the right of assembly and freedom of speech—are staging grounds for civil society and for democracy in action (Habermas 1996). As Judith Butler (2015) has argued, the significance of this aspect of public space has been powerfully illustrated in political demonstrations from the Arab Spring to rallies caused by European Union austerity measures. The same can be said for FEMEN, a feminist protest organization where women protesters command visibility via political slogans written on their exposed breasts. Taking one's concerns to the street is perhaps the most basic expression of democracy.

Unlike private spaces, public spaces are accessible to—and to some extent owned by—the public. Users of this space are expected to abide by a public code of conduct. Moreover, pedestrians and others who use this space ensure the civility of conduct and its reinforcement through what Jane Jacobs (1992) has called the "eyes on the street." Public space thus carries with it an expectation of legitimacy and civility: what is seen in public and what one expects in public is civility. At the same time, public space and the public order are of course highly contested and marked by a constant intrusion of competing interests, of which advertisement is but one (Habermas 1996). In his *Practice of Everyday Life*, Certeau (1984) juxtaposes the repressive strategies employed by organizational power structures—whether municipalities, corporations, or private owners—against the tactics of those targeted and subjugated by these strategies. As Certeau emphasizes, the tactics available to the urban flâneur, the pedestrian, or the customer are always more restricted than the spaces and contexts created and organized by more powerful entities. Even the illustrious advertiser Howard Gossage (1995) complained about how outdoor advertisement imposes itself on the user: it forces itself into the viewer's field of vision.

Visual representations that inform our sexual imaginaries often operate on a subliminal level, barely brought to the surface of conscious reflection, noticed only when implicit rules are violated or when unfamiliar sexual images jolt us into tangible discomfort and emotional dissonance. This is particularly the case in advertisement, which is also a critical element of our social reality (Goffman 1979; Hellmann and Zurstiege 2008; McLuhan 1970; Zurstiege 2008).

Contemplating and analyzing images in Neuburg's public spaces, I situate them within the contemporary debate about the "sexualization of culture" (e.g., Attwood 2006, 2014; Gill 2012) and "pornification of society" (Jensen 2007; Paasonen, Nikunen, and Saarenmaa 2007), as it has been articulated by a number of media critics. As these scholars argue, sexual and pornographic imagery has become ubiquitous in our everyday lives and constitutes an objectification of women, which harms and humiliates them as public actors and degrades our society with the commodification of sexuality and intimacy. There are, however, a number of problems with this argument. First, implying a generalized, global sexualization and pornification, these studies often overlook the specific cultural contexts in which such images are placed, generalizing from an American mediascape to locations beyond US borders that are not further specified. This obscures the cultural contexts in which such images are placed. While it is readily understood that obscenity laws in a conservative or theocratic society—for example, Iran—will differ from those in a secular modern democracy like the United States, it is less obvious how cultural imaginaries differ between the United States and Germany, which have a considerable degree of overlapping media space.

This leads to my second point. Studies of sexualization of culture do not differentiate between the virtual public space on one hand, in which print, television, video, and internet media are predominantly consumed, and the tangible public space in which outdoor advertisement is encountered on the other (Jacobs 2007; McNair 2013; Ray 2007). This is an important oversight. The Australian feminist Lauren Rosewarne (2007, 2005) has argued that sexualized images encountered in outdoor advertisement follow a different logic from similar images consumed in private spaces. For example, virtual porn sites visited on a personal computer or laptop presuppose a degree of privacy where the rules of public behavior do not apply. When we are browsing the internet, we are not engaging in a face-to-face public interaction, in a social space that, as Goffman (1972) argued, commands a deliberate set of rules and has its own dynamics. When using the internet, we are either in private or not expected to behave as if we are in public. Even if we use the internet in public spaces, common courtesy demands that we treat others' digital screens as extensions of their personal privacy. In public spaces, face-to-face interaction with others is unavoidable; we are keeping up appearances (Goffman 1959b, 1972) to avoid revealing too much about ourselves. As pedestrians walking through the city, we put on our public masks, steer toward our destination, and interact with others and the world around us in a carefully orchestrated and disciplined way.

Outdoor Advertisement and Slogans

The ubiquity with which women were objectified in Neuburg's public spaces—like in other cities in Germany—stood in sharp contrast to the cityscapes with which I was familiar in the United States. If the tolerance of sexualized advertisement was surprising, the nonchalance with which sexual commerce was advertised to the broadest possible audience was astounding. With ads for photography studios offering erotic shoots placed next to ads for mega brothels, the boundaries between commercial and noncommercial sex were blurred.

Nudity in Germany was not limited to advertisement, however. American students whom I took on a trip to Germany were puzzled by the not uncommon sight of nudity of real people in real spaces. Public nudity, accepted in both East and West Germany before 1989, became even more common after reunification. Public swimming pools sometimes featured a "textile-free" section, and modest saunas had transformed into grand water parks featuring a multitude of culturally themed sauna experiences all to be enjoyed naked. Saunas, a mainstay of leisure and wellness activity in Germany, have always been decidedly nonerotic. In fact, nudist environments generally tend to have an unspoken etiquette to avoid any behavior that could be construed as erotic.

However, while nudity was unspectacular and often not eroticized, ads featuring nudes were a different story. Unlike the ordinary bodies of real women and men visiting public swimming pools, tanning themselves in the park, or steaming in saunas, the naked bodies depicted in advertisement— whether in store windows, on banners, or on construction scaffolding— were young, attractive, female . . . and overwhelmingly sexualized. Women's breasts, their buttocks, or both were featured in a wide variety of product ads for everything from coffee machines, cell phone plans, and cigarettes to cold cuts and frozen dinners. They covered the walls of bus stops, subway stations, and house fronts. Had I just never noticed them before?

As I reacquainted myself with the city, I noticed that commercial venues were not the only spaces that featured sexy young women. Neuburg's tourist information center—situated next to the train station and functioning as the city's official welcome hub—greeted me with a poster of a woman posing on all fours. Dressed in a pink bikini, she was balancing a ball on her behind while a soccer player lunged from the background, reaching for the delicately balanced ball. Then I noticed the title "What Men Love" and realized that the poster advertised a new book about soccer, Germans' favorite sports. I thought about my niece, a rising soccer star, and wondered how she would feel about this poster. Unlike in the United States, where sports and eroticism are deeply culturally linked—for example, in the institution of cheerleaders or the spectacular advertisements of the Super Bowl—I had

Figure 1.1 "What Men Love." Advertisement poster for a book on soccer displayed in Neuburg's Tourist Information Office.

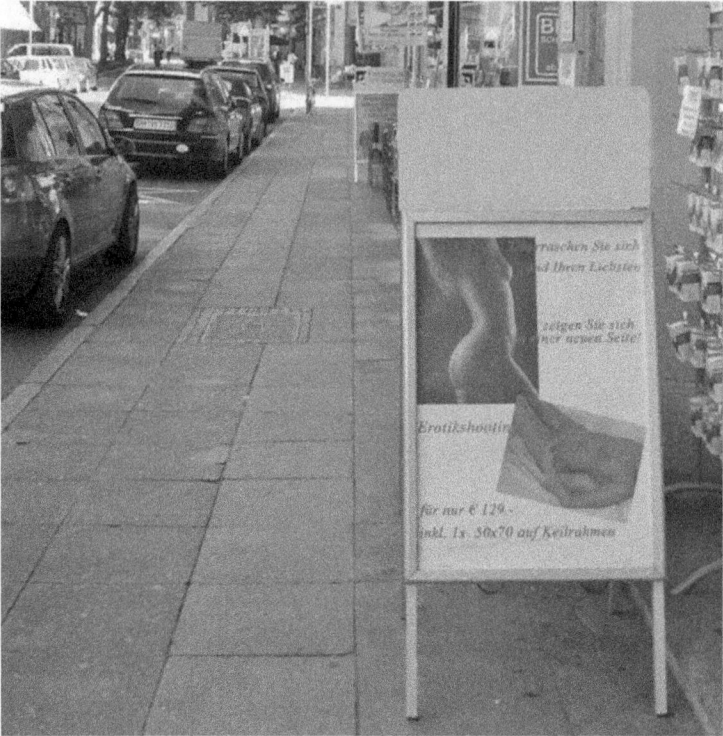

Figure 1.2 Advertisement for erotic photoshoots.

never before noticed the sexualization of soccer in Germany. The fact that this was placed at a tourist information center, as if put up in the name of the city, suggested an even greater stamp of public approval.

Strolling down a busy thoroughfare, I came across a large photo of a nude woman lying on the floor, displayed on a tripod on the walkway: it was an advertisement for a photography studio's offer of "erotic photo shoots" as Valentine's Day gifts. Making a quick stop at a pastry shop to grab a bite to eat and getting in line for my turn, I noticed two chocolate bars on the display counter: one featuring the naked body of a young woman, the other a clean-cut face of a middle-aged man. Another suggestion for a Valentine's present, I realized.

Many of the images featuring nude or seminude women were ads for consumer items, but there were also ads for sexual services. Although individual sex workers could be cited for violating public decency if their ads

Figure 1.3 Taxicab advertising a strip club.

were too explicit, ads for brothels were not particularly hidden. Eye-catching diminutive smart cars covered with images of a seductive bikini-clad blonde darted through the city advertising a new Club Love. Hefty Hum-vees, strategically placed at sites notorious for traffic jams, announced in great pink letters the grand opening of a new flat-rate sex club. Across the street, a Mercedes Benz from the local taxi fleet displayed the logo of the Flamingo, the new sauna club brothel I would eventually study, similar to the taxicab advertising a local strip club. Most baffling, maybe, was the large banner for a local eros center that hung from a ten-story building at the entrance of a busy pedestrian area. Not limited to the red light district or adult-only areas, such ads for sexual commerce throughout the city merged with the themes and tone of advertisement more generally: the "sex sells" marketing model looked barely distinguishable from the "sex for sale" advertising model. While I considered myself a staunch defender of an open approach to sexuality and prostitution, I could not help but find such blatant sexism in public spaces irritating, if not infuriating . . . and disappointing.

Sexual messages were not limited to visual ads but were also prominent in advertisement slogans. In fact, the use of sexual double entendres and ambiguity in advertisement was as boundless as it was creative. There was the big-box electronics retailer Saturn, whose long-running advertisement slogan "Stinginess is sexy" (*Geiz ist geil*) had been strategically positioned in high-visibility settings, with or without the presence of what looked like a nude and seductive female cyborg and her nerdy male human counterpart. Even more blunt was the slogan of the supermarket chain Real, where the handrails on the shopping carts encouraged the shopper to "Just go and get it for yourself" (*Besorg's dir doch einfach*), using the colloquial slang for masturbation, thus linking the act of consumption to sexual release.

As sociologist Irving Goffman has argued in his seminal book *Behavior in Public* (1963a), public space calls for a public demeanor: a limited revelation of the self and a comportment of respect for the privacy and personal space of others. However, the allusions to sexual arousal that I encountered in advertising seemed to grossly invade the privacy of the persons using public space. Moreover, by adopting the lingo of youth culture and its generalization of sexual arousal as being cool, Saturn's "Stinginess is sexy" managed to blur the meanings of the desiring subject and the desirable object (*geil* meaning both "sexy" and "horny," but also "awesome" or "great"). While neither of these meanings was particularly convincing, "Stinginess is sexy" worked on a number of fronts. First, it stunned the audience because of its liberal use of the slang expression for "sexy" or "horny," more typically associated with adolescent language. Secondly, it extolled stinginess and associated it with sex appeal and sexual arousal. And finally, by doing so, it created an association between the brand name, its products, and desire. Whether the gratification was to come in the form of a purchase, in the heightened sex appeal the purchase would bestow on a new owner, or through the sexual arousal of the purchase itself was left up to interpretation. Implied in this all, however, was that the electronics retailer managed to seamlessly weave together desire and desirability into a discourse of consumption.

City institutions also participated in this game of sexual double entendres. On the central square, placed between posters for a DJ party and a new nightclub, the office for cultural affairs invited the onlooker with "Book me!" (*Buch mich!*), a phrase used more commonly by escorts. A poster in the public bus suggested, "With the night ticket you can last longer!" (*Mit der Nachtkarte kann man länger!*). Contemplating what the beaming faces of the couple in the ad might have to do with "lasting longer" (was this a Viagra ad?), I realized a few moments later that it was an advertisement for the newly available night buses. Last but not least, a huge banner hanging from a high-rise building visible from a main highway artery advocated for a controversial public works project: "Neuburg 21 is coming! Are you coming too?" (*Neuburg 21 Kommt! Kommen Sie auch?*)—an allusion often used in sauna clubs and brothels when they tell their clients, tongue in cheek, "You should come more often!"

What was striking about these slogans and ads was how blatantly they transgressed the rules of interaction that are supposed to govern behavior in public. The advertisement voice adopted a stance of intimacy between the ad and its audience that would be utterly inappropriate between actual people. Double entendres are convenient rhetorical devices in advertisements, as the sexually explicit connotation can always be blamed on the fantasy of the observer (Holtz-Bacha 2011). Similarly, for the city to adopt a stance of double entendres and sexual intimacy with the passersby, just as commercial sex venues did, signaled a new rule for interactions in public: that such messages were legitimate and appropriate. To the extent that such ads enjoyed broad acceptance, they also facilitated a new status quo of normalizing transgressions of public behavior and invasion of privacy from above.[3]

As I was learning my way around the city again, I could not help but find such invitations to sexual gratification irritating. This did not look like the sexual enlightenment I had expected—not from the Germany I had grown up in during the '70s and '80s, nor from the Germany that had passed a law making sex workers eligible for the same labor protections as other workers and no longer subject to discrimination in the name of morality. Some people were surprised or even alarmed when I pointed out this blatant everyday sexism, admitting that they had never noticed it or paid any attention to it. Others were blasé about it, like the agent at the Public Transportation Authority's customer service, who quipped, "For every person complaining about sexist advertisement, we have ten callers complimenting us on such ads."

Encounters Underground

While such ads and slogans were a serious damper on my notion of a sexually enlightened Germany, the following excerpt from my field notes illustrates the consequences they had on me and my interactions with others. They made me relive experiences I'd had as a teenager and fall back into automated reflexes I had developed to dodge uncomfortable situations in

Figure 1.4 Outdoor advertisement in downtown Neuburg.

public: avoiding a stranger's gaze or the chance of uninvited eye contact; making way or getting out of the path when someone was walking toward me; keeping my knees close together when sitting on the train; and a range of other deeply gendered and internalized behaviors. If the visual cues that I describe in the following passage had such an effect on me, what kind of effect did they have on those who had become accustomed to them?

I hurried down the stairs to the subway station when I heard the train approaching and arrived in time on the platform. Once in the train, I squeezed through the aisles as I made my way past people to the only available seat next to a window and sat down. Opposite me sat a nondescript middle-aged man in a shabby suit, his legs spread open wide in a gesture that has recently been termed manspreading.[4] *I knew this posture. And how I dreaded it! My only option was to sit with my knees wedged between his legs, leaving me with the balancing act of not touching his thighs at every turn the subway made. A déjà vu of anger and entrapment overcame me.*

The new train ran very quietly. Some people were reading books. The man across from me was reading Bild—*the infamous German Boulevard paper, read by millions of people every morning on their way to work. With its bright-red logo, huge format, and oversize lettering and also because it was advertised excessively in the streets,* Bild *was hard to miss. The man opened* Bild, *burying his face behind its six square feet and presenting to me the full glory of the front and back of the paper. Of course, my eyes were drawn immediately to the seminude blonde on the lower part of the front page, wearing a silky negligee, her nipples clearly visible under the transparent fabric. I didn't know it yet, but Page One Girl had been a staple of* Bild's *layout for almost three decades.*[5]

I couldn't resist continuing to read. Her name was Jenny: "She likes it wet. . . . She likes to spray herself with water. But she likes it even better if someone brings her some juice." Jenny's dimensions were included: age—twenty-four; eye color—blue; cup size—65B ("firm to the touch"). Her preferences were "quickies, dirty talk, and fellatio," and Jenny's dream man was "passionate, faithful, eloquent." While her arousing image was not lost on me, I wondered whether Jenny looked for a boyfriend or for customers.

As the train moved on, I continued to scan discreetly the large front and back pages of the paper with its huge headlines: "Lawyer threatens parents with lawsuit." Right next to it was a picture of a young couple. Below it, the subtitle: "Because they left Maddie alone in the apartment." A smaller headline informed, "This is the price of whores and sex tourism!"—apparently a story about the CEO of Volkswagen, who had become embroiled for rewarding union reps as well as employees with free all-inclusive "sex tours" to Budapest's famous spas.

As the train started the descent into the city, it provided spectacular views of an urban landscape surrounded by picturesque hills. With every turn, the thighs of the man sitting across from me came precariously close to my own. It took effort to avoid touching them. It was very quiet in the train, everybody absorbed in a private cocoon of silence. All of a sudden, the man across from me dropped the paper and looked straight at me. Instinctively, I turned my head to look out the window, blushing. For whatever reason, I felt it was impossible for me to withstand his gaze. It did not help that a week earlier I had caused a stir for calling out a subway rider for staring at me.

As we got closer to the next station, he pushed the stop button at the middle aisle and said, "Excuse me." As he got up to exit, I drew my legs even closer to my seat. He had left the finished paper behind. A few minutes later, I picked it up inconspicuously. The articles were short, about three lines of text under the headlines, before the reader was referred to pages elsewhere.

Leafing through the paper, I noticed a page entitled "Hello in Neuburg." About a hundred or so small sex ads covered the lower part of the page, with women in provocative postures and nipples blocked out with stars—ads of individual sex workers, local brothels, nudist clubs, wellness oases, erotic arenas, and housewives "ready to spoil you":

"Vicky—new, home and hotel, from Poland." With phone number and URL.

"Tiwa—everything possible." Address and phone number.

"'Harem,' Nudist Club on 3,000 square meters. New: with large open-air range. Sundays two hours for 30 €, Saturdays, three for the price of two, Mondays, two for one."

"Susi, horny for her and him."

"Swinger Club Wednesdays from 10–2pm, Mondays and Wednesdays, new."

"Linda, 30 yrs., from Lithuania, without taboos. The first time in Neuburg East."

"Erospark Mindelsheim. 21 international models, starting at 30 €."

Oddly enough, in this mix of commercial sex ads, some seemed generic romance ads.

The train now went underground. Billboards and large-scale advertisements magically attracted my eyes in the dark tunnels. A glass-encased, illuminated billboard advertised the new cover page of Der Stern *(a liberal weekly news magazine comparable to* Time *magazine), which announced its new cover story: "Love around the world," featuring a collage of couples each in a different exotic surrounding and revealing different positions and degrees of nudity.*

Unpacking Relations in Public

The experience left me seething with anger. Why was I, at fortysomething, moving my legs out of the way to make room for his, even though I was perfectly aware of the manspreading he was engaging in? And what—if anything—did *Bild* and Page One Girl have to do with this?

Walking past large-scale outdoor advertisements alluding to sexual desires was one thing. Encountering sexual depictions in the enclosed space of the subway was another. What was displayed in front of me inside the subway was not fleeting but hard to escape. The windows provided a limited

Figure 1.5 Cover of the newspaper *Bild* with Page One Girl.

visual refuge. They were transparent but also reflective, even more so once the train went underground and the windows became mirrors. Add to this the unspoken rules for women versus men of how to behave in public and occupy public space: the customary manspreading, amplified by the narrow stalls and a seating arrangement that makes riders sit face to face, eye to eye, and thigh to thigh. In this tight public space, what did the presence of *Bild* add to my interaction?

Figure 1.6 Seating arrangement in the subway.

Bild, a tabloid that mixes political news with celebrity gossip, sports, explicit sexual images, and sex ads, does not have a counterpart in the landscape of American newspapers. With a circulation of about four million, *Bild* is one of the most visible newspapers for shaping public opinion at its most basic level (Schrag 2007). It is the newspaper both men and women read—on their breaks at work, at fast-food places, or while on public transportation—and leave behind after they are through with it. The fact that few women who read the paper seem to object to its misogyny might well be an indication of how normalized and invisible it has become to most of them. *Bild* is sold in convenience stores, in supermarkets, and at newspaper stands in busy city streets and subway stations. As a Boulevard Press, mostly sold on "the boulevard," it has much greater presence in public space than other newspapers, an impression reinforced through its excessive branding and ubiquitous outdoor advertisement, with headlines such as "*Bild* educates!," "Daddy—I am gay," "Are these boobs real?," "Boss, your jokes are not funny," and "Somebody has to tell the truth—*Bild*!" These headlines, complete with *Bild*'s well-branded logo, make it likely the newspaper with the widest brand recognition in Germany.

The online version of *Bild* is one click away from the erotic portal *Bild Plus*, an app wherein past Page One Girl pictures and stories can be downloaded for a fee: its slogan, "Get her down on your cell phone" (*Hol sie Dir*

Figure 1.7 Advertisement column with the branded *Bild* logo and slogan. "'Daddy, I am Gay.' Every Truth Needs Someone Courageous to State It."

aufs handy runter), conflates the colloquial phrase for masturbation (*sich einen runterholen*) with downloading the app. From the *Bild* Plus app, the reader can easily follow links to other forms of erotic entertainment. Underscoring its association with sexual commerce, *Bild* also runs regular reports about prostitution and "girls next door" working at local brothels— a strategy some of the mainstream newspapers call a blatant case of covert advertisement.

In fact, *Bild* is a major advertising outlet for commercial sex; three times a week, it dedicates most of page three to sexual commerce in the paper's local distribution area. *Bild* regularly uses sexual depictions of women to sell products and stories, and with its half-page sex ad section— "Hello in Neuburg" (or whatever city the edition is sold in)—it also plays an important role in the marketing of sexual services. Thus, it acts as a conduit between sexual arousal and commercial sexual satisfaction as a normalized fixture in everyday life. In that regard, *Bild* plays a very different role from underground newspapers, sexual weeklies that may be found in big cities in the United States or elsewhere, or sex ads on the internet. *Bild* nurtures sexual arousal, conditions its readers to associate news with eroticism, and cultivates a visual and verbal vocabulary of a distinct type of sexuality, of a specific form of erotic consumption, and all of this on the boulevard. The paper's ubiquitous accessibility and circulation both reflect and prescribe molds for sexual imaginaries and for commercial and heteronormative sexuality at large.

Counterpublics, or How Democratic Is the Public Space?

It would be wrong, however, to regard such representations of sexuality as monolithic facades. In her critique of Habermas's concept of the public sphere and its importance to democracy, Nancy Fraser coined the term *subaltern counterpublics* (Fraser 1990) to refer to sites of engagement of subordinated groups wherein critiques, identities, and interpretations are articulated, contested, developed, and disseminated. However, sexist advertisement, with its objectification of women and its constant appeal to the sexual imperative of gratification—what others have called the sexualization or pornification of the media—did not stand unopposed. Neuburg's public space also entailed representations that challenged the imagery offered up in commercial and public venues. In the following, I discuss three examples that illustrate such counterpublics and their influence on

Figure 1.8 A common advertisement board for *Bild* in Neuburg's commercial downtown.

sexual imaginary: the feminist Alice Schwarzer and her magazine *Emma*; the writer Charlotte Roche and her debut novel, *Wetlands* (*Feuchtgebiete*) (2013, 2014); and the publicity stunts of FEMEN activists. Such counterpublics challenge the imaginary of sexual norms in advertisement and public slogans that I have described so far.

Alice Schwarzer, one of the most prominent voices of a feminist counterpublic in Germany, has long been a household name for calling out and fighting sexism in the media. Inspired by second-wave feminists such as Gloria Steinem as well as radical feminists such as Andrea Dworkin, Schwarzer started the feminist magazine *Emma* in 1977 and remains its editor in chief as of this writing. In 1978, Schwarzer and her colleagues organized a lawsuit against the so-called men's press: they sued the weekly magazine *Der Stern* for notoriously portraying women in sexually humiliating postures on their magazine covers. The lawsuit attracted enormous attention, but Schwarzer ultimately lost. In 1988, she revived her antisexism and antipornography efforts with the PorNo campaign and remains a vocal critic today. In 2006, Chantal Louis wrote in the magazine *Emma*, "The constant bombardment [with sexualized images] by the media has tangible motives. They are called number of copies sold, viewer ratings, and revenue" (cited in Schwarzer 2007, 187).[6]

Emma has been outspoken on its positions on sexism in the media and prostitution. As was written in one of its issues, "*Emma* stands for: solidarity with the prostitute—but war on prostitution. Prostitution destroys not only the body and soul of women who prostitute . . . but it turns all women into the purchasable gender" (2007, 187).[7] Buoyed by the growing critique of the Prostitution Act of 2002 by prominent politicians such as Ursula von der Leyen—then minister for Family Affairs, Women, Families and Youth (BMFSFJ)—Alice Schwarzer wrote in 2007, "The disastrous reform of 2001, which hurt prostitutes and benefited Zuhälter, brothel operators and traffickers, will be reversed, at least in part. A law to punish clients of victims of sex trafficking is in the making. *Emma*'s often lonely fight in this matter is paying off, a rethinking is happening" (Schwarzer 2007).[8] Her optimism was premature, but the Prostitute Protection Act of 2017, which introduced new regulations for sex workers and brothels, would eventually be passed. Needless to say, Alice Schwarzer has been at odds with sex worker rights organizations and sex-positive feminists as well as others on the political left. Her credibility received a further blow in 2009, when she was featured, larger than life, in *Bild*'s extensive advertisement campaign entitled

"Someone has to speak the truth: *Bild*." She had tirelessly fought against sexism in the media, of which *Bild* had been a prime example, and it was not clear why she suddenly seemed to be advocating for this paper.

When I visited Neuburg in 2008, Alice Schwarzer's giant tome *Thirty-Year Anniversary of Emma* (2007) was displayed prominently in Neuburg's largest bookstore. The following year, the same bookstore featured Charlotte Roche's novel *Wetlands*, piling up hundreds of copies of the book on the floor. Roche's feminism—her embrace of the female body and its fluids and the pursuit of men as objects of desire—broke radically with Schwarzer's focus on sexuality as a staging ground for women's oppression and victimization. In fact, as much as Roche challenged sexist dictates of the female body, she toyed with *Emma*'s critique of sex as a transactional bargain when, in an interview with German president Christian Wulff, she allegedly offered to have sex with him if he voted against the extension of nuclear power.[9] In her enormously successful debut novel, *Wetlands*, where the female protagonist breaks every taboo about feminine body hygiene, Roche offered a critique of the feminine mystique 2.0. Her protagonist explores and describes in detail her hemorrhoids, her menstrual blood, and her dislike for shaving while at the same time relentlessly pursuing the object of her sexual desire. Roche's novel struck a nerve with a new generation of young women and men who saw in her and her protagonist liberators who tore down outdated notions of proper femininity. The impact of Charlotte Roche's message was apparent not only in the phenomenal sales of her book but also in the large and ecstatic crowds of young people who attended her public readings and the numerous talk shows that featured her as a special guest. Roche had clearly become the beacon for a new generation of sexual consciousness and female self-confidence. Her success, however, did not translate to the other side of the Atlantic, where her book and the feature film based upon it (Wnendt 2014) made barely a ripple.[10]

FEMEN activists (Ackermann 2014; Scharff 2017) presented yet another facet of Germany's sexual counterpublic in the first decades of the new millennium. FEMEN originated in Ukraine in 2008, with several national chapters emerging in the succeeding years, including a German branch in 2013. FEMEN activists have staged a series of strikingly effective publicity stunts by unexpectedly exposing their breasts—on which they write political statements—at critical moments in public or political life.[11] The targets of FEMEN stunts have ranged from female objectification in pornography and popular culture to the religious oppression of women, sex trafficking,

Figure 1.9 FEMEN activists protesting the brothel Geiz Club (*Miser Club*). Source: Getty Images.

and unfair labor conditions in brothels. FEMEN activists have organized events against sauna club mega brothels such as the Pascha in Cologne (2012), the Artemis in Berlin (2013), the Paradise in Saarbrücken (2014), and the Geizclub on Hamburg's Reeperbahn. Following a maxim of "taking back our breasts" rather than exploiting their breasts for commercial purposes, FEMEN activists use them as a canvas for their political messages, ideally amplified by the media. The gaze of the viewer is thus automatically attracted to where the activists want it to go: to the political messages written on their breasts.

These three examples of counterpublics illustrate how advertisement's representations of sexuality are challenged in public. If advertisement and public slogans propagate a sexual imaginary favoring a male gaze, where attractive seminude or nude women are used as bait for sexual arousal and appeals to sexual satisfaction abound, these counterpublics challenge such sexual imaginary and offer a counterimagery, including Alice Schwarzer's antipornography and antiprostitution agenda, which presents a focal point of opposition in the public discourse of commercial sex; Charlotte Roche's novel, which offers a collective recalibration of female sexuality and identity; and FEMEN activists, who, although they seem ideologically more in line with the abolitionist politics of Alice Schwarzer, use the sexualization of their bodies for their own political purposes. If the dominant discourse of sexuality casts women as inviting objects for the sexual desire of men and puts everyone on a hamster wheel of sexual pursuit, the openness in which this discourse is staged also produces a repertoire of counterimages, causing openings for oppositional messages, visions, and imaginaries.

Conclusion

Ethnographies often start with a tale of the author's entry into the field (Bradburd 1998). In a process described as culture shock and alienation, we ethnographers must familiarize ourselves with new cultural mores, a different language, and unfamiliar patterns of interaction. While we are busily observing, adapting, and trying to understand what is going on around us, we are particularly sensitive to the stimuli of this new environment and their effects on our minds and bodies. This process of cultural immersion, of learning to live and operate in a new culture, is an intensely personal and subjective process, and often an intensely emotional one (Behar 1997; Davies 2010).

To me, this cultural immersion into the collective sexual imaginary of contemporary Germany and the heightened sensitivity that goes along with it was most palpable during my first five months of research. Its novelty did not survive the second leg of my fieldwork the following season, by which time my initial sensitivity to all things sexual in Neuburg's cityscape had vanished. As a new returnee to Germany, not quite used to this repertoire of explicit sexual imagery tailored to heterosexual men, I saw a world of erotic invitations and endless appeals to orgasm, where rousing sexual appetites and suggestions on how to satisfy them were as unspectacular as fast-food advertisements. By the time I returned to the field again the following winter, the novelty had worn off, and my internal barometer for registering erotic messages had been recalibrated.

What does this excursion into the cityscape of Neuburg tell us about prostitution or about the collective sexual imaginary in Germany more generally? Charting the visual landscape of my stroll through the city revealed a public space saturated with salacious images. Sexist advertisement, abundant and versatile, focused on a narrow male heterosexual gaze featuring young, slim, and attractive women in seductive poses. This iconography of sexualized advertisement merged rather seamlessly with sexual commerce, with women placed in the role of erotic bait. Almost four decades ago, feminist philosopher Luce Irigaray, in her influential essay "This Sex Which Is

Not One," described such a gendered positioning through the concept of the male sexual imaginary (1997):

> Woman, in this sexual imaginary, is only a more or less obliging prop for the enactment of man's fantasies. That she may find pleasure there in that role, by proxy, is possible, even certain. But such pleasure is above all a masochistic prostitution of her body to a desire that is not her own, and it leaves her in a familiar state of dependency upon man. Not knowing what she wants, ready for anything, even asking for more, so long as he will "take" her as his "object" when he seeks his own pleasure. Thus she will not say what she herself wants (Irigaray 1997, 364).

Irigaray's analysis still fits the inviting smiles and alluring gestures of the uniformly attractive young women in the ads of Neuburg's visual landscape today, which serve as objects of desire for men and subjects of identification for women.

There is a new message in this sexualized space, however: the many verbal allusions to sexual gratification. Rather than limiting the message to sexual arousal, these messages seem to appeal to an unspoken right—if not obligation—to orgasm. Finally, we see an intrusion of such imagery into urban space beyond a dedicated red light district. Considering urban zoning laws, this is surprising. As I show in the next chapter, such zoning restrictions are based on very concrete definitions of where sexual commerce can be placed, where it is prohibited, and which populations must be protected.

My experience of riding the tram illustrated the intensification of space as an intersubjective arena. Its semipublic space entailed a texture, a code of conduct distinctly its own. Placing pairs of riders vis-à-vis each other set the stage for highly gendered face-to-face interactions. Through the presence of *Bild*, the gendered aspects of this intersubjective space became turbocharged. By disregarding the privacy of other participants, *Bild* imposed on me a heterosexual male gaze, independent of whether the man sitting across from me reading the paper was even aware of this fallout. If public space and its sexist advertisement position women automatically as sexual bait, the subway encounter turned this scenario from a hypothetical possibility to a seemingly inescapable proposition. The examples of counterpublics, however, also remind us that sexist representations in public do not stand unopposed. Thus, even though sexual advertisement is a recurrent theme in the everyday landscape of the city, it is also intensely opposed. This was illustrated in Alice Schwarzer's enduring feminist voice, in Charlotte Roche's rewriting of femininity, and in FEMEN activists' use of their bodies as canvases for political messages.

At the beginning of this chapter, I posed a question: What does the visual landscape of the city reveal about a common sexual imaginary and a collective stance on prostitution? The representations examined here present Germany as a society less squeamish about nudity, public sexuality, and sexual gratification than the United States. However, legalizing prostitution obviously did not mean a greater alertness about sexism in the media. The realization that Germans no longer viewed prostitution as immoral—which had been the justification for the Prostitution Act of 2002—did not mean they had become collectively more aware about how mainstream media relegated women to the position of sexual lure. Luce Irigaray's comment from 1977 about the prominence of a male sexual imaginary that positions women as sexual objects was alive and well in Neuburg's outdoor advertisement and slogans in 2010. If anything, it seemed that the visual language of advertisement, its merging with a more general representation of commercial sex, and its ubiquity in spaces beyond the red light district had saturated all aspects of public space, even though there also were counterpositions.

In conclusion, then, what looked like a relatively liberal legislation in regard to prostitution was accompanied by a form of antiquated sexism, which—to my Americanized sense of interaction in public, at least—felt uncomfortable and intrusive in regard to both my space and my sexual privacy. At the same time, such a public space enabled a different calibration of sexuality where nudity was ordinary, sexualized poses were the norm, and sexual commerce was publicly marked, thus paradoxically making sexuality both more and less visible.

Many media scholars have criticized what they call the sexualization or even pornification of society. Challenging these notions, media scholar Brian McNair (2013) has embraced what he has termed *porn chic*. Leaning on Habermas's concept of the public sphere and its central role in democracy, McNair makes a parallel argument about what he calls the *pornosphere* as crucial to advancing a sexual democracy. Like the public sphere, McNair argues, the pornosphere—the public space comprised of porno videos, internet sex sites, erotic performances, and sexual services, to name but a few—provides a space for dialogue and contestation where positions are advocated and challenged and new societal positions on sexuality are advanced. While this is readily evident in the growing movement toward lesbian, gay, transsexual, and queer rights, he argues, it is also reflected in the growing ability of women in Western democracies to self-confidently enjoy their sex appeal and market it for their own financial gain—as, for example, in the case of Madonna, Kim Kardashian, or Paris Hilton, who have managed to use their sexualized bodies for their own financial gain.

Notes

1. For example, this was seen in public slogans inviting the onlooker "to come" or "come more often," which is synonymous in Germany with "cumming" and frequently used in a sexual context.

2. *Flânerie* is a French term that describes the practice of strolling through a city in a leisurely manner. The term has undergone a significant change in meaning among cultural theorists of urban space, from "loitering" to a distinct experience of the city and urban life (see Certeau 1984). One reason why this term is used regularly in French but lacks a precise translation in English might be that French cities—and European cities generally—are more pedestrian-centered than their American counterparts.

3. This astute observation was made by the literary theorist Lisa Propst, my friend and colleague at Clarkson University.

4. *Manspreading* is a term that was coined in 2013 on social media sites in the United States, criticizing the way some men tend to sit in subways, spreading their thighs wide open and thus invading the space of others—usually women. Compared with the manspreading in New York City subways, where the phrase originated, manspreading in Neuburg was even more invasive, as seats on the tram were arranged in stalls of four on either side, one pair of riders facing the other pair across from them.

5. Page One Girl was discontinued in 2012, after twenty-eight years (*Telegraph* 2012).

6. "*Der mediale Dauerbeschuss hat handfeste Motive, und die heissen Auflagenhöhe, Einschaltquote, Umsatz. Wie praktisch wenn die Zielgruppe für Handys und CDs. . . . immer jünger und damit grösser wird*" (Schwarzer 2007, 187).

7. "*Für Emma gilt: Solidarität mit den Prostituierten—aber Kampf der Prostitution. Denn sie zerstört nicht nur Körper und Seele der sich prostituierenden Frauen . . . sie macht alle Frauen zum käuflichen Geschlecht*" (excerpt from Chantal Louis from the magazine *Emma*, cited in Schwarzer 2007, 187).

8. "Die fatale Reform von 2001, die Prostituierten geschadet und von der Zuhälter, Bordellbetreiber, und Menschenhändler profitiert haben wird rückgangig gemacht, zumindest zum Teil. Ein Gesetz zur Bestrafung von Zwangsprostituierten ist geplant. Emmas oft recht einsamer Kampf in dieser Sache hat sich gelohnt, ein Umdenken beginnt" (Schwarzer 2007, 269).

9. *Der Spiegel*, November 14, 2010. AKW Debatte.

10. That the book became a runaway success in Germany but not in the United States indicates cultural differences. However, it might also be an expression of US hegemony in regard to media, as cultural products travel more easily from the United States to Germany than the other way around.

11. See femen.org; Fetz 2013. Femen Aufschrei in der Herbertstrasse.

2

THE DECLINE OF
THE RED LIGHT DISTRICT

A Night Out

The Maxxim was my last destination for the night. A striptease and hostess bar in the heart of the historic red light district (RLD), the Maxxim was small, nestled between similar bars. With its bright-red neon lights and quaint exterior, it looked inviting. A glass vitrine near the entrance listed the beverage menu on yellowed paper. Tacked below the menu was a series of small, faded four-by-six-inch prints of past striptease performances. Not a particularly high-tech advertisement, *I thought.*

I walked up the six or seven steep steps and entered a small bar with a low ceiling and the bright-red plush decor so characteristic of red light establishments. I sat down in one of the booths, from where I could observe what was happening at the bar as well as on the pole-dance stage without appearing too conspicuous. The bartender was a woman in her late fifties, short and stocky, with black hair and a ponytail. She looked a bit perplexed as she came to my booth and asked me what I wanted to drink. I ordered a glass of mineral water for the stiff price of €10.

It had been an eventful evening so far. I had visited a video porn shop, where I'd chatted with a young attendant at the counter, who quickly put away his sandwich when he saw me walking up to him. I asked him about the video booths in the back of the shop, a technology I had thought would be long gone by now. He told me there were still men who came to borrow videos and watch them on site, in these booths. "And after each use, the booths have to be cleaned," he said, ending with a meaningful pause.

After the video porn shop, I braved an attempt to enter the oldest Laufhaus in the city, a hotel brothel spread out over three floors and several houses.

Figure 2.1 Display case outside of a strip club with "dollar bills" required to tip dancers.

Before I could get up the stairs to the second floor, however, a tall middle-aged woman in a white lab coat intercepted me. Pointing to my outfit—a T-shirt, a midlength brown skirt, and Birkenstock sandals—she shook her head and told me in no uncertain terms that I was not going to go upstairs. My outfit and age probably made it clear to her that I was not working there, and thus I had no business being there.

I had also gone into a large multistory erotica building that featured a porn shop on the first floor, a porno cinema on the second, a gay porno cinema on the third, and a Laufhaus on the fourth. I built up my courage and decided to go into the porno cinema. The attendant at the turnstile entry generously waved me through without asking for the obligatory €10 entrance fee. Immediately, I found myself lost in a maze of dark rooms connected by see-through windows and glory holes. I heard ecstatic moaning but was uncertain whether it was coming from the loudspeakers or live action. After making out the silhouette of a man fondling himself, accompanied by a soundscape of eerie, ecstatic shrieks, I decided I was not quite ready for it and moved on.

The small bar of the Maxxim, although it was almost abandoned, was comforting after my excursion in the porno cinema. A large TV positioned above the bar ran a short clip of a woman in a hot tub. Her hand was resting on the chest of a man sitting next to her while he looked at another woman glancing at him seductively from a distance. I soon realized it was on an endless loop but could not stop myself from looking at the screen again and again.

Three or four women were sitting or standing at the bar, waiting for customers to entertain, I assumed. One couple sat at a small table. This was obviously not a regular bar, and I felt somewhat out of place here. Selma, as the barkeeper later introduced herself, came back to my booth half an hour later, asking whether I wanted something else. Still sipping on my expensive water, I declined but asked her whether there would be a striptease performance. "That will cost extra," she said, shrugging her shoulders as she walked away.

Another twenty or thirty minutes went by, during which the women at the bar talked to each other in low voices while the couple at the table seemed engaged in something other than a romantic conversation. Then, a woman in a sheer negligee walked toward the pole dance stage. I realized that she was one of the women who had been standing at the bar. Music started to play, and she began to dance. The other women, including the bartender, followed and sat on the benches around the stage. As the dancer began to sway and pirouette in her high heels, her movements revealed her ample, firm body. Stretching her leg up along the pole, she exposed her smooth muscular thighs. The women and I cheered her on, and both the dancer and her audience began to get absorbed in the performance. At one point, I noticed a man peeking in from the outside, but he was gone when I looked again. Meanwhile, Selma had gotten a stack of what looked like American one-dollar bills, but they had a depiction of a naked woman rather than a president; she handed them out to us and then put one of them in the dancer's thong—the customary form of tips that was also an invitation to reveal another piece of clothing. Diana, as the dancer would introduce herself later, smiled at her and began to take off her white negligee, slowly revealing her curves while looking at us. Our little crowd got more and more enthralled, clapping and screaming with excitement. Diana got closer toward her audience, presumably her fellow hostesses, with a seductive look in her eyes. One of the women raised her fake one-dollar bill to attract Diana's attention and then tucked it into her thong. In one skilled move, Diana opened her bra and took it off, cupping her breasts with her hands. Her dance became ever more seductive, and both performer and audience were visibly immersed in her erotic performance. After she took off her thong, the last piece of clothing, which revealed her shaved pubic area, she ended with a split-leg performance on the floor. We applauded enthusiastically. By then, I noticed that the only man who had been in the bar had left.

The shared intimacy of Diana's performance had broken the ice among us. Selma sat down at my table, followed soon by the other women, and told me about how hard it had become to run a striptease club. It was not in demand at all anymore, and here in Neuburg, the men were particularly prudish. By then, all her dancers had become hostesses. Her boss used to own three clubs, including one in Cologne, she said. In the past, the business had always been great. But now, nobody came to see striptease anymore, much less wanted to pay for one.

A few minutes later, Diana came back in her regular clothes and sat down at our table. Still radiating from the excitement her performance had generated, she explained that she had not danced in a long time and in the beginning did not feel like dancing at all. But after Selma asked her and after she saw how excited we got, she found her old passion rekindled.

Field notes, May 2009

My visits to Neuburg's red light district left me with the feeling of being in a time warp, of plunging into a bygone era. My experience at the Maxxim, its dreary emptiness, and Diana's nostalgic performance for her fellow hostesses and me rather than for a paying male clientele hinted at drastic changes, if not the decline of the district. This chapter explores the gradual disappearance of prostitution venues from Neuburg's historic red light district and the emergence of new and larger brothels at the city's periphery and in its surrounding cities. Many of the people I would meet in the district referred to the 1970s and '80s as "the golden years" (*die goldenen Jahre*) of the RLD. In this chapter, I trace the decline of the red light district and the spatial reorganization of the sex industry that emerged in the periphery and show the processes by which this transformation happened.

The landscape of prostitution in Neuburg had changed dramatically since the 1990s. In tandem with the city government's tightening grip, there were larger structural transformations. The gradual closing of US military bases since the end of the Cold War in 1990 meant the disappearance of a substantial number of clients, while growing mobility had made decentralized destinations in the periphery more easily reachable. The internet was another new development that helped to direct clients to a variety of new venues, both online and offline. At the international level, the expansion of the European Union led to a dramatic shift in the demographics of sex workers in Germany, as a high proportion of international labor migrants were now women from Eastern Europe (TAMPEP 2009a and 2009b; Staiger 2009).

While the RLD shrunk, sexual commerce moved increasingly into other areas. Apartment brothels, the least noticeable kind of erotic establishments, had emerged in the city at large, while new mega brothels had set up shop in the city's periphery. With this process of restructuring, prostitution had paradoxically become both less and more visible: less because fewer such businesses remained in the red light district, the walkable center where pedestrians intimately experienced city life up close, and more because new venues such as eros centers and sauna clubs had opened up in the industrial urban fringe and in neighboring cities. They became larger in scale and, with oversize pink and red signs, were visible even to motorists on nearby freeways. Nevertheless, inside these new spaces, sexual commerce had transformed into a more discreet and private experience, unlike in the red light district, where clients could barely avoid rubbing shoulders with others.

Sexual Commerce and Its Spatial Context

Although prostitution is legal in Germany, the geography of prostitution varies greatly from city to city and state to state, as cities and communities have considerable freedom about how to manage and regulate it. Some states, such as Bavaria and Baden Württemberg, altogether prohibit prostitution in communities under thirty thousand inhabitants. Cities such as Frankfurt, Cologne, Hamburg, and Stuttgart have designated red light districts. Some cities, such as Berlin, despite being dubbed the "sin city"[1] during the interwar years, don't have any dedicated red light areas at all.

Scholars who study the geography of prostitution have observed two seemingly parallel trends: the move of commercial sex from outdoor to indoor prostitution and from red light districts to decentralized locations (Hubbard and Whowell 2008; Bernstein 2007). The newly dispersed "contemporary markets in sexual labor" (Bernstein 2007, 2) escape the public scrutiny of law enforcement and city officials. Brents and Sanders's (2010) argument about the mainstreaming and upscaling of sex industries also helps to explain this trend of new sex markets situated away from traditional red light districts. They show the ways in which Nevada's sex industry has undergone many of the same trends as other sectors of the tourist industry, from rationalizing to the emergence of theme parks and the focus on emotional labor in order to create authentic and satisfying leisure services, mostly performed by freelancers. By making commercial sex more mainstream in regard to its economic and social integration, sexual advertisement also becomes more acceptable and marketable, thus exposing a larger audience to this industry. In this mainstreaming, Brents and Sanders (2010, 43) argue, "sex-industry businesses can adopt traditional business forms such as corporate structures, vertical and horizontal integration, chains, franchises, and marketing techniques and traditional forms of financing" and include "horizontal integration of sex and non-sex related business."

Trends toward mainstreaming and upscaling have been described not only in locations where prostitution is legal, like in the Nevada brothels described by Brents and Sanders (2010), but also in locations where prostitution is criminalized (Agustín 2007; Hubbard and Whowell 2008; Scoular 2010). Bernstein writes, "What is arguably most remarkable about the disparate array of legal strategies that Europeans and North Americans have implemented in recent years is how singular they have been in effect: The overarching trend has been toward the elimination of prostitution from city streets, coupled with the state-facilitated (or de facto tolerated) flourishing of the indoor and online sectors of the sex trade" (2007, 164).[2] To what extent does this trend hold true for Germany, where prostitution had already been tolerated for decades before the Prostitution Act in 2002, and for Neuburg, where sexual commerce had a home in its small but centrally located red light district?

Neuburg's Red Light District

Of all the cities in this densely populated region, only Neuburg had a designated red light district and a police unit on prostitution, colloquially called "the morals" (*die Sitte*)—short for *morals police*, as this unit was called in the 1920s. With the detailed records Neuburg's police department kept about all things related to prostitution and the city's assortment of urban regulations, Neuburg offers critical insight into the development of the geography of commercial sex since the 1980s.

Historically, the red light district in the heart of Neuburg had been the center of sexual commerce in the region. Despite its ongoing shrinkage, about one-fifth of prostitution-related businesses were still located there in 2009,[3] concentrated in an area barely half a square mile in size. The remaining sex-related businesses were spread out over the rest of the city while large-scale mega brothels had emerged in the periphery of Neuburg and the smaller cities surrounding it.

The sociologist Ronald Weitzer defines a red light district (RLD) as a "setting containing a cluster of visible sexually-oriented businesses [that] include strip clubs, porn shops, bars offering sex, peep shows, massage parlors, and brothels" (2014, 703). Such RLDs are "not confined to street-level transactions" (Weitzer 2012, 106). He distinguishes between "single purpose" RLD, where one type of business predominates or exists exclusively, and "variegated" zones, where sex-related businesses exist next to non-sex-related businesses and other vice-related industries such as gambling (106). According to this definition, the RLD in Neuburg was the variegated type. Small striptease and hostess clubs like the Maxxim were situated close to hip restaurants and bars but also next to clubs that served as contact areas for clients and sex workers and where the latter rented out rooms upstairs to take their clients to. One of the table-dance bars, the Las Vegas, which had been popular with American soldiers in the past, still attracted a younger international crowd on weekends. Most such bars, however, had gone the way of the Maxxim, populated by only a few hostesses who waited the better part of an afternoon and evening for clients willing to buy expensive drinks in exchange for their company. Between these aging clubs and brothels were gambling halls with slot machines, the latter also being a common feature in many prostitution businesses. Wedged in between hostess bars, striptease clubs, and brothels was a semiprivate Hells Angels club, another fixture I had noticed in red light districts elsewhere. Hells Angels were a potentially troubling presence, as they had a reputation for being the single largest organized crime group associated with sex trafficking and extortion (Herz and Minthe 2006; Herz 2006). At the edge of the red light district were convenience stores that sold everything from cigarettes and international calling cards to packages of instant soup and liquor. The district was also home to social intervention services such as a needle exchange program and a café for drug users, a secondhand clothes store run by a Christian charity, a church that offered free food to the community once a week, and a café and resource center for sex workers called the Night Owl, which would become the entry point for my contact with the women working in the district.

The Sausage Quarter, as the district was called locally—after a famous late-night sausage stand there—had its own rhythm, with long periods of quiet during the day, when the only people to be seen were the occasional pedestrians taking a shortcut through the district. Sex clients tended to come in shifts: in the early morning hours before work, during lunch breaks, or after work in the evening. On weekend nights, groups of young men cruised the area as the streets became more crowded. Police were never far away, though. Controlling the district in their white and green patrol cars or on foot, they either worked with a vice squad, checking brothels to see whether workers there had valid work and residence permits, or as traffic police, writing tickets for illegal parking or solicitation in public. The latter was particularly confusing, as this was the dedicated red light district.

However, the district did not feature only vice-related commerce and social intervention services. Other attractions included small eateries, cafés, restaurants famous for their local cuisine, and bars with a living room character, drawing in the hip, young, and wealthy. Two of the more popular bars were owned by former Zuhälter. Those in the older generation of ex-Zuhälter were respectfully called *Altluden*,[4] as in OG. These were men who had been active in the area in the 1970s and 1980s, when they had acquired a reputation as local legends, but by now they had retired. Savvy entrepreneurs, they recognized the desirability of the area as an authentic, historically grown district with a certain underworld charm unmatched by most other parts of the city. In fact, one of the new bars owned by an ex-Zuhälter used to be a contact area for a small Laufhaus, the bare-bones type of brothel consisting of individual rooms rented out to sex workers. Instead of clients in search of sex, the bar now attracted intellectuals, bohemians, and others thrilled by a walk on the wild side, for whom mingling in the RLD provided a flair of genuine urban adventures. Even the occasional local dignitary could be found in the tiny bar, as one of the visitors introduced himself to me as the chief of the local fire department.

Visiting the RLD in the evening often turned into an unexpected adventure. At first, I felt a bit uneasy walking into the bars or nightclubs by myself, but I was often surprised by how easy it was to get into conversations with people. Both women and men were gregarious in a way that was uncharacteristic for the locals, who had a reputation of being grumpy and reserved—something even locals themselves readily acknowledge. I was also surprised by the variety of people I met at the clubs—from once-famous prize boxers and bodybuilders to musicians; from erotic event organizers to sculpture artists; and from photographers to retired Zuhälter. Although as a single woman I could have easily come across as being in search of customers, I was approached for sex only once, when the man with whom I had engaged in a friendly conversation suddenly asked what I was charging for the hour. As I learned later, such questions were clearly a form of solicitation, which was prohibited in the district.

While the center of the RLD was for pedestrians only—a feature common to urban downtowns in Germany—the streets in its perimeter were moderately busy and included one where street prostitution took place. During the day, young women mostly from Romania and, according to police officers and social workers, often underage, stood next to the flower shops or in front of the small hotels. Occasionally, a car stopped, and a driver rolled down the window, trying to talk to a young woman, after which either she got into the car or he drove off by himself. Police and social workers watched the district with some concern; some local politicians were outraged.

This street prostitution was regarded as particularly notorious. According to police officers and social workers, it was controlled by Zuhälter who trafficked underage girls from Eastern Europe. Although one might expect that the district would be an appropriate locale for street prostitution, it was officially banned in this area. The city had closed off roads, created one-way streets, and put up no-parking signs but had not been able to eliminate the trade.

Many of the names of the bars and clubs in the RLD were in English, as they had been when I'd visited the district in the early 1980s. Generally, English-language signage is common in Germany. Its ubiquity in the RLD, however, hinted at the strong presence of US soldiers who had been stationed on nearby bases for several decades, as they had been in many other parts of the country since the end of World War II. The concentration of brothels in Germany generally used to be a good indicator of US military installations and their personnel (Enloe 1989; Höhn 2002). While the bases and their soldiers had gradually disappeared after the end of the Cold War, the names of the clubs remained, as well as a cultural affinity for all things American in the RLD.

Other signs that Neuburg's RLD had intimate relationships with American things and people were the clothing and equipment stores featuring American labels, such as Alpha Industries (a former supplier to the US military), Magnum, and Dickies, including bomber jackets and other somewhat militant-looking apparel and accessories favored by bouncers and security personnel working in nightclubs. Then there were the fake one-dollar bills I had noticed in the Maxxim, which were used as scrip money to tip dancers. Another manifestation of Americana was the decor of the wedding party of a former Zuhälter and his significantly younger bride, both local celebrities of Neuburg. A crowd of guests dressed in rather unconventional wedding outfits—including a middle-aged man wearing an unbuttoned orange Hawaiian shirt and a necklace of predator teeth—and curious onlookers had gathered at the local square to see the bride and groom arrive. Eventually, the newlyweds drove up in a huge 1960s Oldsmobile decorated with a US flag attached to the passenger side and a Confederate flag attached to the driver side.[5] As the Oldsmobile came to a stop, the groom—dressed in a US general's uniform—emerged and escorted the bride out of the car. Then both of them handed out glasses of champagne to guests and onlookers alike. A group of Roma musicians from Bulgaria provided musical entertainment.

Less conspicuous but no less important was the presence of Americana in the memories of the women in the Night Owl, a café for older and impoverished sex workers. Some of the women I met there told me fondly of their experiences with American GIs as their lovers and husbands.

Regulars at the Night Owl

Staff of the Social Services Department, whom I had visited at the beginning of my fieldwork, had suggested the Night Owl as a good place to meet women who worked in the red light district. Starting in the spring of 2008, I visited the Night Owl several nights a week for several months, getting to know some of the women who had been working there for many years. They had grown old together with the bar and hotel owners from whom they had rented rooms. Some were so well-known in Neuburg—cherished rather than maligned—that they were regularly mentioned in the local newspapers as the people who gave the Sausage Quarter its unique and personable character. A surprising number of women at the Night Owl were over fifty, and this was not a coincidence. The staff at the Social Services Department considered old-age and poverty prostitution a central problem of the district and had worked hard to be able to offer these women a safe space, protected from the elements, where they could get hot drinks, warm food, donated clothes, condoms, and medical exams and counseling while also enjoying companionship with other women. Men were not allowed here. The Night Owl was quite successful in attracting these older women getting by on scarce resources but much less so in attracting younger women working the streets.

The regulars at the Night Owl did not greet me with great enthusiasm when a social worker introduced me as someone from the United States who wanted to write a book about prostitution in Germany. As I would learn later, many had grown tired of providing yet another life story to help out someone else's career, as they had done with generations of social work students. They were also a bit perplexed about why I claimed to be from the United States when I spoke the regional dialect. The easiest way to relate to each other turned out to be our experiences with American men and the romantic relationships we had with them.

Elisa was a regular at the Night Owl and a legendary figure in the district. In her matching pink outfit and bright lipstick that emphasized her thick, blond hair, she stood out. Elisa was in her seventies. I never would have guessed her age. She looked like she was in her fifties at most, attractive and well taken care of. She was also gregarious and friendly, making sure newcomers to the café had chairs to sit on and plates to eat from. Often she would act as peacemaker, calming down others and appealing to reason in an environment that was habitually ripe with tension. Elisa was also extremely frugal. She carefully checked that no one gorged themselves at the expense of others; she would often wrap leftovers in a napkin and give them to other women to take home, and she took some home herself as well. "That way I have something to snack on at night, when I get hungry," she explained when she saw the surprised expression on my face.

Like others, Elisa was not eager to share details of her experiences as a sex worker with me and conveniently ignored my questions about her work. She was always eager, however, to tell me about her American husband and her years in the United States and proudly showed me time-worn photos of the two of them that she kept in her wallet. Only in conversation with others at the table did Elisa talk about her long experience of working in the district.

One of the recurring topics at the Night Owl was that things used to be much better in the '70s and '80s, and even in the '90s. Back then, the women insisted, sex workers were professionals who had been trained by experienced prostitutes. The women at the Night Owl were adamant that in the past, you did not actually have sex with clients but only practiced "pretend sex" (*Falle schieben*) instead and were sure to charge a client for any additional services, such as taking off clothes, showing breasts, or letting a client touch you. Kissing on the mouth, or even French kissing, which had become standard in the sauna clubs, had been totally unheard of. Customers also rarely complained about a sex worker or her service, Elisa explained, as they knew they would have to deal with her Zuhälter then. But all that was now out the window, they said. Their young and untrained colleagues from Eastern Europe started out working in the nude, offered genital sex as a standard practice, and did it for less than they had been paid in the old days for pretend sex. Worst of all, many complained, was that these naive newcomers were willing to provide sex without a condom, thus messing up the business for the rest of them and endangering them all. This was an argument I would hear regularly, and it was voiced not only against migrant sex workers.

Bettina, a regular at the Night Owl who was in her early sixties, was suspicious of the others and cautious of revealing too much about herself. As she later confided in me, she thought of the other women at the Night Owl as highly dysfunctional and volatile, ready to explode at any moment. At some point Bettina invited me to her home, located half an hour away by tram. In her small two-bedroom apartment that she shared with her estranged husband, she told me her story: about growing up in the harsh postwar years and about her marriages and the time she spent in the United States with her soldier husband. She said she began sex work only at the age of forty, when she was pregnant with her fourth child, after her husband had not brought home money for the family in a long time. "In the beginning, I could not believe how easy it was to earn money. I could make one thousand DM[6] a night effortlessly," Bettina said. "But I never planned to be doing this kind of work at the age I am now. I promised myself to stop it when I turned sixty, and I did. But now, I need expensive dental work. How am I supposed to pay for it with my social security income alone?" After Bettina had stopped working, the Internal Revenue Service charged her a hefty fine for not claiming her earnings from sex work while receiving welfare benefits. Bettina did not want to have to relive that experience again.

She had maintained connections to the landlord of a brothel in the district, an old lady who rented out rooms to sex workers in one of the houses near the Night Owl. "The landlady must be ninety years old," Bettina said. "She always wears the same cheap clothes, always wants to be paid in cash, and always carries all the money she collects to the bank herself. In that same old plastic purse she always has used," she exclaimed, shaking her head. The landlady had given Bettina a special deal, a small room on the top floor of the building for fifty euros a day. But it was very hot now in early summer. More than once, Bettina arrived at the café frustrated and miserable because she had been waiting in her sizzling room since noon and had not had a single visitor by the time she came to the Night Owl for dinner. Bettina suspected that her age was not the only reason why she had so few customers but that her colleagues in the rooms next to her offered sex without a condom.

Sheri, a smashing cross-dresser who referred to himself as "he," had a strikingly different story. With his tight skirt, skimpy top, and high-heeled boots, he was a stunning contrast to most of the other regulars of the Night Owl. Sheri was the center of attention whenever he came. His modest personality as much as his stunning feminine appearance made him a coveted neighbor at the dinner table. Even Joanie, a loud and boisterous old-timer who was feared by most for her rough edges, made sure Sheri spent some time at her table. Given Sheri's popularity, I was very surprised when I realized that he was more willing than most others to share his experiences with me. Over a long dinner in one of the historic restaurants in the district, he told me that he was a registered nurse who came to work in Neuburg only once a week. His territory was the street at the periphery of the RLD. To Sheri, standing on the street and garnering the attention of men was a thrill. Sheri loved to wear sexy clothes and actually found that coming to work in Neuburg once a week offered him an outlet for his sexuality while also providing a nice side income. On the street, he was courted and sought after by men. Most of his clients, he said, were in fact regulars who scheduled dates with him in advance. "This is much better than looking for one-night stands in discotheques,[7] as I used to do when I was younger. In those days, I often got my feelings hurt by guys who left me after having had sex with me. Now, men are looking for me. They beg me to be with them, they want to make dates with me, and they even pay me for it." While the district was also home to a legendary gay nightclub, Sheri was rather unique at the Night Owl and, as far as I could tell, the only cross-dresser in the district. Working independently on the street, he had a degree of autonomy not shared by women who rented the upstairs rooms of the hotels. His story shows that the district offered people with a variety of gender identities the opportunity to engage in sex work—something I would not find in the sauna club brothel I will describe later.

With the exception of Sheri, the accounts of the sex workers at the Night Owl painted a stark picture of their experience over time. Having spent their prime in what they regularly referred to as "the golden years" (*die goldenen Jahre*) of the district—when sex workers worked less, had more control over their bodies and their clients, earned more, and, with or without Zuhälter, often lived a fast and fancy lifestyle—they now found that the working conditions for sex work had grossly deteriorated: clients expected more, paid less, and acted empowered in a way they had not dared before. And yet the RLD still offered these older sex workers, who were accustomed to a different mode of work, a familiar place, a network of people they knew, an infrastructure they could deal with, and the memory of good times.

Public Resentments

Not everyone shared the image of the district as a small piece of old-town authenticity, underworld flair, and gregariousness. In fact, at least since the early 2000s, tensions had been brewing between the encroaching residential neighborhood and city officials on one hand and sex-related business owners on the other. Residential neighbors and newspaper reporters had complained about "kerb crawlers" who were cruising the perimeter of the RLD in search of sex, about the used condoms that they would find on the street, about clients who approached students from the junior high school mistaking them for sex workers, or about the Albanian, Bulgarian, and later Romanian young women, most of them under eighteen and therefore below the age where prostitution was legal, who worked the streets under the tight control of Zuhälter. The zoning officer, who had witnessed decades of debates over the district, described its ambiguous reputation: "There are those who say the historic district has to be wiped clean entirely, that it is an eyesore. And then there are those who say you have to leave it alone, it just got a character that you cannot reproduce by design. But the city had to do something to prevent the district from going down the drain. So we decided that no more than thirty percent of businesses should be sex related. And it was the job of the zoning office to keep an eye on them."

The district's city council representative—a well-groomed middle-aged woman from the Green Party whom I met for lunch to talk about the current situation in the RLD—told me that she was "determined to clean up" the district and that she and her constituents regarded it as an "offense to decency." Following her suggestion, we walked together through some of the streets of the district, during which she pointed her finger at a young woman standing at the street corner and said, with unconcealed contempt in her voice, "Look at how she stands there, in her miniskirt, just opposite the school!" While street prostitution next to a junior high school is problematic for a number of reasons, the city council representative's undisguised hostility and look of disapproval toward the young woman, who probably had not selected this location herself, were painful to watch as well as embarrassing and made me regret that I had ever agreed to accompany her on the walk-through.

Less public were the concerns of brothel and club owners, who felt encroached upon by residents and commerce not compatible with the adult industry. Following a roundtable discussion between business owners and city representatives, one of the brothel owners who agreed to talk to me summarized his frustration: "How can you place an antique store in the middle of the red light district and then have the antique store owner complain about sex workers and their clients in the neighborhood?" Similarly, the regulars from the Night Owl were often demoralized if they got yet another ticket for solicitation in public, wondering why they were even issued tickets for prostitution in the red light district. As I will show later in this chapter, the paradox of sex workers being fined for soliciting in an area specifically dedicated as a RLD illustrates the interplay of laws and regulation and the historic influence of police departments in engineering local geographies of such districts. Putting it simply, the city had deliberately contained the red light district within a "restricted zone" area, which gave police and city officials maximum control over sex workers, even though prostitution as a whole was legal.

Prostitution Statistics

Neuburg was not only the largest city and the only one with a designated red light district in the region. It also had a long history of regulating prostitution and a police department that over the years had amassed detailed statistics on sex workers and prostitution establishments. The surrounding cities, in contrast, had seen a rise in prostitution only since the millennium, and therefore, as Neuburg's police chief put it, they had no tools in place to curb this trade in their communities. Not so in Neuburg, where the number of prostitution businesses remained roughly the same—from 165 in 1990 to 180 in 2015 (see table 2.1).

One problem with Neuburg's statistics was that prostitution businesses differed vastly in the numbers of women who worked there. While brothels and brothel-like venues such as apartments might have between three and seven workers on-site, Laufhäuser might have as many as fifty or even hundreds. This was also the case for eros centers—the more contemporary version of a Laufhaus—and sauna clubs, which typically had between twenty-five and eighty sex workers. Merely looking at total number of establishments without taking into account their size did not, therefore, provide a good picture of the size of the industry. Another way to gauge it was to look at the number of sex workers about whom the police kept records. This showed a different trend: between 1990 and 2013, first-time registered sex workers increased from two hundred to almost one thousand, a fivefold increase.[8]

Yet another way to count the number of sex workers was to add up the number of women police found working in brothels during their checkups. Using this method, I discovered a close to 50 percent increase between 2000 and 2007, paralleling the spike in the number of prostitution businesses and sex workers during the same time period, and possibly reflecting the uptake in business after the Prostitution Act of 2002.

However, the greater increase in newly registered sex workers over those already registered requires an explanation. The discrepancy between the rapid increase of first-time registered sex workers and the comparatively slower increase in the total number of sex workers might say more about migration patterns than absolute numbers of sex workers. In fact, one of the most striking trends revealed in Neuburg's prostitution statistics was the growing proportion of international migrants. As described earlier, this trend, which to a significant extent was linked to the expansion of the EU and the new labor migration opportunities it entailed for citizens of member states also held true for Germany (Staiger 2009). In Neuburg, however, this trend was particularly pronounced. By 2001, only 40 percent of sex workers were foreign, a number that grew to over 90 percent by 2015. The rapid increase of both categories—first-time registered sex workers and foreign sex workers—suggests that many were in the city for only a short time before leaving to work elsewhere or return home. Rather than a drastic increase of sex workers in Neuburg since the new millennium, the higher rate of first-time registrations might indicate that sex work became a niche filled increasingly by foreign sex workers moving from one city to another. However, all of these numbers should be taken with a degree of caution, as the Neuburg Police Department also had an interest in presenting statistics that showed that their efforts to control prostitution were effective, even if some critics questioned the legality of their procedures.

Statistics about sex workers are generally hard to come by and notoriously inaccurate (Kavemann et al. 2007). Neuburg's detailed records were in reality the result of Neuburg's police protocol for prostitution management that forced sex workers to register with the local police before they were able to work in the city.[9] On their regular patrols, plainclothes police would ask for IDs and work permits to check for legal age, proper residence, and work authorization. New and foreign sex workers had to hand over their IDs and go the police station in order to register before they could get their IDs back. Chief Ringelnatz, director of the prostitution unit, explained that the reason behind this procedure was that allegedly, special equipment was necessary to detect forged IDs. "But more importantly," he said, "having the ladies come to the police station and tell us why they want to become a sex worker gives us a chance to find out if they are doing this on their own free will, or whether they are working for a Zuhälter. That is also the reason why we do not allow them to bring along others. We don't want their 'boy-friends' or coworkers to make explanations for them." Once registered as a sex worker, a person would remain in the police database for up to three years after the last time they were identified during a checkup.

Chief Ringelnatz defended this method as one of the most effective interventions to detect sex trafficking and other forms of foul play. As the director of his unit, he had decisively contributed to this particular procedure. His critics, however, pointed out that it was unlikely to reveal women who were linked to traffickers and constituted a violation of privacy for sex workers and discrimination against them on the basis of their work, as no other form of labor required such a registration. Many women considered having to be registered as a sex worker an invasion of privacy. One owner of an apartment brothel recounted how horrified she was when she received a letter from the Police Unit on Prostitution two years after she had stopped being a sex worker. The letter, sent to her old address at her parents', clearly marked the sender as the Police Unit on Prostitution and thus revealed her past to her parents. Finally, the requirement to get registered constituted a form of search and seizure, as it gave the police a means to check sex workers for petty offenses. A local police officer described such a scenario when he told me that checking sex workers and their papers also provided an opportunity to check their records for outstanding warrants and other problems.

This regime of surveillance also had ramifications for brothel owners. They were not required to let police enter their establishments, but not doing so could raise the ire of the police officer and cause retributions later on. I witnessed another way in which police used soft power to coerce brothel operators to comply when I accompanied a police officer during a checkup of a small apartment brothel. He explained, "If they don't cooperate with us, they know we can just come not as plainclothes police but in our uniforms. This quickly scares away all the clients who don't want the risk of exposure."

TABLE 2.1 Overview of data about prostitution collected by Neuburg Police Department, 1990–2015.

Year	1990	2000	2004	2007	2011	2013	2015
Sum of all Prostitution Venues[1]	160	186	203 (209)[4]	202 (259)	186	183	165
Apartment Brothels[5]	N/A[2]	83	120	117	119	117	107
Total reg. sex workers[3]	N/A	2700	3027	4101	N/A	N/A	N/A
Newly reg. sex workers	213	512	787	1057	987	912	702
% of foreign sex workers	N/A	39	51	68	79	85	91

Notes:
[1] Prostitution Venues: Neuburg lists a variety of indoor prostitution venues: striptease bar, hostess bar, brothel, Laufhaus, massage parlor, domina studio, flophouse, and apartment brothel. These categories are not always clearly distinct or applied consistently. Therefore, I concentrate on the largest number.
[2] Empty cells or N/A means no information is available.
[3] All numbers refer to female sex workers only. For consistency, I left out numbers on male sex workers because they were negligible and, after 2000, were no longer collected in the original data.
[4] Numbers in parenthesis indicate discrepancies in records.
[5] Apartment brothels are the largest segment of prostitution venues. Escort services and domina studios as well as street prostitution constituted only minor segments of prostitution markets in Neuburg.

With the legal changes to prostitution in the so-called Prostitute Protection Act of 2017, registration of sex workers had become mandatory for sex workers in all of Germany. Neuburg's invasive and unpopular management of prostitution had thus prefigured what soon would become the new law of the land.

Making Legal Prostitution Illegal: Restricted Zone Ordinances and Zoning Laws

Another factor influencing prostitution in Neuburg was a set of state rights and community ordinances that limited how and whether prostitution could be practiced in a particular setting. As Weitzer (2017, 366) cautions, "Some national laws give discretion to provincial and municipal authorities to implement the spirit of the law as they see fit. And even if a national law contains clear mandates for local officials, the latter may vary in the degree to which they implement such mandates. As a result, national law often has at least some geographically uneven effects at the local level. These points are crucial for a proper understanding of the operation of any legal prostitution system. It should not be assumed that laws on the books are fully reflected in the law-in-action."

Unlike its neighboring cities, Neuburg had a restricted zone ordinance (*Sperrbezirksverordnung*) in place that designated areas where prostitution could not be practiced. While prostitution, indoors or outdoors, had not been illegal in Germany even before 2002 and the passing of the Prostitution Law, restricted zone ordinances were a legal tool for states to give communities the possibility to control sexual commerce. Based on a federal law in effect since 1974, restricted zone ordinances allow cities to designate spaces where prostitution is prohibited in order "to protect youth and public decency," a phrasing consistently used in such ordinances.[10] Restricted zone ordinances can prohibit prostitution entirely in communities with twenty thousand inhabitants or fewer and may demand special regulations in whole or partially in communities of twenty to fifty thousand.[11] This ordinance, which in a similar form had already provided a legal back door to curtail legalized prostitution in the Anti-Venereal Disease Law of 1927,[12] was also unaffected by the Prostitution Act of 2002, despite protests from sex worker rights organizations.[13]

Restricted zones typically include schools and other public institutions and spaces, and the ordinance stipulates specific streets, public areas, and buildings where and times of day when prostitution is not allowed. As I learned from Chief Ringelnatz, Neuburg's restricted zone covered nearly all of Neuburg's downtown and wholly engulfed its red light district. While prostitution within buildings was legal, sex workers caught violating this ordinance—for example, by soliciting in public—were subject to fines: €180 for the first offense, €300 for the second, and up to thirty days in jail for the third. Clients could also be fined if they were found soliciting sex workers, although with lesser fines, from €100 for the first offense to double the amount with each subsequent offense.

Designating a restricted zone that covered the entirety of an established red light district seems facetious at best. When I asked Chief Ringelnatz about this apparent paradox, he smiled. "That was our intention," he said. "The Restricted Zone Ordinance is the reason the police can control the district and keep a close eye on it." The zoning officer confirmed this assessment: "This is a deliberate policy." As it turned out, the restricted zone in the RLD was not the only one in the city. Another zone comprised a narrow strip around a US military base that was well known for street prostitution. Thus, while prostitution was theoretically legal, restricted zone ordinances de facto made it illegal in many areas, including those where sex work had already been well established, and thus were means for the police to take control over prostitution.

For sex workers in the downtown area, the restricted zone ordinance was a nuisance, if not an insult. Sheri, whom I described earlier, came to the Night Owl frustrated one evening, wondering why he had gotten another ticket for soliciting in public even though he was working specifically within the red light district. Women at the Night Owl often commiserated about the repeated fines they were getting from police for soliciting, although they thought they had done everything by the book. While this ordinance did not forbid prostitution per se, it did make it punishable to solicit in public for both buyers and service providers, a rule that provided ample room for ambiguity.

Another tool in the arsenal of police controls over the red light district was their ability to issue parking tickets. Chief Ringelnatz stated matter-of-factly, but with a twinkle in his eyes, "The parking tickets that we send home include the street where the car was parked illegally. So their wives get an idea about what their husbands are doing."

Finally, zoning laws (*Bebauungspläne*) were a governance tool to regulate prostitution at the city level. Zoning laws designate areas as residential, commercial, industrial, or mixed-use. By assigning an area to such a designated zone, a city determines what kinds of buildings can be built and for what purpose they can be used. This gives the city another means to prevent the opening of new prostitution businesses, although already existing ones in newly defined zones had to be grandfathered in. Sometimes, the zoning officer explained, police and the zoning office worked together to try to eliminate undesirable businesses. "If police find a brothel that looks suspicious, they send me a note to see if we can find some problems, and if we do, we can start pressing charges. This might not be according to the letter of the law," he said, "but how else can we keep the upper hand over the sprawling city and our responsibilities with an understaffed office?"

The issuing of a new zoning map in 2010 prevented the opening of new brothels in the RLD. At the same time, the city closed down several existing ones, thus reducing the number of brothels in the RLD substantially. Another of the city's strategies to reduce prostitution was to buy up more of the properties as they became available and refuse to resell them or give out new building permits. But, as the local newspaper reported, brothel owners also had become savvy in fighting back: some managed to drag out legal

Neuburg City

Downtown Area

Red Light District

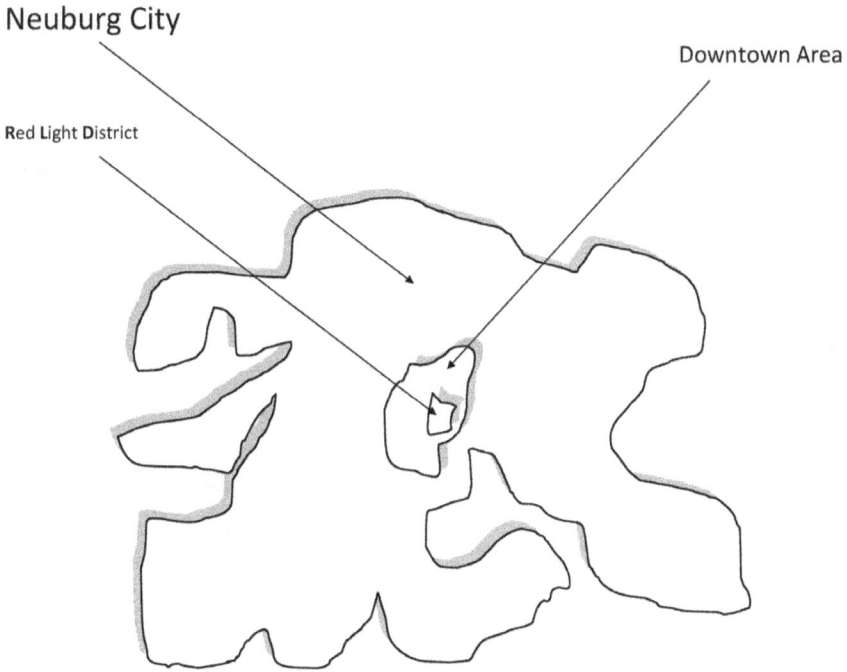

Figure 2.2 Map of Neuburg City, its downtown, and its red light district.

procedures against having to close down for many years, during which they could continue to earn money from prostitution, while other brothel owners decided to sublet their space to third parties who were not targeted by the city.

Beyond the Red Light District:
The New Geography of Sexual Commerce

Neuburg's RLD comprised a mere 1 percent of the city surface, but almost one-fifth of all identified commercial sex venues. Sex-related businesses in Germany are, however, not typically limited to RLDs.[14] Neuburg's larger downtown area also offered strip clubs, sex shops, and adult cinemas. Such businesses were not hidden away but freely visible and accessible to pedestrians. One striptease bar, for example, shared a building with a dentist and a real estate office and was in close proximity to the police department; a franchise of the legendary Beate Uhse porn shop sat in a busy pedestrian section between a health food store and a discount drugstore.

As conditions in the traditional RLD became increasingly difficult for brothels, new business models emerged elsewhere. The first were small apartment brothels in commercial and residential areas and large eros centers in industrial areas of neighboring cities. At the turn of the millennium, the new FKK sauna clubs emerged. None of these types of business venues were represented in the RLD, suggesting the emergence of a new prostitution regime.

Of these new venues, apartment prostitution was the least visible from the outside. Hidden away in residential or commercial areas, they usually were discreet, without signs giving any indication of the nature of the business. In the 1990s, prostitution venues grew larger and moved into industrial areas. The new eros centers that emerged in the periphery were a modern version of the Laufhaus of an earlier era, a dormitory or hotel-like structure where individual rooms were rented out to sex workers. The number of eros centers opening up in the cities surrounding Neuburg indicates how popular they had become within little more than a decade: between 2003 and 2015, in a twenty-mile radius from Neuburg, ten new eros centers had sprung up, each with an average of twenty to thirty service providers.

Unlike eros centers, the FKK sauna clubs that started to emerge in the new millennium were a radically new business design that had not existed in Germany in this form and magnitude before 2000. If eros centers were the low-cost version of large-scale prostitution, sauna clubs were entirely different establishments, where clients paid almost one hundred dollars just to get through the door. Made possible by the greater financial securities that the Prostitution Act offered brothel owners and helped by the growing number of women from Eastern Europe seeking to work in the German sex industry, sauna clubs quickly became very popular and grew rapidly in number. Located in industrial areas, sauna clubs were often lavishly remodeled factory buildings, with state-of-the-art spa facilities and a large bar and contact area where between thirty and a hundred nude workers mingled with clients in a bar-like atmosphere.

Conclusion

A number of processes occurred to transform the traditional red light district into a backwater of sexual commerce while a new prostitution regime emerged elsewhere. Some of the observations made about sexual commerce in other countries hold true for Neuburg as well. Sexual commerce became decentralized by moving out of the traditional red light district and into the city at large and the periphery; it became upscale, in particular in the sauna club brothels, as I will show in the subsequent chapters. While in this regard Neuburg reflects trends in other cities in Europe and the United States, there has not been a process of mainstreaming, as sexual commerce to some extent was mainstreamed before, and it was a familiar feature outside of the red light district as well.

However, what is striking in Neuburg's case is the extent to which local governance structures, particularly the restricted zone ordinance, could be used to make some aspects of prostitution de facto prohibited. By declaring the historical red light district, with the highest concentration of sex-related business in the city, an area where sexual soliciting was illegal, the city had de facto put police in charge of prostitution—a practice occurring in other cities as well and widely criticized by sex worker rights organizations[15] and sex work scholars (Kontos 2009; Löw and Ruhne 2011; Ruhne 2006; Pates 2012).

In addition to the restrictive zone ordinances, the city used another effective legal tool—new zoning laws—to limit the number of sex-related businesses and reduce the red light district in its downtown area. Over-regulated by the police, squeezed into a restricted zone, and increasingly regarded as an eyesore and a violation of decency, sex-related businesses and their patrons in the RLD had come under growing pressure. The increased surveillance and the hassle it entailed made the district less desirable for workers, owners, and clients and led to ongoing friction between various stakeholders: between neighboring residents and sex-related business owners, and between the latter and non-sex-related businesses. Meanwhile, the tightening of police surveillance created an environment increasingly hostile to brothels, sex workers, and their clients. Those who stayed in the historical RLD were those with few options to go elsewhere, like Selma from the Maxxim; old-timers like Elisa and Bettina, who had built a community in the district and were too old to move elsewhere; and prostitution businesses that had lost their competitive edge.

This gradual decline of the district as a site for erotic industries went hand in hand with the emergence of a new red light geography, consisting of apartment brothels in the city at large and mega brothels in neighboring cities and the industrial urban periphery. On online platforms, clients were wondering why anyone would still frequent these overpriced, over-controlled, and underpopulated brothels in the RLD when more modern facilities and cheaper options could be had in more discreet locations else-where, and when full genital intercourse could be had for the same price as oral sex and without risking public disclosure as in the heavily populated red light district downtown.

Restricted zone ordinances are a time-tested strategy of urban prosti-tution governance in Germany (Kavemann et al. 2007) and exist in many cities. For real estate, non-sex-related businesses, and nearby residents, the governance regime of the RLD was a means to keep the district orderly: a mixed business clientele would ensure a more diverse population in the district, keep rowdy nightlife crowds at bay, make it attractive for real estate owners to invest in their properties, and maintain a livable residence and an attractive destination in the dense Neuburg downtown business dis-trict. Others, however, see in it an overregulation of a legal industry not matched in other sectors. The urban sociologist Renate Ruhne (2005, 2006) has shown that Frankfurt's RLD, not unlike Neuburg's, was fully engulfed within such a restricted zone and had declared "tolerance zones" for several brothels within them—a policy that German gender studies scholar Silvia Kontos (2009) described as de facto sex worker internment politics, as it discourages sex workers from leaving the premises.

The spatial location of prostitution, however, must be seen not only in light of the economy, urban planning, and development but, as Ashworth, White, and Winchester (1988) have argued, also as an indicator of its place in the social and moral hierarchy. As prostitutes during the Middle Ages in Europe were forced to make themselves easily identifiable so they could not be confused with "respectable" women, the spatial marking of spaces of prostitution produces a similar effect of social demarcation. In their study of the red light district in Frankfurt, the urban sociologists Martina Löw and Renate Ruhne (2009) show how the stigmatized shadow world of prostitu-tion is embedded in gender relations but also reproduces them. Building on such a framework, the political scientist Silvia Kontos (2009) shows how spatial policies can become means of "locking in" sex workers and others associated with the red light industry while simultaneously "locking out" other segments of an urban population—that is, "respectable women." The verdict here, however, is ambiguous. One could argue that the decline of the red light district and the sex industry's move out of Neuburg's visible cen-ter and into the social invisibility of the industrial wastelands of the urban periphery signal the low place of sexual commerce in the social and moral landscape of Neuburg. This, however, is juxtaposed by the spread of sex-related business throughout the general downtown business areas in Neuburg and a generalized, if not surprising, public tolerance for sexual commerce in the public space. In regard to the growth of prostitution venues in the periphery, however, there was a clear trend toward further isolation of sex workers combined with a growing trend toward greater privacy for clients.

As I show in the next chapter, the new business models of prostitution that emerged in the periphery offered a new prostitution culture where clients were more secluded from the general public, brothels offered more modern facilities with a more transparent business structure, and sauna clubs promised an upscale experience of unprecedented possibilities for titillation. While these new locations offered a drastically new prostitution culture, with variety and unprecedented possibilities for socializing, they also brought increasingly labor-intensive earning strategies for sex workers, particularly in sauna clubs.

Notes

1. Berlin is portrayed as sin city in the acclaimed Netflix series *Babylon Berlin* (Tykwer et al. 2020), in the erotic sketches of illustrator Heinrich Zille, and in Mel Gordon's book *Voluptuous Panic* (2006).

2. See also Bernstein 2014, where she explores this question further.

3. According to statistics provided by the Neuburg Police Department.

4. *Lude* is another term for Zuhälter, commonly used by people in the milieu.

5. The fact that they used these two contradictory flags side by side suggests that they had no understanding of their meaning in the United States. Instead, it seemed to signal a belief common among the postwar-generation Germans of America standing for everything progressive, rebellious, and hip.

6. DM stands for deutsche mark. The DM was replaced by the euro in 2002. At the introduction of the euro (€), one DM was valued at €0.50. The purchasing power of the euro, however, decreased rapidly so that DM1 in 1980 was equivalent to the purchasing power of €1 in 2010 (see the inflation calculator at https://www.inflationtool.com/euro-germany?amount =100&year1=1980&year2=2010).

7. A discotheque is a nightclub where people dance, usually to recorded rather than live music.

8. The number of male sex workers had been small and declined drastically between 1990 and 2000. After that, Neuburg's police department no longer counted them in its statistics.

9. The actual number is presumably higher, as some sex workers are likely to work without wanting to be registered because they don't have work permits, are underage, work for third parties or traffickers, or just resent the idea of having to reveal to the police the nature of their work.

10. For example, the Ordinance of Friedrichshafen, entitled "Ordinance of the Regional Administrative Council of Tübingen about the Prohibition of Prostitution in the City of Friedrichshafen" (*Verordnung des Regierungspräsidiums Tübingen über das Verbot der*

Prostitution in der Stadt Friedrichshafen), of June 18, 1984, declares it necessary "for the protection of the youth and public decency" (*zum Schutze der Jugend und des öffentlichen Anstandes*). Landtag von Baden-Württemberg, "Gesetzblatt für Baden-Württemberg," August 10, 1984, 511–512, https://www.landtag-bw.de/files/live/sites/LTBW/files/dokumente /gesetzblaetter/1984/GBl198416.pdf.

11. Restricted zone ordinance (*Sperrgebietsverordnung*) is defined in Artikel 297 as "Prohibition of Prostitution." The law gives "the state the right to limit the practice of prostitution in order to protect youth from public indecency." The law states:

> 1. that a community with a population of up to 50k can prohibit prostitution for the entire area; 2. a community with a population over 20K can prohibit it partially; and 3. independent of the size of the population, a state can prohibit prostitution on public streets, paths, plazas, enclosures, and other locations, which can be seen from there, in the whole area or in parts of a location or community or an unincorporated area through laws. The state government can limit Nr. 3 also to specific times of day. The state government can transfer this entitlement to other state or local authorities [author's translation of Section 297 of the Introduction to the Criminal Code about the Prohibition of Prostitution (Restricted Zone Ordinance), 1974].

In short, this means that since this law came into effect in 1974, state, county, or city governance could use it to limit prostitution in certain areas and at certain times, even though prostitution overall was not prohibited.

12. See Hunecke (2011) and Roos (2002, 2017) and the discussion about the introduction of the so-called church tower ordinance (*Kirchturmparagraph*), which was introduced with the liberalization of prostitution laws in 1927 and provides the blueprint for the current Restricted Zone Ordinance.

13. See, for example, Hydra e.V. "Hydra fordert die vollständige Entkriminalisierung der Prostitution in Deutschland, vor allem die Abschaffung der Sperrbezirksverordnungen, des Werbeverbots und der polizeilichen Sonderrechte" ("Hydra demands the complete decriminalization of prostitution in Germany, particularly the abolition of Restricted Zone Ordinances, Advertisement Prohibitions, and Special Laws of the police"; author's translation, Hydra e.V. 2015, 11).

14. As described in chapter 1, the mainstreaming of sexual commerce (Brents and Sanders 2010) as it has been described for anglophone countries such as England, the United States, and Australia has been much more common in Germany, where sex shops (Heineman 2011) and female nudity in advertisements and on television have been commonplace for decades.

15. Such as Hydra e.V. in Berlin, Madonna e.V. in Bochum, and the German-language sex worker forum sexworker.at.

3

THE NEW RED LIGHT GEOGRAPHY AND CHANGING REGIMES OF PROSTITUTION

WITH THE SPREAD OF PROSTITUTION BUSINESSES INTO ADJACENT cities came different governance systems. While Neuburg's police chief was proud of engineering the paradox of a red light district enclosed by a restricted zone, the neighboring cities had their own strategies—though, according to Neuburg's police chief, much less effective ones because the cities had less experience in dealing with prostitution. The new prostitution ventures occupied different niches of the market, in regard to not only their locations but also business structures, client experiences, and working conditions. How did these new venues operate? Which actors benefitted from them? What cultures of commercial sex did they establish? What kind of client experience did they offer? Last but not least, how did these new establishments position sex workers vis-à-vis clients and managers? Comparing these three prominent types of business models a decade after legalization illustrates the new forms of prostitution cultures they created and the new forms of sexual labor they entailed.

Most scholars argue that indoor sex work provides better working conditions than street prostitution, as it allows sex workers and clients to engage in longer and thus less objectifying sexual relations with more affluent clients (Bernstein 2007, 2010; Brents, Jackson, and Hausbeck 2010; Sanders 2008; Weitzer 2012). In his comparative study of legalized indoor venues in Antwerp, Amsterdam, and Frankfurt, three cities in Western Europe, Weitzer (2012) described a growing professionalization of indoor sex workers, which gave them greater control over their work environment and their management of self. Pointing to the promise of legalized prostitution in creating better working conditions, Weitzer (2012, 25) writes, "When prostitution is legal and regulated by the authorities, much of the regulation is designed to control third parties who run brothels and other indoor businesses, forcing them to improve working conditions, and more generally, empowering workers vis-à-vis managers and owners." Studying legalized indoor prostitution, he argues, can provide a best practice model where all stakeholders—that is, sex workers, brothel owners, clients, residents, and city authorities—win.

Describing legal brothels in Nevada, Brents, Jackson, and Hausbeck (2010) argue that sex workers report greater satisfaction about their work as they provide both "surface" and "deep emotion" work (Hochschild 1983) to clients who more and more demand emotional experiences and fantasy play. Researching the escort and indoor sex market in San Francisco, Amsterdam (Netherlands), and Stockholm (Sweden), Bernstein (2007, 2010) describes a growing demand for emotional and physical authenticity in commercial sex that remains bound in time and personal intimacy—a type of exchange characteristic of a market exchange. Offering a more comprehensive theoretical framework about the kind of sexuality and sexual ethics characteristic of postindustrial societies, Bernstein offers the concept of a recreational sexual ethic. She writes, "The recreational sexual ethic derives [as opposed to the preceding 'relational' model of sexuality and prototypically procreative orientation of preindustrial society] its primary meaning from the depth of physical sensation and from emotionally bounded erotic exchange—what I here term *bounded authenticity*" (Bernstein 2007, 6, italics in the original). This new paradigm of "bounded authenticity," she argues, is linked to a new form of engagement between clients and sex workers, expressed in the demand for the so-called girlfriend experience. She continues, "In postindustrial cities throughout North America and Western Europe . . . a brave new world [has sprung up] of commercially available intimate encounters that are subjectively normalized for sex workers and clients alike" (2007, 7). Bernstein argues that this phenomenon—in colloquial language referred to as *girlfriend experience*—is the expression of a new paradigm of sexuality in postindustrial societies, where monogamy and procreative relationships are increasingly fragile and replaced by intense, affective, and authentic relationships that are nevertheless bound in time and personhood (see also Illouz 1997; Giddens 1992).

How does this play out in Germany, a postindustrial society par excellence that has arguably one of the most liberal prostitution legislations within Europe and a population largely tolerant of legal prostitution? More specifically, what does it look like in Neuburg's new geography of sexual commerce? This chapter explores this brave new world of normalized and presumably fully commercialized intimate encounters by comparing three of the most common new business venues: apartment brothels, which feature discretion; Laufhäuser and eros centers, which offer efficiency and low prices; and FKK sauna clubs, the most striking new establishments, which promise upscale facilities, extended socializing, and a service structure where girlfriend sex is club standard.

My central argument here is that instead of a labor of *bounded authenticity* that emphasizes the market exchange aspects of erotic services, there has emerged a new labor of *boundless intimacy* in which sex workers' labors are open-ended, in terms of both time and physical and emotional autonomy. As I will show, temporal boundedness is in question for sex workers in sauna clubs, as the performance of authentic feelings does not begin with the purchase but is an essential part of sex workers' client recruitment labor. It is also does not end with when the purchase is completed, since sex workers routinely perform emotional and physical labor after they have sex with a customer to secure future business with him and to cultivate or keep him as her regular.

This chapter looks at how different venues stage interactions between service providers and clients, explores what working conditions they offer, and probes to what extent sex workers and their clients, particularly those in the upscale prostitution venues, subscribe to the notions of sex as a fully commodified form of transaction, free of lingering love attachments yet emotionally and physically authentic.

To understand which niche of the market each of these prostitution venues had carved out, what new cultures they produced, and what labor conditions they offered to sex workers, I focus on four aspects of indoor prostitution: (1) the location of a particular venue and how it affects its economic niche; (2) its income structure and management style, such as whom clients pay, how sex workers get paid, and the economic relationship between manager and service provider; (3) the client experience: what kind of client is targeted and attracted to this venue, what they seek there, and in what kind of relationships are they engaging; and, last but not least, (4) the perspective of sex workers—their working conditions and the advantages and disadvantages a particular niche of indoor prostitution provides (see table 3.1, at the end of the chapter).

Location was critical in regard to urban governance but also had implications for the privacy and convenience of sex workers and clients. Income structure and management styles describe the ways in which money is generated, whom clients pay for the services they buy, and how sex workers are paid. Looking at brothels through the eyes of clients provides insight into new cultures of commodified intimacy while exploring the perspective of sex workers illustrates the labor regimes and living circumstances they encounter in different venues.

Price Decline and Service Inflation

The question of working conditions and modes of interaction in different types of brothels must be set against the backdrop of a pervasive discourse on price decline and service inflation in commercial sex. I first encountered this argument with the women in the Night Owl, who complained about their young competitors from abroad working for very little money and offering any service, with no regard for personal boundaries or for the well-being of their fellow sex workers. If their complaints might be explained in part by them having surpassed the zenith of their earning careers in prostitution, this argument was by no means limited to them. Brothel owners and sex workers, law enforcement and former Zuhälter, and sundry other industry insiders old enough to remember agreed that the golden era of prostitution was a thing of the past. In a conversation with the chief accountant of the Flamingo about the earning potential in prostitution, he told me that the price for sex had gone down to one-third or one-fourth of what it used to be thirty years ago. Similar stories about the '80s, when a sex worker would make in a night what she could earn at another job in a month, were a regular staple of conversations with entrepreneurs. Several of the smaller brothel owners I interviewed, most of them women, explained that they had to cut prices in order to attract clients, sometimes by up to 50 percent. Most attributed this drastic decline to a number of circumstances: an oversaturation of sex markets; the general economic downturn since 2008, which made customers less generous; and, last but not least, a heavy influx of sex workers from poorer countries within the EU and elsewhere, as mentioned earlier (TAMPEP 2009a). In the Neuburg region, which had a relatively high percentage of foreign-born residents, the number of sex workers from abroad was even more accentuated than elsewhere, growing from 39 percent in 2001 to 87 percent in 2013.

Younger sex workers made similar observations. Tina, a German woman in her thirties whom I met when visiting an eros center, had entered sex work in the late '90s. During the ensuing ten years, prices had gone down drastically. Notwithstanding such price cuts, customers were sporadic, she said.

Figure 3.1 Sticker on Tina's locker in her room in the Laufhaus, reminding clients to use condoms.

It was a buyers' market, and those who came often demanded sex without a condom. As she said that, I pointed to a locker room across the bed from where we sat, which featured an eye-catching sticker of a condom-covered penis. "Yes," she said, "that's why I put that there." Another woman, Rosa, who was in her midthirties and came from the Dominican Republic, had been working in one of the sauna clubs for the last eight years. She said, "As recently as five years ago, it was not rare to make a thousand euros in a weekend. Now I would be happy if I could make half of this."

If price decline was one common complaint, inflation of services was another. This was also the subject of a discussion on a sex client forum dedicated to the larger Neuburg region, the NR9. The discussion below about the concept of *girlfriend sex*, as it is called there rather than *girlfriend experience*, illustrates the conflicting expectations between clients and sex workers. On the forum, Elvira spelled out her frustration about clients' demands for a girlfriend experience and why that was unacceptable to her:

> I belong to the ladies who do not offer unprotected oral sex, French kissing, cum in mouth, or the new and popular bare-backing [i.e. sex without a condom, author's explanation]. . . . On top of that, [clients] want everything for very little money. . . . I decided to work in an eros center, where I do not have

to act as the loving girlfriend. Unfortunately, the trend goes toward men expecting a hot wedding night for fifty euros. If men don't realize that sex with a prostitute will feel different from sex with a girlfriend, then more and more women who want to provide a solid and honest service will leave the business.[1]

Leaving a fancy sauna club for a drab eros center might have seemed like a step down for Elvira, but it meant more freedom and self-determination for her, as she was not under pressure to provide the girlfriend experience her customers and management had expected in the club.

A number of men on the forum responded to her comment. Johann answered, "The real experts in this profession don't let you know the difference between a girlfriend and a professional. So much so that one actually almost feels pity for them [grinning emoticon]." Another commentator chided Elvira: "Even bare-backing will become more and more popular." A third revealed his negative attitude toward German women more generally: "This is exactly the kind of brainy and uptight attitude I hate and the reason why I stay clear of German and German-assimilated whores."

In a more conciliatory tone, one forum member explained the difference between quickies and quality girlfriend sessions: "In a brothel, a visit costs fifty euros. That is standard. And no one should demand oral sex without a condom or kissing for that. But I pay close to two hundred euros per meeting, and I want no goddamn low-class sex but (pretend) girlfriend sex with unprotected oral sex and kissing." To this, Elvira responded, "You will get girlfriend sex, you will just get it as safe sex, and without kissing." Another member then responded sarcastically, "Do you know what a paradox is?"—implying that girlfriend sex is not compatible with safe sex and no kissing. This exchange shows how clients in Neuburg equate girlfriend sex with kissing and unprotected oral sex, and some with any and all forms of unprotected sex.

Tanya, a well-known, beloved, and experienced sex worker I later met during a social gathering of clients, also joined the forum discussion and defended Elvira's position: "When I started, I fouled my own nest, because kissing and unprotected oral sex were crucial to me and the service I offered. At the time, a Polish coworker confided in me, 'Don't do this, or we all have to do it.' A few years later, to my surprise, I reacted almost the same way when I realized that some of my colleagues offered unprotected sex. Seriously, I was disgusted by them and their clients."

These online exchanges point to the growing expectations in regard to the kinds of sexual services clients demand and some sex workers are willing to provide. They also point to the growing health risks that such demands entail. In this context, girlfriend sex—understood in Germany generally as kissing, unprotected oral sex, caressing, and full nudity—is expected by customers in upscale sauna clubs, where it is usually understood to be club standard. Increasingly, it is also expected in other less upscale versions of indoor prostitution.

Earnings in prostitution are notoriously hard to assess (Cusick et al. 2009; Heberer 2013; Kavemann et al. 2007). Sex workers might be biased toward overestimation, while tax records might invite underestimation. Of course, prices also vary widely by establishment, location, and the particular services offered. Price decline and service inflation were common topics in sex worker forums. One participant on sexworker.at, a forum for sex workers in German-speaking countries, stated that in the late 1980s, a monthly income of DM20,000 (€10,000) was common in Hamburg and Berlin.[2]

Kreuzer, a physician who conducted a detailed study of sex workers in the Frankfurt area in the 1970s, found that ten minutes of "pretend sex" cost DM30 while showing breasts would cost an additional DM50 (Kreuzer 1989, 229). Oral sex, consisting of rubbing the penis against the cheek, also cost DM50 with condom and DM100 without condom. Women could earn substantially more if they offered what was then called "perversions," such as anal sex (260–261).[3] In a more recent study, Kavemann and Rabe (2009) found that sex workers' average monthly earnings was only €1,500—a rather modest income, though not impossible to live on. Even the Association for Erotic Trade Entrepreneurs (UED) estimated a 23 percent decline in the cost of sexual services between 2000 and 2012, from €73 average per encounter in 2000 to €56 in 2012. While the numbers are difficult to compare from one source to another and in different time periods, there is an unmistakable trend toward the decreasing value of sexual labor. What led to this price decline? Was it the growing availability of sexual services, or was it market forces associated with legalization and the decreased cost of a trade no longer deemed immoral? While the ethnographic material does not provide an easy answer to these questions, it does show a new culture of sexual commerce and a changed labor demand in sex work.

Notwithstanding these perceptions of price decline and inflation of services, owners and managers of the large eros centers and luxurious sauna club mega brothels were proud to state that the future of the pay sex industry was theirs, that they had moved it out of the crime-infested red light milieu and turned it into a clean, modern, transparent, and law-abiding business.

In fact, the sauna clubs and eros centers springing up in the industrial areas branded themselves as self-confident, law-abiding, and socially progressive. Appropriating the wellness concept that had been sweeping through Germany's marketing campaigns—encompassing everything from healthy living and exercise to spa products—they presented their establishments squarely as wholesome and healthy. Owners and managers of eros centers and sauna clubs told me proudly that the sex workers in their brothels approached their roles as professionals and saw it as part of their work ethic to provide the customer with a satisfying experience. Pay sex clients, as they called themselves, had voted with their feet, leaving the traditional RLD in droves for the new opportunities elsewhere and informing each other on client forums about the attractions outside of the traditional RLD. But how did women workers perceive these changed working conditions?

Price decline and service inflation thus provide a backdrop against which to evaluate the new prostitution venues beyond the RLD.

Apartment Brothels

Apartment brothels were the least visible form of prostitution. They tended to be located in residential, mixed-use, or commercial areas, often nestled inconspicuously between other businesses or residences. Commonly, apartment brothels were rented or owned by women who worked and lived there themselves or by madams who used them as working and living spaces for sex workers.

According to retired chief Naumann, the rise of apartment brothels in Neuburg was a product of the 1980s and something for which he partially blamed himself. He was a man with a reputation for being tough. "Maybe I was too successful in making the district 'Zuhälter-free,' as I used to call it," he reminisced. "The new apartment brothels that started to crop up throughout the downtown area were much harder to recognize and therefore hard to keep an eye on." If an apartment brothel was located in a residential area, it could be closed down for zoning violations. But the line between business and residence was hard to draw, illustrated in the numerous legal decisions about this matter.[4]

Location

Apartment brothels were located all throughout Neuburg and its adjacent cities. In residential areas, they were inconspicuous and often went unnoticed by neighbors, ranging in size from small two-bedroom units to entire buildings. Of the nine apartment brothels I visited, most were in residential, business, or mixed zones; one was in a stately turn-of-the-century house in an affluent residential area, two were in well-maintained houses near Neuburg's business district, and another was in a quiet suburban residential area, while the others were more hidden in the commercial or mixed zone areas. They often consisted of single-floor units but sometimes spanned multistory buildings. From the outside, none gave much indication of the nature of the business going on within and thus provided more privacy to the clients and to the women working there, as I will show below.

Apartment brothels did not depend on foot traffic and the presence of other sex-related businesses to draw customers—two advantages of the red light district. Instead, they relied on ads in local newspapers, designated internet sites, or advertisement and client reports in online client forums. Because they were located outside the RLD and often outside the restricted zone, they were usually not subjected to police surveillance, and there were no nuisance complaints from neighbors. Police did keep a close eye on these businesses, though, in both Neuburg and the fringe cities, but checkups were done only sporadically and usually by plainclothes police. Although brothel owners were not legally required to open their doors to police, as the zoning officer had explained to me, many did because resisting the authorities was likely to produce complications, if not retribution. Maria, a middle-aged woman who ran a small apartment brothel in a residential downtown area, explained to me that she usually opened the door for police and let them in, although she knew she was not legally obligated to do so. If she did not, she would likely have problems with them sooner or later. I also noticed this kind of coerced cooperation when I accompanied a vice officer on a control visit to an apartment brothel. We were met by a visibly nervous receptionist who apologized profusely for her inexperience and readily showed the officer the facilities and the documents he requested.

Revenue and Management

Apartment brothels were typically owned or rented by women, who often also played the role of madam (*Hausdame*). Out of about twenty-five apartment brothels I contacted, all but one were run by women, and all had been in business for a decade or more. Ultimately, only ten of the owners—all of them women—agreed to be interviewed.

In such establishments, a madam was both manager and business owner. Madams would manage advertisement, cultivate relationships with clients, recruit and manage sex workers, and provide a place for them to work and sleep. They were also in charge of decorating and maintaining the apartment, a task that was decidedly domestic. Madams managed relationships with police and the zoning office, ensured that workers had proper work authorization, often collected the daily pretax that sex workers had to pay, and dealt with the occasional complaints of neighboring residents. Usually present during business hours, madams often played the role of receptionist and acted as a liaison between clients and sex workers. During sporadic police checkups, the madam would be the brothel's public face. Some apartment brothels were run by sex workers jointly, but none of those agreed to an interview.[5]

In addition to placing ads on a variety of websites, madams usually maintained—or paid someone to maintain—sophisticated websites of their own where they featured photos of their apartments' tasteful interiors, services offered and their prices, and etiquette rules so their clients knew what to expect and what was expected of them. Often they hosted profiles of their weekly lineup of workers, including photos and sex workers' particular services and expertise, as well as their work hours. The cost of sexual services in these brothels tended to start at €100 for a one-hour booking. The apartment brothels were thus among the more expensive venues of sexual services, even though these were newly discounted prices to retain customers, I was told.

Madams typically sought women who worked for a week or less at a time, as many clients expected a new lineup of sex workers regularly. Many sex workers favored this time frame: it was long enough to get some familiarity with the place but short enough for clients not to get tired of them. Some madams, however, managed to maintain a more stable team; as one madam I interviewed stated proudly, "My girls are permanent and have been with me for years."

Several madams complained about the drastic decline in customers they had observed over the past few years, as clients had left in droves for the large and fancy sauna clubs that had opened elsewhere. Claudia, a slim, very attractive women in her early forties and the owner/manager of a well-established apartment brothel, had been in the business since the late 1980s. She and her two co-owners owned several brothels and had also managed to open a sauna club in the region. Over time, they could keep the apartment brothel open only by balancing its loss in revenue with revenue from their new sauna club. Eventually, however, they had to close the apartments down. Susanne, another madam who owned an elegant apartment brothel elsewhere in the city, offered drastic discounts to get at least some business back during the global financial crisis following the collapse of the subprime mortgage market in 2007.

From a madam's perspective, finding reliable team members was critical for the success of the business. As apartment brothels catered to a wealthier clientele that expected to engage in conversations with service providers, madams preferred women with the ability to speak German or English. However, this was not always the case, as the majority of sex workers were immigrants from Eastern Europe (TAMPEP 2009a). Language skills— German or English—were important for communication and for the kinds of girlfriend experiences apartments promised, but so were other attributes, such as looks, body style, character, personality, and nationality. From a madam's perspective, it was quite convenient to have sex workers return regularly for weeklong work stints.

Some owners of apartment brothels were worried about unknowingly doing business with traffickers or Zuhälter. Concerned about the integrity and safety of the women working in their establishments, madams emphasized that they never allowed boyfriends—who might well be the sex workers' Zuhälter or traffickers—on their premises, for example to pick up or drop off a worker. Some madams insisted they did not respond to male phone callers who inquired about working conditions for girls. Madams also managed conflicts among workers and stepped in when there was a disagreement. Developing good relationships with the girls and fostering good relationships among them was a key labor management madams engaged in.

In apartment brothels, the madams usually collected client payments before services were rendered, although I also witnessed some instances where sex workers collected money from clients first and then handed it over to the madam. Depending on whether sex workers also lived on the premises or only worked there, the service fee was split 60/40 or 50/50. Madams also scheduled client bookings, with clients choosing girls on the basis of what they saw advertised on the internet or after calling ahead of their visit to find out who was present. Lineups where sex workers introduced themselves to the clients were limited to larger apartment brothels. Many customers were regulars who already knew most of the girls and tended to return, often scheduling appointments with individual workers once they knew the girl they wanted was back in town.

Screening customers was another of the madam's tasks, as it was important to cultivate a particular clientele. As Susanne said, when a customer came in dirty clothes, looked unkempt, or appeared drunk or otherwise intoxicated, she had no problem telling him to leave or that she did not have any girls available at the moment. When there were suddenly too many customers, a madam had to be strategic and resourceful to make sure the men did not run into each other, as discretion for her clients was paramount. In that case, a client might be sent to hide in a restroom or closet until his chosen lady was free. In addition to maintaining good relationships with city officials and generating a flow of acceptable customers, reliable sex workers, and seamless work, a big part of a madam's responsibility was to organize the domestic labor involved in running a brothel—for example, making sure there were fresh towels, clean sheets, and an attractive ambience.

Different trajectories led these women to become brothel owners and madams. Two of them described how they entered the business when they were young mothers with small children, after their husbands had abandoned them. Two women said their husbands had more or less pushed them into the industry, in one case because of debts the husband had acquired. Two women began their entrepreneurship after divorce. While a majority of them had been sex workers themselves before they became businesswomen, there were also a few who had entered from different venues. Elisa, the middle-aged manager of several apartments and an escort service, explained that she had a master's degree in psychology. "But it was impossible to work as a counselor with four small children at home," she said when we met in one of her apartments, "and my divorced husband barely supported us." Before she adopted the apartment brothel enterprise, she had run a marriage agency where she put clients in contact with women in Russia and Eastern Europe. "Many of my clients 'returned' their potential spouses after a few months because supposedly it did not work out," Elisa said. "When I realized that they had just used them essentially for free sex, I got out of that business and started an escort agency, which I think is a lot more ethical."

Regardless of any past financial troubles, all the brothel operators I interviewed seemed to live financially comfortable lives. But many insisted they had to be extremely guarded about their personal lives and separate their work personas. This meant they maintained limited social relations outside of the social networks of prostitution. Susanne, who had a daughter in a prestigious private elementary school, was very careful not to give anybody not affiliated with her business any indication of how she made a living, as she worried it would damage her socially, and especially her daughter. For example, just a few months earlier, she had declined an offer to become a parent representative at her daughter's school, fearing that this position would make it difficult to conceal her business and threaten a scandal in the upscale social circles she had established with her husband, a pediatrician. Another brothel owner, Marlene, said she hated the nosy questioning from other parents at school gatherings and therefore avoided social interactions with people outside of her business circle.

However, the intimate links many had established with regular clients sometimes opened networks with influential men, which to some extent offset the social isolation, stigma, and disenfranchisement they experienced in the world outside of their businesses. Although apartment brothels faced steep competition from sauna clubs, their promise of discretion filled a particular client niche. However, the discretion might also have contributed to the degree of social isolation these madams described.

The prominence of women as owners of apartment brothels was hard to overlook. One possible explanation for the relative absence of male owners was that the model of shared earnings could bring an entrepreneur precariously close to trafficking, defined as profiting from the earnings of a sex worker. For Neuburg's authorities, the notion of a woman owning and running such an establishment was much less troubling than a man doing the same because it was easier to imagine a male brothel owner as a trafficker or Zuhälter. But Neuburg's social workers disagreed vehemently about whether women entrepreneurs treated sex workers categorically better than any male entrepreneur. The sociologist Silvia Kontos made a similarly cautious statement about the assumption that women brothel owners were automatically more benign than male brothel owners: "The suicide of a Colombian prostitute, who jumped out of a window on the fourth floor of a brothel, illustrates that . . . pimps were not always men and apartment prostitution was not always the Eldorado of self-determined prostitution" (Kontos 2009, 336, author's translation).[6] Unfortunately, the question of whether sex workers themselves had gender preferences for their managers never came up in my conversations with them.

Client Perspectives

Members of online client forums widely agreed that apartment brothels provided the client a maximum of discretion, although at a high price. A client could park his car anywhere in the vicinity without drawing attention to himself and enter the apartment without running the risk of facing other customers, as madams would go to great lengths to avoid exposing the men to each other. Intending to establish repeat customers, the madam welcomed new clients warmly and offered a gentle introduction of services, prices, and house rules, while established customers were greeted with a peck on the cheek and small talk about recent happenings, as I observed during my conversation with Susanne. Clients would be presented with the weekly lineup of sex workers, also available on the business's web page, or look for established acquaintances, as many women worked a regular circuit in a number of cities.

Some clients maintained friendly relationships with a madam and stopped by once in a while for coffee. Some offered their expertise or professional services to madams in what seemed like a friendship and trust relationship: among them were lawyers who provided legal support, physicians who examined workers on-site, and accountants who gave tax advice. Some even made substantial loans to madams. Susanne, for example, proudly told me that she just had finished paying back the €100,000 business loan that two of her long-term clients had provided her. The bank had denied her a loan when she'd disclosed that she owned and ran an apartment brothel.

The drawback of apartment prostitution for a client was that it offered only a limited number of sex workers and prompted men to choose[7] from a lineup or based upon recommendations, without the opportunity to get to know the service provider in a more relaxed atmosphere. Martin, a client I interviewed, explained that he had tried out a number of different kinds of establishments but eventually decided against apartment brothels because he found the lineups stressful and unnatural. The pressure to decide in a few minutes which woman he wanted to have sex with was intimidating, even overwhelming.

Sex Worker Perspectives

Apartment brothels provided a small, homelike environment where women could not only work but also live, rest, and eat. In between appointments with customers, women could relax in private, without having to be constantly on display for clients. This made the long working hours—usually from the opening at around eleven in the morning until past midnight—a less stressful environment than in other forms of sex work. In addition, customers tended to be well groomed, financially well-off, and concerned about their reputation, as they were always under the supervision of the madam. Appointments were booked usually for an hour or longer and thus guaranteed a fee per encounter of one hundred euros or more.

As apartment brothels were not identifiable as such from the outside, sex workers enjoyed a degree of anonymity from neighbors, if not from the local police department. For example, they could run errands during the day without outing themselves as sex workers. This provided a much more stress-free situation than working in inaccessible industrial areas at the edges of cities, away from stores and public transportation, or in the red light district, which granted no anonymity. On the other hand, the greater discretion these conditions afforded also brought customers with more unusual tastes and requests. Income possibilities for sex workers fluctuated significantly. While the greater client selectivity and discretion provided a wealthier clientele, there was comparatively little traffic, and it was often not clear in advance whether business would be good or bad on a given day.

One of the most common experiences of women working in apartment brothels were the long periods of waiting for clients. If business was going well, appointments were scheduled throughout the day. But there were also many occasions where sex workers were tied to apartments for long periods of time, waiting for potential customers. Sometimes, they could socialize with each other in semiprivate living rooms, lounging on the sofa wearing just a robe. As Sabine told me, early on in her career as a sex worker, she had started to take up knitting, a very conventional women's hobby in Germany, and became very adept at it. This surprised her clients, she said, and many complimented her for it.

While long periods of waiting and inactivity were boring, they were good opportunities for me to engage in conversations with sex workers. For example, one day when I was visiting the madam Sabine, I met Martina, a young woman with a small nose ring and a muscular body. We were sitting at the small kitchen table in Sabine's apartment brothel, drinking coffee together, when she told me about her professional plans. Martina worked as a vet assistant in training, and her goal was to become a vet herself at some point. "I am almost finished with my vet assistant training, and when I am done, I will work on the entrance requirements for the university," she said.

Martina enjoyed sex work but worked only a few hours a week, which helped her earn some extra money. Her boyfriend was very supportive, she said, but "he never allows me to buy him anything that is expensive. Because he absolutely does not want me to spend any of the money that I earn here on him."

Eros Centers and Laufhäuser

Laufhäuser and eros centers consist of multistory dormitories or hotel-like structures where individual rooms are rented out to sex workers. Like apartment brothels, which had existed before but became more widespread in the 1980s and 1990s, Laufhäuser have existed since the 1950s (Feige 2003; Weitzer 2012); eros centers were a more recent reincarnation of the latter. Unlike apartment brothels, Laufhäuser and eros centers offer some of the lowest prices for indoor sex and often have between twenty and fifty or even hundreds of women working there. Clients freely enter these brothels and walk through the corridors in search of sex workers. As Claudia, the owner of a well-established Laufhaus explained, city officials had approached her husband, a real estate investor, about opening such a brothel in the 1970s. The city was concerned about US soldiers stationed on a military base nearby and the large number of male guest workers from Greece, Italy, and Turkey in the local factories; officials were afraid these foreigners, many of them single men, would be a threat to the women and girls in the area. Rather than leaving this business vacuum to entrepreneurs rooted in the established world of red light businesses, they hoped that by recruiting an outsider, they would have a more trustworthy businessman to work with.

Location

While the older Laufhäuser were limited to Neuburg's red light district and downtown area, eros centers had begun to crop up in the neighboring cities in the 1990s and soon became predictable features of industrial zones, as I noticed when driving through the outskirts of cities. They were usually located outside restricted zones, so police surveillance was minimal, and outside pedestrian areas, so there were no clients to stumble upon the establishments haphazardly. Surrounded by industrial lots and factories that emptied out in the evening also meant there were no residents who would object to the type of business, be bothered by the suggestive neon signage, or complain about the heavy traffic of clients coming and going. Most of the newer eros centers were former industrial buildings; others were hotels

Figure 3.2 The inside of an old-fashioned Laufhaus with 1970s décor. The sign on the wall reminds clients and sex workers to use condoms, which was made mandatory with the Amendment to the Prostitution Act of 2017.

that had gone out of business. While apartment brothels were inconspicuous from the outside, eros centers—more so than Laufhäuser—were usually painted bright red, alerting drivers on nearby streets and highways to the nature of their business. The location of eros centers also indicated the rise of a mobile and independent clientele, different from the soldiers and factory workers of the '70s and '80s, who likely had been dependent on public transportation and thus restricted to more central locations.

Revenue and Management

The central features of both eros centers and Laufhäuser are the large number of sex workers—between twenty and one hundred—and the relatively low costs for sexual services, starting at €30 for twenty minutes of oral or genital intercourse. One owner of an eros center described them as the "Aldis of prostitution. Like the food discounter, they offer good quality for a great price, but no extra frills."

The modern eros centers differed from the older walk-through Lauf-häuser in that they offered a cleaner and more contemporary appearance, with up-to-date showers in the rooms, a uniform and recognizable architectural layout, and easier access. While milieu insiders had predicted that Laufhäuser were destined to lose out to the new sauna clubs emerging in the late 1990s and 2000 (Feige 2003), Laufhäuser have held their market share steady, especially in the new form of eros centers.

With the exception of Claudia's Laufhaus, most eros centers I contacted were managed and owned by men. There were no madams to cultivate relations with customers or screen them for safety or desirability. Instead, there were cameras monitored by security personnel—young men with body-builder physiques—and panic buttons in the rooms that sex workers rented as their work and living spaces.

Eros centers and Laufhäuser offered little or no common living or recreational spaces. Sometimes there was a small contact area and maybe a vending machine for beverages and snacks. Some eros centers had slot machines in their contact areas, which seemed to be used primarily by the women. Some had kitchens where sex workers could cook meals or cafeterias that offered food and drink, although usually at high prices.

Managing an eros center or Laufhaus meant keeping up the facility, advertising, and maintaining websites with profiles of current sex workers and their services. There was very little investment in marketing, securing clients, or providing for the daily needs of the workers. Alex and Albert, co-owners of an eros center in the vicinity of Neuburg, had come up with the idea of posting so-called current health checkups on the center's website for each of the sex workers who rented rooms on their premises. A green dot on a profile indicated an up-to-date health check while a red dot signaled an overdue health exam and thus a warning to potential customers. Although customers often assumed that a green dot meant a clean health check, it merely meant that the sex worker had seen a doctor. This practice aimed primarily to gain a tangible advantage over competing businesses and to help the eros center become popular among clients as a trusted service provider.

The staff of the local health department explained that of course doctor-patient privacy laws prevented any further disclosure about a sex worker's actual health status to the brothel operators. If a sex worker contracted any contagious disease, an up-to-date health check was no guarantee that she actually received treatment or that she stopped working. This collusion between brothel operators and the local health department was problematic, and health care providers elsewhere who knew about this practice regarded it as a violation of the Prostitution Act of 2002, according to which sex workers were no longer required to submit to mandatory health checkups.

Laufhäuser and eros centers made money primarily through renting out rooms to sex workers, who worked as independent contractors.[8] This setup was an adaptation to the prostitution laws before 2002, under which a brothel owner could be charged with trafficking if he or she provided conditions to sex workers that encouraged them to remain in prostitution. By merely renting rooms to sex workers, owners of such establishments could not be directly linked to sex worker earnings and could not be charged with pandering or pimping. Eros centers' primary customers, then, were sex workers, who paid €100 to €150 per day for the use of the rooms, or an astronomical sum of more than €3,000 per month for a small room with no or limited housekeeping services. At the rate of €30 to €50 for a twenty-minute service, a sex worker had to have six or more clients just to cover her daily rent. A sex worker who could not pay the rent would be blocked and could come back only after she paid off her debt. In this business plan, owners needed only to attract enough male clients to make their brothels lucrative enough for sex workers to want to work there.

Client Perspectives

Eros centers provided a very different atmosphere from the more upscale apartment brothels. With no entrance fee and no obligation to purchase sex, they provided low-threshold access to prostitution for newcomers, which regularly included loud and boisterous groups of men. Client privacy was not exactly part of the offer, as there was often heavy traffic, particularly at night and on weekends. Some owners of eros centers complained that many of the men who cruised the hallways had little interest in making a purchase. Since many of these buildings did not have elevators or air conditioning, which was still rather rare in Germany, climbing the stairs to multiple floors could be literally breathtaking, especially in the summer.[9] However, eros centers had clear advantages for clients—namely the large number of sex workers in one location and the relatively low cost of sex.

Without a madam as broker, the financial success of a sex worker depended primarily on her own skills to attract customers, her youth and beauty, her willingness to provide particular services, and her ability to successfully negotiate. With this type of customer recruitment, women had to be fast and explicit to gain attention. Some men on client forums complained about being overly pressured or feeling as if they spent more than they had initially negotiated, as once in the act, women would charge incrementally for extra services. This practice was disparagingly called a rip-off (*Abzocke*) and reminiscent of the negotiation practices favored by an older generation of sex workers.

Sex Worker Perspectives

Sex workers in eros centers and Laufhäuser enjoyed a degree of independence not offered by other venues. They decided when to work, for how long, and when to leave. They had private rooms they could personalize according to their needs and preferences and could close the door when they did not want to work. However, the rooms I saw in Laufhäuser and eros centers were rather depressing—small and close to each other, with a sink or a small shower, and often with the curtains and windows closed; they were stuffy and made me feel claustrophobic. Some were equipped with industrial-style lockers. There was no sign of luxury, yet the rooms were exorbitantly expensive. Unlike apartment brothels, eros centers practiced no control over who entered, so the clientele tended to be ruder, more boisterous, and—on weekends, when men came in groups—often drunk. Violent assaults in eros centers were not uncommon. This was the reason why Nena, a young woman from Latvia, decided to leave the eros center in Cologne for work at the Flamingo, where, she felt, the common lounge areas and the close proximity of others provided a safer work environment.

Despite the relative autonomy and privacy that came with renting a room of one's own, this type of brothel offered few possibilities to get away. Located in industrial areas, far away from commercial shopping areas and with no easy access to public transportation, such locations were often rather isolated. To get daily necessities, women depended on taxi services, informal relationships with men, or gopher services (*Laufbursche*) that provided small deliveries for a fee. Some of the larger, older Laufhäuser I saw in more central city locations, with their closed and darkened windows and their shabby exteriors, looked like the most depressing workplaces for sex I had seen.

A conversation with Wanja, a sex worker introduced to me by her gopher, illustrated some aspects of these working conditions. Wanja was a German

Figure 3.3 An older Laufhaus in another city.

woman in her late twenties who had worked in various Laufhäuser for
about a decade. During our conversation, which she encouraged me to tape,
she seemed unusually tense, even trembling at times. I did not understand
whether I made her nervous or what the reason for this was. The man who
had introduced me to her asked me later whether I had noticed how nervous she was and explained that this was because she still had not had a
single customer that day and did not know how she would pay for her room
expenses. It was peculiar to hear this from him rather than from her. But I
assumed that revealing this about herself would have made her feel uncomfortable and appear vulnerable.

The relative isolation of sex workers in eros centers and Laufhäuser was
combined with a very competitive work environment. Cecilia, a thirtysome-
thing woman from Spain on a three-month work stint in Germany, told me
that she found the proximity to other sex workers stressful. Some customers, she said, tried to play one worker against another by demanding special
acts or a lower price or both, saying that the girl next door had offered them
or offered them cheaper. Another source of conflict was shared bathrooms,

which were seen as places of potential contamination. Some women worried that their neighbors might harbor contagious diseases—especially those they suspected of working without a condom or engaging in other high-risk services. Yet another challenge of working in eros centers was the psychological stress that could lead to so-called *Puff Koller*, which could be translated as *cathouse rage*—a nervous breakdown attributed to the merciless competition and lack of opportunities to escape (Berlin 2012; Dücker 2005). This was exacerbated by the high traffic of largely anonymous men and by the fact that eros centers did not have intermediaries between clients and workers, a role played by madams in apartment brothels and sauna clubs.

FKK Sauna Clubs

Sauna clubs occupied the opposite end of the spectrum from eros centers and Laufhäuser. They featured state-of-the-art spa and sauna facilities in addition to luxurious bar and lounge areas. Sauna clubs differed drastically from the other establishments because they offered an environment where sex workers and clients could meet and interact and have the possibility to get to know each other over an extended period of time, similar to a real bar.

The first club of this kind was the Artemis in Berlin, which opened its doors in 2002. Sauna clubs are often very large in scale, with upward of twenty women on-site, a number that can go up to eighty or more. Since the opening of the Artemis, such mega brothels have conquered Germany, growing from very few in the early 2000s to well over one hundred by 2017. Three such clubs were within a fifteen-mile radius of Neuburg alone.

Location

Sauna clubs were spread out all over Germany but were more concentrated along the borders with France, Belgium, and the Netherlands. Most likely, this reflected an interest in attracting international clients from well-off neighbors. Sauna clubs were noticeably less prominent in the former East Germany, possibly due to the lower standard of living there and the proximity of the Czech Republic and Poland, both favorite destinations for German sex tourists (Rundschau 2019; Süddeutsche.de 2018).

Sauna clubs were often strategically placed in the vicinity of airports or convention centers in order to draw business travelers, who were predominantly male and had money in their pockets to spend. Flyers on the walls in the sex workers' living quarters at the Flamingo advertised upcoming trade

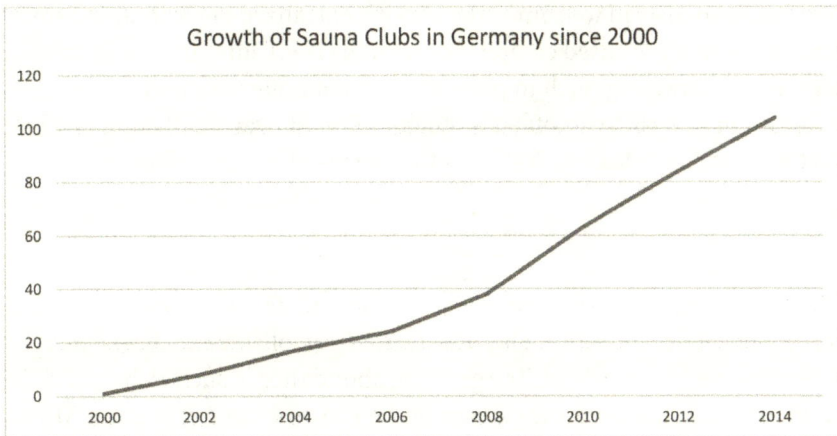

Figure 3.4 Rise of Sauna Clubs in Germany. Source: https://www.fkk24.de/fkk-saunaclubs, accessed July 31, 2018.

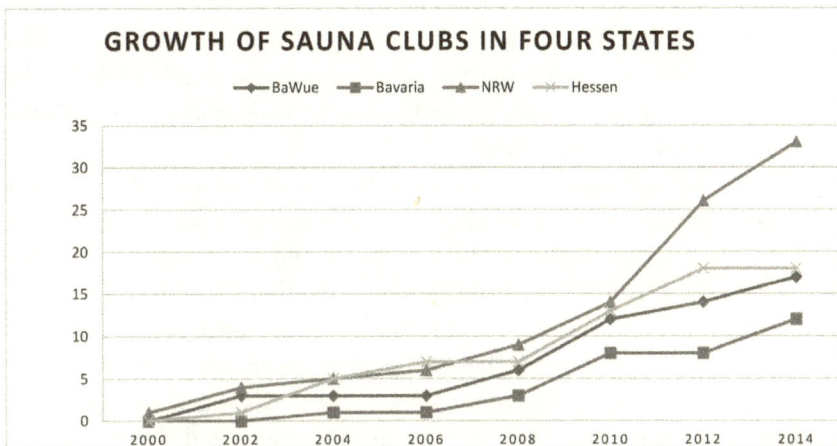

Figure 3.5 Rise of FKK Sauna Clubs in Baden Wurttemberg. Bavaria, North Rhine Westfalia, and Hesse. Source: https://www.fkk24.de/fkk-saunaclubs, accessed July 31, 2018.

fairs and conventions as lucrative times to work at the club, as they promised larger than average numbers of clients. Some sauna clubs managed to be close to freeways, where their large neon signage offered an invitation to people miles away.

Like eros centers, sauna clubs were often located in industrial settings and thus offered many of the same advantages, although they catered to a more upscale clientele. There was little scrutiny from police and city officials, who instead welcomed the idea of centralized and contained erotic businesses that promised compliance with the law. Clubs like the Flamingo, with their marketing pitch to proactively collaborate with authorities, provided an option that city officials much preferred over small-scale brothels that were prone to tax evasion and other forms of noncompliance.

Revenue and Management

FKK sauna clubs, with their lavish decor and fanciful amenities, exist mostly in Germany, although a few similar establishments have emerged in Austria and Switzerland. The growing abundance of such elaborate clubs seemed to coincide with the passage of the Prostitution Act of 2002. Milieu insiders argued that the sudden emergence of such fancy clubs had to do with the greater financial security the Prostitution Act offered to brothels and the de facto decriminalization of brothel owners. As a result of this greater stability, these insiders maintained, brothels became desirable investment objects. According to the chief financial manager of the Flamingo, they offered a profit margin of 10 percent—a sizable profit in the years following the 2008 downturn, when banks in Germany provided only minimal interest for investments.

Sauna clubs generated revenue in a number of ways. First, there was the €60 to €80 entrance fee for clients—which was also mandatory for sex workers. "The girls are guests like the clients and pay the same entrance fee," stated the Flamingo's website, emphasizing that the club could not be held liable for their services. In addition to the entrance fee, sex workers also had to pay €25 to €40 for the hotel part of the brothel—that is, a dorm room shared with up to five other women—if they needed a place to live while they worked at the club. Sauna clubs also generated significant revenue from the bar, which featured excessively priced beverages that were part of a scheme of conspicuous consumption built into the sauna club experience, as I will describe in chapter 6. Another source of revenue came from slot machines and ATMs with excessive fees. What further underscored the sauna club as a high-traffic and multifaceted economic entity of its own were the numerous secondary services offered there, including hairstyling, manicures and pedicures, tattooing, or nonerotic massages from trained massage therapists. In addition to services there was also a range of products offered for sale, such as lines of cosmetics in glass vitrines and designer-label jeans such as 7 For All Mankind.

Sauna clubs capitalized on a popular feature of German culture—saunas and nudity—and used it to market themselves as *wellness* venues—a term that had become a trendy marketing slogan. Unlike their small-scale predecessors of the 1970s—spas that targeted primarily gay men—their contemporary reincarnations featured an elaborate and exotic ambience not unlike other theme-based entertainment outlets. Sanitary conditions were a critical feature of brothels in general, and complaints about hygiene could quickly drive away clients and sex workers. By offering spa and sauna services, which proved popular in their own right, the club could conveniently levy sanitation expenses on the customers, who in turn could rationalize the high entrance fee by comparing it to an actual sauna or spa visit and produce a wet towel to prove it.

The entrance fee provided a client one-day access, which included the use of a sauna, shower facilities, a whirlpool, an ice room, and an around-the-clock buffet with nonalcoholic drinks as well as access to the lounge, porn theater, and bar area. For sex, a client had to negotiate directly with a sex worker about the services and price. The standard rate sex workers demanded—as suggested by management—was €60 for half an hour and €100 for an hour, with extras negotiated individually. A sex worker would then take the client upstairs to one of the available bedrooms and collect the money from him afterward. This was another novelty in the industry, as clients elsewhere paid before the delivery of services. Fiona, one of the top madams, explained that management calculated that on average, a sex worker would service between five and six guests and take home €150 to €200 a night after paying about €150 in expenses to the club for entrance, room, and mandatory pretax. If the expenses sex workers paid to the sauna club owner seem extensive, they were. But sauna clubs here were no different from the lowly Laufhäuser and eros centers, which charged similar fees for their daily room rentals.

Madams were an integral part of this business setup, although at the club they were employees, not owners or managers. Some madams lived on-site, next to the sex workers' sleep quarters. They signed up the sex workers; took care of their paperwork; collected entrance fees, pretax, food coupons, and deposits for lockers and rooms; and made the work plans. They checked the workers in, made copies of their work permits and IDs, and explained the rules and the facilities. Madams were also responsible for making sure the morning shift was ready to work on time and well groomed. On the floor, madams ensured sex workers were friendly to clients and that there were always enough service providers present for and visible to the clients. Madams also played a disciplinary role, reminding women to sit on their towels and to wear their towels around their chests when they went to the dining area, and reprimanding or fining them if they used their cell phones in public areas. At times, madams intervened in arguments between the women or in conflicts between the women and clients. However, madams were careful to not give the impression that they were involved in any kind of training of sex workers, a task performed by American madams (Heyl 1977), as that would put them perilously close to violating the limited right to issue directives in prostitution stipulated in the Prostitution Act of 2002.[10] While madams in apartment brothels trained their service providers how to wash a client's penis and inspect it for venereal diseases, how to best accommodate a client's demands, how to deescalate situations with clients, and how to improve their services to gain better reviews, madams in sauna clubs stayed clear of any such tasks. When I asked Flora, the senior madam at the Flamingo, whether she gave the women any advice on how to go about sex work, she shook her head. "No, that is not our job. Girls that come to us have experience, and they know what to expect." Sauna clubs also were spared unexpected police controls. Rather than having to deal with unannounced visits from police, which were common in apartment brothels, sauna clubs just sent lists of workers and information about their legal status, work permits, and passports or IDs to the police once a week.

The revenue stream in sauna clubs was radically different from eros centers or apartment brothels. The bulk of a club's income came from the entrance fees that both clients and sex workers had to pay. Large numbers of clients were desirable, but a minimum number of sex workers was critical for the club, or else clients would stay away. At the Flamingo, a full 20 percent of revenue came from the bar, the club's financial manager estimated, which also played a significant role in the club culture, as I will show in chapter 6.

Calling sex workers *guests* and treating them as independent contractors was a convenient strategy for sauna club entrepreneurs not to have to pay employment benefits. It also freed the establishment from having to be responsible for settling disagreements between sex workers and clients. One evening I overheard two clients complaining to Flora about a sex worker who had charged them both when they'd had a threesome, but Flora just told them, "This is between you two and her. All the women here work for themselves." The men received a sympathetic nod, but no more. However, many aspects of the club-worker dynamic—such as suggesting specific service fees, demanding a sex worker be present during her shift, requiring a uniform of nudity, and advertising her services on the club's website—were more indicative of an employment relationship than the freelancer contract they de jure had.

From the perspective of the sauna club operators, their business model had outperformed and even put out of business many of their competitors, particularly smaller apartment brothels. As the public relations manager at the Flamingo stated, "We are the modern face of prostitution. Our business is clean. We cooperate with local governments, politicians, and lawmakers. We want to take prostitution out of the sleaze corner. We even make generous donations to local charities, to children's funds, to women's rights organizations and NGOs, and try to work with politicians to develop retirement plans for sex workers." Such emphatic statements were a mantra that the public relations officer and the financial manager repeated regularly and were part of the larger image they wanted to create for themselves. However, not all targets of their alleged charity were eager to let themselves be used as a foil for the Flamingo's management. One women's rights organization, for example, vehemently rejected the club's offer of a donation.

The Flamingo, and other sauna clubs like it, generally advertised aggressively in well-known media outlets such as *Bild*, on dedicated internet platforms, and in marketing clips on YouTube. They also invested considerably in outdoor advertisement on city cabs or other eye-catching vehicles in high-traffic areas, as I described earlier. Sauna clubs also received media publicity through numerous television talk shows about the pros and cons of prostitution, where club owners were sometimes invited as featured guests. Some sauna clubs employed dedicated public relations managers that provided constant feeds to the news media extolling not only the sexiness of the women working in their clubs but also the supposedly superior working conditions, including the availability of on-site gynecologists, accountants, and retirement specialists and even women's representatives, although some of these services were made out of thin air, as I would soon learn.

In the end, as the mayor of Newtown's neighboring city, where the Flamingo was located, told me in an interview, this business model had proven to be very beneficial to the city. It had put out of business the smaller brothels, which sometimes had caused neighbors to complain about drunken guests and abusive Zuhälter. In addition, sauna clubs brought in significant revenue in the form of leisure tax, which was collected conveniently in one yearly lump sum.

Client Perspectives

Sauna clubs provided a bar atmosphere mixed with sauna possibilities, where clients could socialize with sex workers and other clients, use the spa facilities, dine on delicious food, and enjoy elaborate drinks. This setup allowed clients to stay for extended periods of time, as they could rest and recover between trips upstairs to have sex. Although the entrance fee was high, clubs had a clear advantage, as they offered clients the opportunity to engage and flirt with a large number of young, attractive women from many parts of the world—a majority from Romania and Bulgaria—and get to know them casually in a relaxed atmosphere at no additional expense. The more sex workers there were, the higher the competition among them and the more intense flirting a client could expect.

Many clients went to sauna clubs by themselves for a short trip on their lunch break or to spend an evening or even an entire day. Married men traveling away from home had few time constraints in the evening. Some clients went in groups, celebrating a successful business deal or taking out a newly hired employee. Others went to celebrate anniversaries or just have a night out with the guys, as was the case of four men in wheelchairs who had made it a habit to round out their monthly sports competitions with an evening at the club.

After paying their entrance fee at the reception desk, where they received bathrobes and slippers, clients went to change in the locker room. The club manager explained to me the effect having to wear club-owned attire had on clients: "Men can no longer rely on their fancy suits, shoes, or other status markers. They are much less likely to become troublemakers that way." Paying the high entrance fee also created a sentiment of noblesse oblige, where haggling over prices was inappropriate. Someone who paid so much to get in the door was obviously well off. Indeed, one client calculated that a typical night at the club, including two one-hour trips upstairs with sex workers and some drinks at the bar plus tips, would cost him €300 to €400. For a surprising number of clients at the Flamingo, this did not prevent them from coming several times per month or per week, and some even daily—although, as I learned later from clients, financial mismanagement was not uncommon among some of them. Others, however, had to save up for a long time before they could indulge. One young man in his twenties, a carpenter who lived about five hours away, told me that the money he spent in one night there would be enough for a week of vacation in Gran Canaria, a favorite tourist destination for sun-starved Germans. Juxtaposing a one-week vacation at a tropical destination with an evening at the Flamingo, where men could have sex with women who would be out of their reach outside a brothel, shows the enormous appeal the club offered.

For clients, the club's biggest asset was the flirtatious solicitations from sex workers in a friendly and relaxed environment, as numerous men explained to me. Tim, an IT manager in his midforties who had become somewhat of an expert on the pay sex scene, admitted, "Apartment brothels were not for me. You have to make a decision with which girl you want to have sex within minutes. In the sauna clubs, you have much more time to get to know a girl, see if the chemistry is right between you and her." In fact, while girlfriend sex had become a major advertisement feature for apartment brothels, the sauna club atmosphere was much more conducive to such an experience. One client stated in the regional client forum:

> I still remember my first trip to a sauna club vividly. My first impression was that this would cause the extinction of apartment brothels. And I do still believe that. . . . Visiting such a club, particularly in the summer, is like a vacation in the middle of the city. I feel as if I were at a pool, or on a beach, with the difference that I don't have to work hard to get a girl to have sex with me. . . . In addition, in sauna clubs, French kissing and unprotected oral sex are included, which in many apartment brothels are considered extra.

The number of regular clients in sauna clubs was surprisingly high, and regulars often had favorites among sex workers whom they visited over extended periods of time.

While the sauna clubs were certainly a buyer's market in terms of the extended attention and flirtations men could expect there, some men seemed quite aware of the excessive demand on sex workers' unpaid labor that this setup entailed and, as I will show later, sought ways to counteract it.

Sex Worker Perspectives

Women who worked in the sauna clubs often described them as several notches above other types of establishments, which could not match sauna clubs' lavish interiors and modern, luxurious facilities. Leonie, a young woman from Estonia who had just arrived at the Flamingo a few weeks earlier, enjoyed the air conditioning: "The heat in my tiny room in the Laufhaus was unbearable. And I was not allowed to open the curtains and window, so it was impossible to get any air circulation in the room."

Another advantage of working at a sauna club was that women did not have to invest much money in clothes. Except for lingerie night once a week, women worked nude, requiring only the iconic platform stilettos elsewhere associated with strippers. None of the women at the club ever mentioned they disliked working in the nude; in fact, some explained that over time they had come to prefer it because it saved them a lot of money they would rather use for something other than work clothes. Shopping opportunities were limited, though, as I witnessed one day with Jana, a twenty-two-year-old woman from Romania. Jana, who was very petite, with the body of a prepubescent twelve-year-old girl, had arrived at the club with very few clothes. When she came to my room one morning ready to go downtown, she was wearing a dress that was way too long and much too wide for her petite frame. With small scissors and a nail file in hand, we managed to shorten the dress enough for her to be able to walk, which she did by holding the dress up with her hands above her chest. We left the club by 10:00 a.m. and took the train downtown, where she had a routine exam at the health department, then darted to a discount fashion store, where, in the span of five minutes, Jana picked up a T-shirt and sweatpants in the children's section. We had fifteen minutes left to sit down at a McDonald's before we had to head back so that Jana could arrive at the club in time for her early shift.

As about two-thirds of the women working at the club lived far away, either in other cities or abroad, they usually made use of the hotel option that the club offered. This meant they rented a bed in a dormitory for €25 to €40 per night. Providing accommodations for sex workers was common in most of the prostitution venues I had seen. Unlike eros centers, however, where women rented an entire room to work and live in by themselves, sauna clubs offered simple beds in rooms shared with up to five others. The twin-size beds, with their white Formica frames only a few feet apart from each other, with barely enough space for a nightstand between them, were rather basic. Utility lockers rather than closets were provided for personal belongings. Such austere bedrooms were in stark contrast to the luxurious ambience in the public spaces of the club.

Sleeping in such dorm rooms was not easy. Two different work shifts—from noon to 8:00 p.m. or from 7:00 p.m. to 2:00 or 4:00 a.m.—meant that those working early would be woken up by those working late and vice versa. This often led to conflicts and women complaining about never getting enough sleep. Natasha, a woman in her midfifties whom I will introduce in detail in chapter 4, said, "When I am here, I cannot sleep well at all. After three days I have to leave because I don't get enough sleep." I myself rarely managed to spend more than three days at the club before I would end up with a raging headache due to sleep deprivation, as it was notoriously difficult to get any rest. I could not imagine working there for months at a time, as many of the international migrants did.

The Flamingo did offer a spacious dining and living room separate from the customer traffic, where women could socialize and be out of sight of clients before and after work: they could lounge on the sofa and watch TV, iron their clothes, and eat lunch or dinner away from the public areas of the club. Some friendships did in fact develop, despite the extremely competitive environment. However, for the women who had to make the sauna club their exclusive home for extended periods of time, the Flamingo offered little in the sense of real privacy—certainly less than the rooms in a Laufhaus or eros center.

Sex workers spent the majority of the workday recruiting clients—a process they called "going for a walk" (*spazieren gehen*). Women went about this kind of labor in various ways. Some just walked straight up to a man, introduced themselves, and even shook his hand; others made contact in a more playful way, teasing the men or asking if they could sit next to them. Some approached potential clients with a mesmerizing smile and, depending on sympathy, initiated physical contact, from casually brushing a client's arm or thigh to starting to fondle his erogenous zones. It was not uncommon for such contact to go on for some time, with growing intimacy between them, but not always ending in a private session upstairs. Only when she had managed to take him to the bedroom where the actual sex act was supposed to take place did paid-for services contractually start. Sometimes, a sex worker would take a client upstairs within minutes or set up a date in advance, for which a client then did not have to pay a full entrance fee.[11] Some women tried to arouse customers quickly into a sexual state of no return, for example by directly fondling or even fellating them, but this was a risky recruitment strategy, as the client might insist that he had not actually agreed to the service. Without any explicit agreement, there was no guarantee that a client would pay. Moreover, as many customers attempted to have sex with more than one sex worker, they needed a lot more stimulation after their first rounds. The more experienced sex workers learned not to waste their efforts on men who had just come back from the bedrooms.

During the months I spent at the clubs, I had much time to observe these recruiting efforts. During the day, when clients tended to be older, the interaction was more demure, while during the evenings, particularly on the weekend, the atmosphere could become quite lively, with clusters of clients flirting with groups of women, champagne flowing freely, and, at times, women dancing with each other to Eastern European pop songs, with some of their Turkish and Eastern European clients joining in. The later the night, the more risqué the flirting became, and occasionally, a couple did not make it up to the bedroom. But with the growing intoxication, tempers could also flare up, and management and security eyed the crowd carefully for potential trouble. On slow days, when customers were rare, women often spent many hours walking around in search of clients, sometimes not even making back the €150 they had to spend to work at the club.

Watching how often women were turned away by clients, I wondered how they managed to keep up a cheerful attitude. Marie, a young Italian woman who had grown up in Germany, told me it took a lot of effort to get used to this and that it could be extremely demoralizing. Some women learned to cope with the stress by forging close relationships with madams, adopting the role of a daughter; others formed a close-knit group of friends with whom they tried to share a room and work shifts whenever possible, and they spent time together on their free days. Some found ways to escape, at least temporarily, by using the tanning booths.

While it was sometimes hard to get a client, women did not hesitate to reject a client they did not like. No one could force a sex worker to have sex with a client, at least not according to the law. And I observed several occasions where women told clients they needed to wait or to freshen up first or that they were not interested in them.

As discussed above, customers at a sauna club expected girlfriend sex, understood primarily as French kissing, unprotected oral sex, and a genuine and authentic sexual and emotional performance. They also expected social time with sex workers, which customarily preceded the purchase and often also extended after the purchased time. Especially with regulars, this before and after care was indispensable.

Emergence of New Prostitution Markets: Who Are the Winners?

Clients abandoned apartment brothels in droves for the new upscale sauna clubs or the cheaper eros centers. This competition, together with the economic downturn, forced apartment brothels to lower their prices, change their service structure, or get out of business altogether. The rise of eros centers and sauna clubs also ushered in a shift in the relationships between sex worker and client and between sex worker and owner/manager. While apartment brothels still operated by sharing income with sex workers, eros centers and sauna clubs severed such economic entanglements. The clubs' business revenue was not tied directly to the sex workers' earnings, as was typical in the profit-sharing model common in apartment brothels. Instead, eros centers and sauna clubs made money from renting out rooms or charging entrance fees, thus shifting their revenue stream away from sex work and onto their guests—in eros centers by renting out rooms to sex workers and in sauna clubs by charging both male and female guests—as sex workers were called on the Flamingo's page. Sauna clubs achieved particularly striking success by fashioning themselves as oases of "wellness for men," turning a private endeavor into a male-male socializing opportunity and eliminating the need for privacy that was so central to apartment brothels. Offering sauna and spa facilities was also an innovative way to pass sanitation costs on to their guests and justified the high cover charge.

City authorities gained from the upsizing of the brothel industry. With the passage of the Prostitution Act, owners of prostitution venues were much more protected against charges of procurement and trafficking, as long as they complied with police, city, and tax authorities. The sauna clubs were also much less likely to draw complaints from residents about unruly clients or pimps, as sauna clubs are usually located away from residential areas. Clients benefitted from the upsizing because it provided them with newer and cleaner settings and a larger number of women, with emphasis on low prices in the eros centers and on a version of girlfriend sex in the sauna clubs.

How sex workers benefited from the growth of eros centers and sauna clubs is less clear. Many of the more experienced sex workers told me about price decline and service inflation, and it was hard to see any positive development in regard to working conditions, although some described the sauna clubs, with their lavish facilities, and eros centers, where workers found relative independence, as attractive work environments. The changing demographic of sex workers in Germany, with a growing number of labor migrants from Eastern European countries, suggests that these environments were becoming increasingly competitive. Still, some experienced German women chose to work in mega brothels for the long run, as they found the conditions there better suited to their style of working.

Capitalizing on Sex Workers' Labor

While apartment prostitution operated on shared profits, the revenue generated by the larger sauna clubs and eros centers came only indirectly from the labor of sex workers: eros centers rented rooms to sex workers for €100 to €150 a day—an exorbitant rate for the small rooms they offered—and sauna clubs collected entrance fees from sex workers and rent for sleeping quarters. In both these business models, sex workers were ostensibly independent freelancers, thus making management not accountable to customer complaints or responsible for employee benefits. At the same time, brothel owners managed to capitalize on sex workers' invisible labor. In eros centers, the major source of revenue came from the rent sex workers paid for their rooms, while in sauna clubs, the major revenue came from the clients and their alcohol consumption, driven by the presence of sex workers. Without the sex workers—who were described as guests but were there to flirt with and titillate male guests—clients would have little reason to go there in the first place. Sex workers' invisible labor or recruitment and maintenance of customers, with the extensive and uncompensated work of entertaining and flirting with guests and the emotional and physical labor it entailed, became free labor provided to the sauna club owners. This labor was critical to the bottom line of the club, because without sex workers' presence and recruitment labor, there would be no clients. In this regard, the freelancer status of the sex workers could be considered a form of "misclassified labor."[12] And while it was not clear to what extent a club operator would or could enforce the club standard of caressing, French kissing, and unprotected oral sex, it was clear from many posts on client forums that it was a competitive disadvantage for a sex worker not to offer these practices to customers.

Postindustrial Sexual Ethics, Emotional Labor, and Bounded Authenticity

"Bounded authenticity," Bernstein claimed, provides the contours for "the sale and purchase of authentic emotional and physical connection" (2007,

103) bound by the time of the purchase contract, although it is left open whether sex workers engage in a "self-conscious simulation of desire, pleasure and erotic interest" or in "emotional and physical labor of manufacturing genuine (if fleeting) libidinal and emotional ties, endowing their clients with a feeling of desirability, esteem, or even love" (Bernstein 2010, 155). Like the men Bernstein studied, many men I spoke to preferred the girlfriend experience. They emphasized the fact that they wanted a woman who was genuinely enjoying their company, sexually and emotionally, over "fakeness" or mechanical sex performances. As I showed in my ethnographic account of the Flamingo, however, the term *girlfriend experience*, used by Bernstein, does not map neatly onto the concept of girlfriend sex used in the sauna clubs. In contrast to the emotional and sensual authenticity associated with the girlfriend experience Bernstein's escort workers and their clients described, the discourse of girlfriend sex in sauna clubs was more narrowly focused on specific sexual services such as kissing and unprotected oral sex, although it also entailed tenderness and caressing and the implicit expectation of regulars to engage in more enduring relationships with sex workers.

Client recruitment was an important aspect of sauna clubs' popularity. Although men were not categorically denied the possibility of initiating courtship, it remained a labor investment of sex workers to a significant degree, one that was indispensable and ongoing. Here, more experienced German sex workers were at an advantage, as they had the language and social skills to engage in sustained conversations with clients and would use these assets to differentiate themselves from the mostly younger Romanian or Bulgarian sex workers, who were much more likely to engage in ongoing recruitment.

While men were explicit in their demand for girlfriend sex in sauna clubs, the women I talked to were rarely as explicit about the degree of intimacy they wanted to exchange with clients, and as the online exchange described earlier illustrated, they often resented clients who insisted on disregarding their personal boundaries.

Instead of *bounded authenticity,* I therefore suggest the concept of *boundless intimacy* to emphasize the open-endedness of sexual labor from the sex workers' vantage point. Temporal boundedness was in question for sex workers in the sauna clubs, where the insinuation or performance of authentic feelings did not begin with the purchase but was an essential part of sex workers' efforts to recruit clients. It was also not completed with the purchase; rather, it was the labor that a sex worker routinely performed after she had sex with a customer to secure future business with him and to cultivate or keep him as a regular and herself as his favorite. The setup of sauna clubs, where sex workers and clients spent prolonged time in each other's presence, thus created working conditions quite different from the setup described by Bernstein. Just as sexual labor in sauna clubs and the performance of authentic feelings were not bounded by the time of the purchase, neither were physical boundaries maintained during the recruitment and service provision. Here, rather than *bounded authenticity*, the concept of *boundless intimacy* emphasizes the lack of both temporal and physical boundaries sex workers could maintain.

Germany, probably more than any Western European nation, represents the characteristics of late postindustrial society and the recreational sexual ethic suggested by Bernstein. However, the sex workers' labor described in my study differs dramatically from that of the sex workers Bernstein studied in San Francisco, who often were nonmonogamous or unmarried, subscribed to a concept of themselves as "single persons" with no front- and backstage issues about the nature of their work, and were open to not only providing but also purchasing sexual services in the market. In addition, these women, most of them escort providers, chose this work as an alternative to less satisfying and lower-paying jobs in the formal economy. Among the 30 percent of sex workers at the Flamingo who were German, such an outlook on sex work was not altogether absent, as was evident in their frank admission of the pleasurable parts of sex work, their greater ease with communicating and maintaining relationships with clients while also keeping boundaries, and the relative leniency with which they were treated by club management.

However, among non-German women at the clubs, such a perspective was exceedingly rare.[13] Among migrant sex workers from Eastern Europe, where sex work remains a highly stigmatized profession, such a liberal view of sex work and their role in it was less common. These women often supported their extended families back home with their incomes and planned on returning to their countries of origin in the short and long term. For them, it was essential to separate their personal self from their work self. They had limited employment options in the German labor market and often sought marriage or traditional romantic relationships as an alternative to sex work. In regard to this new and more exploitative labor regime of boundless intimacy ushered in through the new sauna clubs and the Prostitution Act of 2002, Germany's brave new world of sexual commerce had serious shortcomings.

TABLE 3.1 Comparison of main brothel types in Neuburg region in regard to location, management, client perspective, and sex worker perspective.

Prostitution Venues	Apartment Prostitution	Laufhaus/Eros Center	FKK Sauna Club
Location and Zoning			
Zoning	Mixed residential, commercial, or business	Commercial	Commercial
Location	Downtown, suburbs, industrial periphery	Industrial periphery	Industrial periphery
Visibility	Low	High	High
Management Structure			
Revenue Stream	50/50 of sex worker earnings	Renting rooms to sex workers	Entrance fees from clients and sex workers
Madam onsite	Yes, usually is owner/manager	No	Yes, but is an employee
Average number of girls	4–7	20–100	30–100
Business revenue detached from sex worker earnings	No	Yes	Yes

Prostitution Venues	Apartment Prostitution	Laufhaus/Eros Center	FKK Sauna Club
Client Perspective			
Cost	€€€	€	€€
Discretion	High	None	None
Male socializing	No	Limited	Yes
Client-sex worker socializing	No	No	Yes
Girlfriend sex expected	Yes	No	Yes
Sex Worker Perspective			
Earning type	Profit sharing	"Freelancer"	"Freelancer"
Recruitment labor	None	Limited	Yes
Price for services	€100 per hour	€30 for 20 mins	€60 per 30 mins
Work expenses	None	€150 per day	€140 per day
Safety	High	Varies	High

Notes

1. Author's translation. All exchanges on the forum were in German.

2. Surprisingly, according to sex workers posting on the Austrian sex worker forum sexworker.at, price decline in the Netherlands did not occur to the same extent as in Germany, although the Netherlands legalized prostitution before Germany and were equally affected by growing immigration from Eastern Europe.

3. Kelly (2008) also found that in Tuxtla, oral sex was more expensive than vaginal sex because it was considered not normal.

4. See, for example, the numerous legal decisions about apartment prostitution on http://www.rechtslupe.de/stichworte/wohnungsprostitution.

5. Informal apartment brothels are often residences where sex workers live, and it is conceivable that the women who work and live there are more guarded about their privacy and advertise more selectively.

6. "*Der Selbstmord einer kolumbianischen Prostituierten, die aus dem Fenster einer im dritten Stock gelegenen Hostessenwohnung sprang, um sich dem Zugriff ihrer Zuhälterin zu entziehen, [machte] deutlich, dass . . . Zuhälter nicht immer Männer sind und die Apartmentprostitution keineswegs das Eldorado der selbstbestimmten Prostitution ist*" (Kontos 2009, 336).

7. According to the Prostitution Act (2002), sex workers always have the right to refuse a client, even after a client has already paid for services. At least legally, the agreement between a client and a sex worker is thus a unilateral contract, binding only for the client to pay, but not binding for the sex worker to perform. Thus, by law, a client who is choosing a sex worker and her services has to rely on her willingness to provide these services (Kavemann and Rabe 2009; see also Law to Regulate the Legal Relationships of Prostitutes [ProstG], 2001).

8. Independent contracting is the most prominent form of labor for sex workers in Germany outside of apartment brothels, just as it is for sex workers in Nevada's legal brothels and for strip club dancers in the United States. As I will show, this type of labor makes sex workers ineligible for employment benefits that the Prostitution Act was meant to afford.

9. See also Weitzer (2012), who commented on this when doing research in Germany.

10. (*Eingeschränktes Weisungsrecht*) According to the Prostitution Act of 2002, employers are not allowed to give sex workers directives on whether, with whom, or how to provide sexual services. The employer therefore has only limited power to give directives (ProstG). For more detailed information, see Section 3 of the Prostitution Act of 2002 (1990), which states that (1) employers cannot give directives about the if, the kind, or the extent of providing sexual services (*Weisungen, die das Ob, die Art oder das Ausmaß der Erbringung sexueller Dienstleistungen vorschreiben, sind unzulässig*) and (2) for prostitutes, the employer's limited ability to provide directives is not in conflict with employment in regard to the laws for social security ("§ 3 ProstG - Einzelnorm" n.d.).

11. As one of the reviewers for this book suggested, it is hard to understand why sex workers would not forgo the club and its exorbitant charges by scheduling outside appointments with clients. A worker named Katharina had in fact worked at the club and at the same time had hotel visits arranged by her Zuhälter. Exclusively working in a hotel meant being responsible for scheduling a steady stream of clients and no contact with coworkers, which provided at least a degree of security, if not friends. For sex workers who remained

for only a limited time at a location, making hotel and client arrangements could mean a significant degree of uncertainty and complicated logistics.

12. The charge of pseudo self-employment or "misclassified labor" (*Scheinselbständigkeit*) has become a hot issue in the state's attempts to regulate brothels. However, the state's primary interest does not seem to be sex workers' loss of labor benefits but the state's and municipalities' uncollected taxes resulting from this misclassification (personal communication with Neuburg city officials).

13. Although half of the women I spoke with in sauna clubs were German, it was not a representative sample. I would learn later that about 70 percent of club sex workers were labor migrants, the majority from Romania. I discovered their real national identities only after gaining access to the clubs' daily attendance lists, after I had finished the bulk of my research. Since so many were from Romania and Bulgaria, some chose to say they were from less common countries of origin, such as Italy or Greece, which was believable in regard to their physical appearance.

4

WORK AND LIFE AT THE FLAMINGO

Portraits of the Girls

"*I* FIND IT WEIRD THAT THE GIRLS HERE *are so squeamish about me taking photos of them naked.[1] I don't get that. They all are so flawless," Paul said, taking a break between photo sessions he had set up with a few of the girls at the club.[2] Paul, a bald middle-aged man wearing khaki shorts and a hippie shirt with a V-neck lace-up, seemed eager to get into a conversation with me. Maybe he was sensing in me an outsider like himself, with whom he could exchange notes about the club and its bewildering world of sexual commerce. We were sitting at the large dining table in the girls' lounge, where I had gone to get a break from the noise and the hustle and bustle of the club downstairs. Paul and I soon got into a conversation about doing photo shoots with sex workers, something the club strongly encouraged sex workers to do as part of their professionalization, although at their own expense.*

In earshot of us was Brigitte, a madam in her late forties, who was ironing her clothes. Brigitte had become a kind of confidante. She had been working in this industry for decades, so I asked her why she thought the girls were so uncomfortable about having nude pictures of themselves taken. "That is typical for the red light milieu. The girls always have to look at other women with perfect boobs. How can they not be self-conscious about themselves?" she answered, slightly irritated.

My conversation with Paul then turned to how the women at the Flamingo might feel about providing sexual services. Brigitte, who until then had not paid us much attention and continued to iron her clothes, interrupted us, now visibly agitated. "Almost all of them hate this job," she said. Looking straight at me, she asked, "Do you think there is one single eighteen-year-old girl who wants to have sex with a seventy- or eighty-year-old man, just for fun?" I countered that not all jobs were pleasant, and a nurse might not like to give someone an enema or wash a patient's private parts. But Brigitte was unimpressed. "That is totally different. To sell your body, that damages your soul. You don't forget about this. You cannot put this away. It stays with you! You and Paul, you have a totally idealized vision of this industry."

Field notes, June 2010

By the time of my conversation with Paul, Brigitte had become more than an ethnographic informant to me. She had introduced me to the routines of the club, and her friendship had been invaluable in helping me become accepted by others. As madam, she was in charge of managing the girls and a point of contact for customers. Brigitte was self-assured, with a great sense of humor and self-irony; she loved to travel off the beaten path by herself, with a backpack, for extended periods of time, and on a shoestring budget. Brigitte was not shy about setting colleagues and clients straight when they behaved inappropriately or made sexist comments. Sex work had helped her to become self-confident sexually and otherwise, she had told me. And yet, listening to Paul and me, two outsiders, she condemned the industry in the strongest terms and called out our naivete.

Brigitte's condemnation of the industry was not the only one of its kind that I would hear from a milieu insider. Nathalie, the owner of a well-established apartment brothel in Neuburg's downtown, who had provided sexual services herself until recently, made a similarly startling comment during the course of our three-hour interview, when she suddenly asked me what I thought about prostitution. Before I could respond, however, she answered herself: "It is an immoral business and should never be allowed to be legal."

Such scathing condemnations from milieu insiders—and successful ones at that—were juxtaposed by enthusiastic comments from others. Eva, owner of a successful escort club and a licensed psychologist, for example, praised the autonomy and experimentation that this line of work offered to women with a high sex drive. Sarah, who was co-owner of a number of different apartment brothels and a sauna club, married to a physician, and mother of a toddler, emphasized the degree of sexual self-confidence sex workers often developed as a result of their work. Sex workers I spoke with in the various establishments I visited also made this point. Lili and Marie, for example, had been doing gigs together in sauna clubs for several years.

Just settling into their work one evening—they usually came together—Lili approached me and said, "We want you to know: We do like this work. Do not think we are victims. This job is okay. It actually gives us a thrill and a sense of power to control men sexually, and they pay us for it." Similarly, Irina, a woman in her late forties from Russia, who was married and had four grown children, made it a point to explain to me that work at the club was an opportunity to satisfy her sex drive as well as make a good living.

Doing Research with Sex Workers

The discomfort that sex workers had about the photographer taking nude portraits of them and the ambivalence insiders felt about the industry are mirrored in the portrayal of sex workers in society at large. In academic discourse, those who look at prostitution through the lens of work and workers' rights and as a labor market comparable to other markets prefer the term *sex worker* (Bernstein 2007; Kempadoo, Sanghera, and Pattanaik 2012; Weitzer 2012), while those who look at prostitution as a form of sexual and gender oppression prefer to use the term *prostitute* or *trafficking victims*, emphasizing the view of sex workers as victims with a lack of agency (Hughes 2000; Jeffreys 2009, 2013; Meshkovska et al. 2015).

Although prostitution was legal in Germany, the stigma associated with it had obviously not disappeared. Most sex workers did not particularly like to talk in detail with me about the intricacies of their work, even if they were adamant about letting me know they were happy with it or even found it empowering. Unlike clients, who were eager to share their impressions with me at the club, sex workers at the Flamingo were more reserved, at least initially, which was consistent with what I had experienced with the women at the Night Owl. Talking with an outsider about their work made some women visibly uncomfortable. Language barriers seemed only to enhance this discomfort.

Up to that point, my experience with sex workers—primarily in the context of the Night Owl and older sex workers in more precarious conditions—had taught me that few were interested in answering mundane questions from a clueless researcher. My apprehension about feeling like an intruder was reconfirmed on my first visit to the Flamingo, when the manager introduced me to Henry, a tall man in his midforties with a big belly, and asked him to give me a tour. Henry was a VIP client, which meant he was a frequent visitor and possibly a personal favorite of the club owner. He was pleased about being considered an expert by the PR manager and happy to help. Showing me the facilities spread out over two spacious floors, he turned out to be an astute observer of the club and a thoughtful connoisseur of the scene. Our tour came to a premature stop, however, when he decided that two women standing at the bar would make a convenient test case for his theory about whether friendship among sex workers was possible. Instead of asking about their experiences, however, he began to lecture them on the psychology of sex work and friendships between workers. As expected, this turned quickly into a divisive conversation between "them" and "us," and I realized what an unfavorable first impression I was giving at the side of this pretentious mansplainer.

My previous experiences had made me careful to avoid cornering sex workers into giving up information that might make them uncomfortable or feel overtaken. Scholars who work with trauma survivors (Sheftel 2013)—a description that is likely to apply to at least some sex workers[3]—have argued that researchers need to respect the silences of their participants and be aware of the moral complexities their research entails and the conundrums it can cause. Taking a "wait and see" approach to conversations with women at the Flamingo was ultimately the only approach I could stomach. Rather than aiming at a comprehensive and representative sample of sex workers and their experiences at the Flamingo and approaching women directly, I would be content with a smaller set of whoever wanted to talk to me. Thus, I decided to introduce myself and my project when the occasion arose but wait until a sex worker was ready to hear about it. Here, I draw on the experiences of more than thirty women who felt comfortable enough to talk with me or decided on their own to talk to me. Many of them I would see again and again during my eighteen months of visits to the Flamingo. However, there was also a good number of women with whom I had little or no interaction and knew nothing about. For example, it came as a surprise to me when I found out, a year after I had left the club, that the majority of women registered at the Flamingo were from Romania.

Intimately tied to the question of representation is the question of reception. What knowledge and assumptions do readers bring to the subject? And does a focus on generalizations and types fairly illustrate the complexities of the relationships and the subjective experiences of different actors? Here, as Susan Dewey (in Dewey and Zheng 2013) has argued, an "ethnography of the particular" (5; see also Abu-Lughod 2000, 262) provides a powerful strategy of anthropological representation "which conspicuously avoids a focus on the theoretical and analytical in favor of recreating the complex nature of everyday life" (Dewey and Zheng 2013, 5). In the context in which Abu-Lughod wanted to introduce Arab women, the subjects of her study, to her American readers, processes of othering had been entrenched, and ethnographic accounts of Arab "culture" were likely to be perceived as flattened categories of others. "In our own socio-cultural worlds, whatever objectification takes place in forms of social-scientific representations is countered by what I called the discourses of familiarity—the way we talk about ourselves and our friends and family in everyday life. We know that everyone is different, that people are confused, that life is complicated, emotional and uncertain. This counter discourse does not usually exist for us with regard to distant communities where all we might have is the social-scientific analysis, the ethnographic description" (262–263).

Sex workers, like Arab women, have become an excessively used subject of othering in a variety of discourses, shaped and bent to represent one facet or another of the reporter's theoretical framing. By employing a perspective of "ethnographies of the particular," I hope to resist such an attempt to flatten stories to fit particular typologies and instead present portraits that allow contradictions and complexities of personal experiences.

Following such an ethnography of the particular, the profiles I present in this chapter are stories of women who invited me into their personal lives; they are stories that revolve around them and our interactions with each other rather than around my questions. Instead of following a deliberate agenda or set of inquiries I had in mind, these stories chronicle the women's lives in the context of their work at the club and reflect the research process and the relationships that developed between industry insiders and an outsider.

There are drawbacks to such a methodology. The four women—Lavinia (forty-four years old, German), Katharina (twenty-three years old, German), Natasha (fifty years old, Russian immigrant), and Ariana (twenty-seven years old, Bulgarian)—were not a representative sample of the demographics of sex workers at the Flamingo, not in regard to age (the vast majority of women were in their midtwenties) nor in regard to their nationalities, as most were from Eastern Europe. But there were also definite advantages. Since conversations took place at the club and predominantly during their work shifts, the nature of our interactions throw light on their work environment and the roles we both assumed vis-à-vis the club, the clients, other sex workers, and staff. The result is a mélange of conversations meandering from the immediate present to experiences in the past and hopes for the future. I was available to talk when they needed to let off steam with someone who was not part of the social fabric of the club. The spontaneous interactions rather than scheduled interviews also avoided the pitfalls of extended narratives in which research participants are sometimes prodded to create rehearsed stories about themselves and their lives or force coherent narratives (Nencel 2014, 2017)—something that had crossed my mind when Bettina from the Night Owl told me what sounded a bit like a rehearsed life history. In contrast, the conversations on which the following portraits are based were rarely linear but comprised a patchwork of narrative selves, structured by the frames of different conversations and moments in action, and embedded in a particular environment and context.

Work Routine at the Flamingo

On the website and in official management parlance, sex workers were referred to as *female guests*. Both sex workers and clients paid about the same entrance fee, and both used the services that the club offered: the bar, the restaurant, the lounge areas that stretched out over two floors, the dining area, the spa facilities, and the bedrooms in which the sexual service was supposed to take place. There was a difference, of course: men came to relax while women came to work. Describing sex workers as guests also obscured the fact that they had to follow rules set by management, although they were technically self-employed.

After paying the entrance fee, sex workers, just like clients, received a hard-to-remove red paper bracelet, similar to those that hospitals use to identify their patients. This was proof that they had paid. At the end of the workday, madams cut the bracelets from the girls' wrists and settled the scores, calculating how much the club owed them for drinks they had been invited to and pole dances they had performed. Sex workers then checked in at the registration desk on the second floor, where a madam took down their names (both actual and performer), passport or ID information, and, if they were not German or did not have proof of EU citizenship, work authorization documents. The information collected was sent once a week to the local police, who checked it for migration status, work permits, and minimum age requirements. Women who came from countries that were part of the European Union required merely a valid passport. Although doing sex work was legal beginning at age eighteen, letting someone work who was younger than twenty-one was risky for brothel operators, as any suspicion of foul play could quickly turn into charges of sex trafficking.

After filling out the paperwork, a sex worker signed up for the shifts she wanted to work—either morning, from 11:00 a.m. to 7:00 p.m., or night, from 7:00 p.m. to 3:00 a.m. during the week or 4:00 a.m. on weekends.[4] She then paid the €50 deposit for a key to her personal locker. If she decided to sleep there overnight, she would pay the additional €25 and receive sheets and blankets for her assigned bed in one of the dorm rooms, which she shared with up to five other girls. Not all women opted to stay at the club overnight. Some preferred nearby hotels, particularly those who wanted to be able to have clients outside of the club as well, recruited through escort agencies or on their own.

In addition to the twenty to eighty or so sex workers who worked there every night, the club had a permanent staff of about sixty employees. Among them were eight madams; three to five of them were present at any time. The madams' job was to register new arrivals and instruct them about club expectations: french kissing and oral sex without a condom were considered standard service, and €60 for half an hour and €100 for an hour were strongly advised as the going rates. Beyond that, a sex worker was free to set her own fees for additional services—an area in which German-speaking women had a decisive advantage. But even among them, significant additional charges were uncommon in this highly competitive environment. Women were required to work nude, except for their high-heeled platform stilettos and maybe a small waistband. On Tuesdays, they had to wear lingerie such as sexy bras, corsets, or boudoir sets. For hygiene reasons, workers were told to use towels in the dining area that were available throughout the club—one for their chairs and another to be wrapped around their chests.

Club management calculated a sex worker would have five to six clients per day so that even with only the thirty-minute services, she would have a daily gross income of about €300. After paying for the entrance (€70), her shared room (€25), the daily upfront income tax (€25), meals (€6 for dinner, €3 for breakfast/lunch), and other incidentals at the club, she would be left, on average, with €170. This was still a sizable income for the average unskilled German worker, although not as much as freelancers, as they had no access to employer-based benefits such as pension plans, unemployment, health insurance, or sick days.

The protocol for using the bedrooms where sex was to take place—sometimes it occurred in more public areas—was highly structured. The sex worker would take a client to the second floor, take a key from a designated board, find a room that was open, and leave the key in the door from the outside. Seeing a closed door with a key stuck in it signaled to others that the room was occupied but presumably also reminded a client that someone could enter at any moment and thus could work as a layer of protection. After finishing with a customer, the sex worker was to close the door and bring the key to the housekeeping crew, who then would go in to tidy up the room and get it ready for the next use. This protocol ensured that clean rooms were easily distinguishable from used ones. Sex workers were instructed to put a large bath towel on the bed when they were with a customer, as bedsheets were not changed after each use. After returning the key, a sex worker followed the client to his locker, where she would get paid. After each customer, a sex worker was expected to use a shower or bidet to freshen up. Those who did not follow this routine could quickly raise the ire of their colleagues, as fear of contagious diseases was widespread.

Cell phone use was not allowed in the contact area. Breaking that rule came with a fine of €10 to €25. While the official reason was that sex workers using cell phones signaled to clients that they were unavailable, another reason was that management did not want workers to make arrangements with clients outside of the club, as this would cut into the club's business and would mean fewer women were available on the floor. However, playing the slot machines, another potential distraction that could signal unavailability, was not forbidden. And in fact, playing the slot machines, which were spread out over two floors, remained one of the main distractions for staff and sex workers alike, and another lucrative source of revenue for the club.

Since mandatory health checkups had been abolished, the Flamingo did not require sex workers to visit health departments. In fact, management gave no formal instructions on how to practice safe sex or how to use condoms, though sex workers could purchase them on-site. I was surprised that all of the work rooms were equipped with large bottles of Vaseline body lotion, a petroleum product that dissolves latex-based condoms. "Oh, these are not lubricants. They are used for massages," one of the women from the housekeeping team assured me. Not all clubs practiced such a hands-off approach to health and what is referred to in Germany as *safer sex*. In fact, some states (Bavaria, for example) require condom use even for oral sex.[5]

Although the club was easy to reach by train and just a ten-minute walk from the subway station to the club, the women who did not live at the Flamingo usually arrived by cab or were dropped off by a friend or, as some clients suspected, their Zuhälter. Only some of the German sex workers owned cars and drove themselves. Walking the short distance from the subway station to the club could turn into a walk of shame, as the club's location in an industrial area without regular foot traffic instantly marked any attractive woman walking in the vicinity as a sex worker. In particular, pulling a wheeled suitcase—indicating an overnight stay in this industrial area—would be a dead giveaway and could lead to annoying catcalling or worse.

In order to maximize their earnings and keep down their expenses, many women opted for housing on the premises, in the club's dorms—euphemistically called the hotel. Some doubled up their shifts and took off only one day per week. As a result, many women spent the majority of their work stints almost entirely within the perimeter of the club. A few of them had lived at the Flamingo for the last six months without ever having gone home.

Some felt that the lack of daylight, the many hours working in the dark, and the constant exposure to people, music, and cigarette smoke were taking a toll on their health, as was the difficulty in getting a good night's rest. Those who lived on-site also complained about getting little privacy; some went to the tanning booths in the basement to get away from it all. This almost total lack of privacy meant, paradoxically, that outside the context of commercial sex sanctioned by the house, sex workers were essentially unable to engage in intimate relationships with partners.

For those without a car, being tucked away in an industrial area could make access to the daily necessities of life difficult. Although the downtown area was within walking distance, many relied on in-house services and merchandise. Thus, the club maintained a secondary economy consisting of niches tailored to the needs of sex workers. For the most urgent daily necessities not provided at the club, a nearby gas station with a convenience store offered everything from toothbrushes to headache pills, snacks, wine, phone cards, and cigarettes.

Many women, especially those living abroad, were on two- to six-month work stints before they returned home. Generally, the farther away they lived, the longer they worked at the club in order to cut back on their travel expenses, although the new economy airlines that now operate within Europe have made international travel faster and cheaper than ever before. While clients were talking to me about sex workers' lengthy bus rides to get

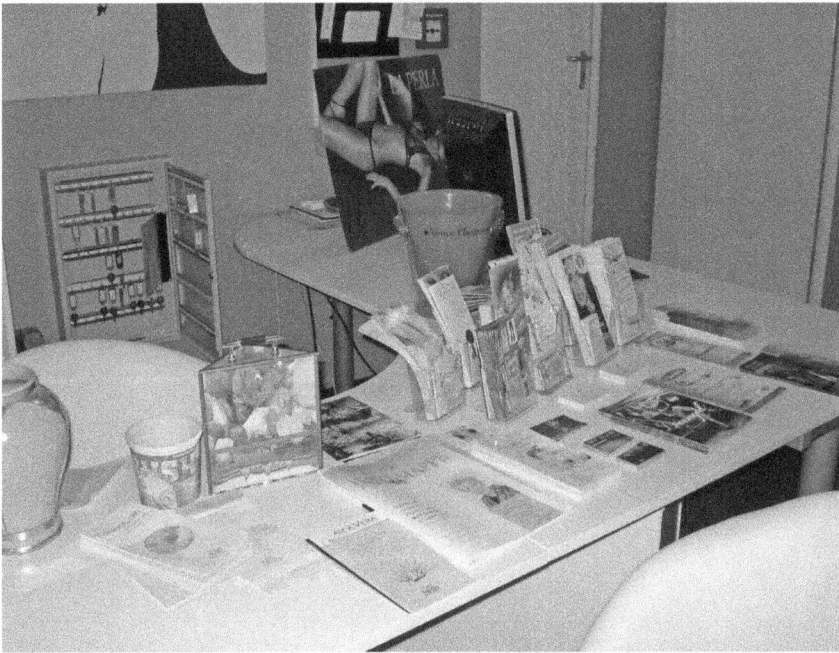

Figure 4.1 Registration desk for sex workers with spread of leaflets for health services, cosmetic institutes, etc.

back home, plane tickets from Germany to Romania or Bulgaria or a variety of other destinations in Europe could in fact be had for as little as €20, less even than most bus rides would cost.

Three out of ten women at the Flamingo were German. That percentage was higher than in most other commercial sex venues I had visited and higher than the 10 percent quoted nationally (TAMPEP 2009b). The reason for this, according to management, was that the club expected sex workers to be able to engage in conversations with their clients in German or in English. The majority of sex workers at the Flamingo were from EU countries in Eastern Europe, following an established trend where women from the newest and poorest EU member states tended to be the most prominent nationalities among sex workers (Staiger 2009). A very small percentage of women were from Latin America and Asia, many of whom were married to German citizens and thus had German citizenship.

Those who lived on their own in the vicinity of the club were more likely to work there only on the lucrative days—Thursdays through Sundays—or

Figure 4.2 Display case with skin care products for sale in sex workers' living quarters.

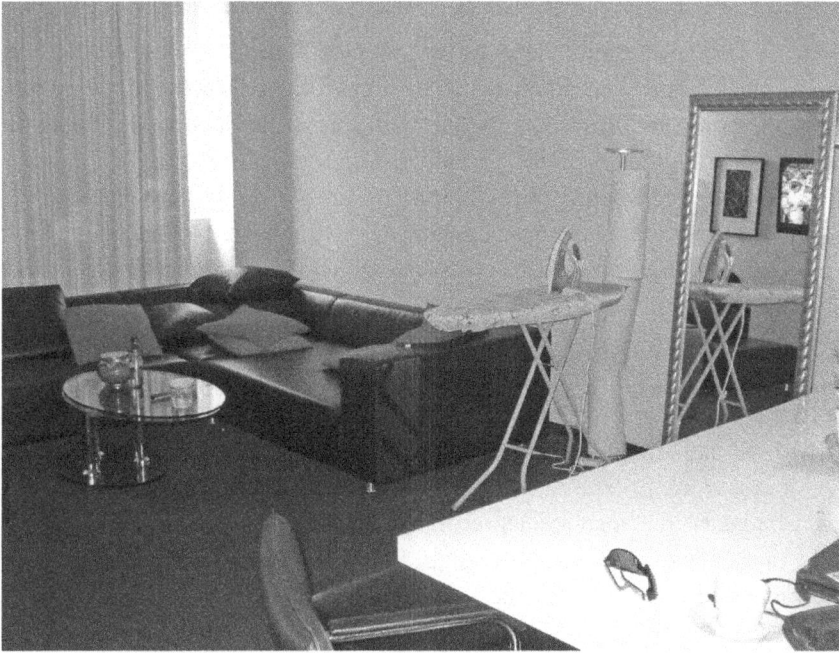

Figure 4.3 Living room in the sex workers' quarters.

rotate between clubs in the area. Working in different clubs or moving from city to city was a common strategy for sex workers to maximize their client base. However, the woman rumored to be the most successful at the Flamingo was a local who worked six days a week and had done so for several years.

While most of the women at the club were in their early twenties, a few regulars were in their forties or even fifties. Everyone at the Flamingo, as elsewhere in the industry, referred to the sex workers as "the girls" (*die Mädels*), often using the English term. Thus, when Lavinia, a woman in her midforties, described herself to the women she shared a bedroom with, who were two decades younger, as "one of the girls," it conveyed a sense of communalism and egalitarianism. Similarly, when madams referred to the "girls," it was a respectful way to differentiate between sex workers and staff. And finally, when clients talked about the girls, it seemed less to infantilize them and more to address them as someone whose favors they wanted to win. Outside of the club context, some clients politely referred to them as "female service providers" (*weibliche Dienstleisterinnen*), possibly in order to normalize the sexual services they purchased and make them comparable to other personal services.

For some, the Flamingo was their first sex work experience. Others had been in the business for decades or had even run brothel establishments themselves. Some worked only on Saturdays, like Jessica, a college student who used her earnings from the club to supplement her college stipend. As she confided in me one night, the club gave her an opportunity to enjoy the attention of older men—father figures, whom she generally preferred over younger men. Sabine, another regular, worked at the club to supplement her job as a salesperson in a bakery while enjoying the glamor and excitement of the club. Some were accomplished businesswomen in their own right, like the silversmith who regularly sold her handcrafted jewelry for €700 apiece to madams and colleagues at the club and hoped to earn €10,000 in a month to buy the materials she needed for her work. Marina, a muscular blond woman from Bulgaria, had been a professional athlete but was left without any job prospects when she got older; another woman from Hungary had earned a business degree in Italy that she hoped to utilize once she had earned enough at the Flamingo. For Sheila, an Afro-Caribbean who was married to a German man, it was just an easy and entertaining way to make money, although, at the age of thirty-six, she played with the idea of settling down and having a child. "I tried that once," she told me. "But I got bored out of my mind and decided, at least for now, to go back to work here." For a good number of women, the work at the club was a means to make a living, sometimes even enough to amass what would be small fortunes in their home countries, although quite a few expressed their intentions to remain in the industry for only a limited time.

The four women whose experiences I am describing in the following have vastly different backgrounds and trajectories and show the diverse experiences of sex workers at the club: Lavinia, a middle-aged German woman who described herself as addicted to the fast-paced and glamorous life of sex work; Katharina, a young divorcée and mother who became increasingly disillusioned with her Zuhälter; Natasha, a Russian woman in her fifties who was married to a German and for whom sex work had become a dead end; and finally Ariana, a bubbly young woman from Bulgaria who supported her family back home.

Lavinia: "I Am a Milieu Junkie"

Flora, the senior madam at the Flamingo, approached me one evening. "Annegret, here is a lady who wants to talk with you about her work." And

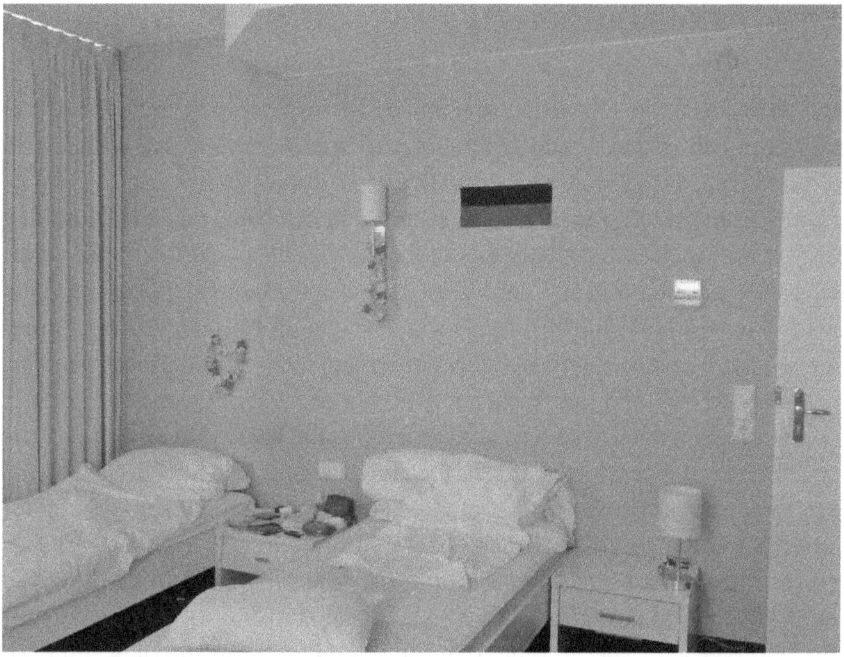

Figure 4.4 Bedroom in the sex workers' living quarters.

Figure 4.5 Nightstand between two beds in sex workers' bedroom.

she introduced me to Lavinia, who looked to be in her early forties. She was tall, broad-shouldered, with ample breasts and a small waist, wearing an unglamorous pink bodice and miniskirt.

After Flora left, Lavinia sat next to me at the bar, and I explained my project and showed her the consent form for her participation in the study. Lavinia was outgoing, self-confident, and easy to talk to, quickly making me feel at ease. Like all the other women to whom I presented the consent form, Lavinia wanted only a verbal agreement. She had no problem telling me about herself and her work, she said, but putting her signature and her real name on a document was not something she wanted to do.

What is it like to work at a sauna club, I asked, and how did she manage the contrast between work at the Flamingo and life outside the club? Lavinia was prepared for this question: "Every time you drive to a club, you go through a kind of metamorphosis," she said. "And this is how you do it." Sitting up straight on the barstool, she continued, "You get in your car, you play your special type of music that puts you in the right mindset, and on the one-hundred-mile trip, you transform from Isabella to Lavinia. Once you are done, you drive home again and return to being Isabella. The long drive helps you get the distance you need between home and work." The ease with which she answered made me wonder whether she had been asked this question before. Lavinia told me about her eighteen-year-old son and said she had to make sure that he would never find out about her work. For his sake, outing herself was not an option.

Being a sex worker was not socially acceptable, Lavinia said, but she herself did not mind the work. In fact, she liked and even needed the party atmosphere, the fast pace, and the naughtiness, and it was good money. She had been in the industry for more than two decades, starting with table dancing in 1989. Then, for fifteen years, she had run a small apartment brothel with her boyfriend. After they broke up, he paid out her share, and with the money, she started a small bistro, which, she said, "had no connections to the milieu whatsoever." But she missed the milieu scene. "You know, I am a milieu junkie. I need the fast pace, the thrill, the raunchiness, the people." For a bit more than a year, she had been working at the Flamingo, usually four days a week, from Thursday through Sunday. She loved the atmosphere at the club. "I have found a family here. There is such a good atmosphere and team spirit. I feel at home here; it is more like coming to have fun than coming to work."

Getting back to her experience of running a brothel—and curious about the persistent rumors I had heard about Zuhälter—I asked whether that boyfriend had been a Zuhälter. Lavinia was unfazed but did not answer directly: "He was always correct with me." I must have looked skeptical, as she added, "A Zuhälter means status and protection. Of course, as in other relationships, sometimes there are marriages of convenience and physical abuse and control. But such relationships don't happen only with prostitutes and Zuhälter."

Lavinia assured me that she was no weak heart and not easily intimidated, as she had a black belt in martial arts. "That helped me to learn how to control my mind. I had to defend my sister once from her husband. Not only did I get him off her, I even broke his ankle. And he is much stronger than I am," she said. While Lavinia did not say that her former boyfriend was a Zuhälter, she did explain the benefits such a companion could provide and at the same time assured me of her ability to stand her own ground. It certainly did not sound as if she considered them to be criminal exploiters of sex workers.

As we were sipping on our drinks, Lavinia kept playing with a little embroidered string purse. This was definitely not a designer handbag, to which, as some clients insisted, so many sex workers were supposedly beholden. Lavinia excused herself to briefly say hello to a guest who had just arrived, leaving her bag on the table. I had watched other women do that and always wondered why they did not seem to worry about their purses getting stolen. After all, theft was not uncommon at the club.

When Lavinia came back, I asked her. "Oh, there is nothing too important in here. Check it out!" And she poured out the contents. "Here is my phone. That is the most important. That is my connection to the outside world. I need this so that I always can be in contact with my son." Then there was a small bottle of hand sanitizer; a small bottle of Weleda rose oil—"for massages," she explained; a little container for coins; and a travel-size tube of Alverde facial cream, an inexpensive drugstore brand, with the end of the tube cut off. She caught the surprise on my face and said, "Of course! I do that with all my cosmetics. That way I get everything out." She also had wet wipes "to clean the penis" and an antibacterial cleaning lotion, "also for the genitals," she said. I was about to tell her how unhealthy such lotions were, as the staff at various public health departments had pointed out to me. Lavinia did not let me: "Of course, when you work here, you need something like that!"

She dug out the rest of her handbag's contents, revealing business cards, a hairband, and a nail file, and looked at me, bemused by my interest in what to her must have seemed like utterly mundane objects. She did not keep money in her purse. That she would always take to her locker right away.

Judging by her purse and its contents, Lavinia definitely did not fit the image of the sex worker addicted to designer handbags and other luxury items, as so many clients mentioned when they complained about sex workers supposedly being incapable of managing their finances. But it was also something I had heard from others. Nathalie and Bettina, two former sex workers, described to me how fast the money had gone through their hands when they'd begun in sex work. Money was easy come, easy go, and something in the nature of sex work, they thought, made consumption an easy outlet to counter frustrations. However true that was, Lavinia's purse and its contents suggested she was rather frugal.

Lavinia explained that she had been at the Flamingo since it first opened and was close to management and the madams. The owner, Hans Hartmann, was a friend of hers, she said. "When I started—or, rather, when the club just opened—we did a team-building exercise, the girls and staff. Everyone got some type of glass stones, and then we sat down and made a large mosaic together. It is still on display somewhere in the building." Since then, staff and management had grown together even more, she said. "Hans is really an asset to the whole sauna club scene," Lavinia said emphatically. "He is just very humane." Also, the madams made sure she would get a good room to sleep in, with others she got along with. Right now, she had a four-person bedroom but shared it with only two colleagues.

A few weeks earlier, her colleagues had organized a birthday party for her at the club. "They gave me a birthday card, with everyone signing it, and everyone was so warm with me. Even some guests remembered me and congratulated me. That was very touching," she added. "And the guests notice it when the girls are having a good time."

When I saw her again the following week, Lavinia told me about having been interviewed at a local TV station about her experience as sex worker. Documentaries about prostitution had become a staple on German television, especially on the many private channels. "They asked me to be available for half a day but interviewed me only for an hour or so. But they paid me five hundred euros." She chuckled. "They promised to blur my face and change my voice, but when I looked at the show, there was just a two-minute segment that had anything to do with me. And even in these two minutes, they did not use my own words but made it sound as if I said that men who go to brothels are afraid of their wives. But that is not at all what I said."

It was obvious that Lavinia enjoyed special status at the club. I often saw her joking with the madams; she was closer in age to them than she was to most of her colleagues. In fact, she was much more integrated into the social network of staff and management than that of her work colleagues. When I asked her about it, she just shrugged her shoulders. "You work with the girls, and you are friendly to them, but you keep your distance. In the end, they are your competitors."

This declaration seemed a contradiction to her earlier statement about the team-building effort she had participated in with the staff. However, it was plausible that the club would be more concerned about the sex workers—their alleged guests—engaging in team building with the staff rather than with fellow sex workers. Particularly without a formal power of directive, staff and madams depended on the soft power of trust relationships to discipline sex workers.

Like other German women at the club, particularly the more seasoned ones, Lavinia was critical of her coworkers from Eastern Europe, who, she said, did anything a client asked for and cared little about how to work safely. "Their low prices, their low expectations, their lack of training, all that is the reason why gonorrhea, syphilis, and AIDS are spreading drastically," she said. I had heard similar allegations from staff at various health departments I had visited.

The special status Lavinia seemed to enjoy was reflected in her work habits. On some weekends, while others were walking around to recruit clients all evening long, sometimes without success, Lavinia was just sitting at the bar. One Saturday, when we had been talking for over an hour already, I finally asked her whether she was going to work that day. Lavinia looked at me. "Why would I waste all my energy now when I know I am going to make good money later just sitting at the bar and partying?" She explained that some VIP had booked her in advance. All she needed to do was sit and drink with him. She would get paid by the bottle and did not have to have sex with anyone. In addition to the Flamingo, Lavinia also worked at another club owned by Hans. And then she had her grandpa (*Opi*), an eighty-one-year-old she had known for over ten years. Once a week or so, she would spend the day with him, but she had not had sex with him in a long time. "It is more like a father-daughter relationship. He gives me three thousand euros per month and occasionally an extra fifty-euro bill."

During the eighteen-month period in which I went to the club, Lavinia and I would often get together and talk about our favorite topic: men. When I first met her, Lavinia had been in a relationship with a gym owner, whom she had been dating for a year or so. And while she insisted she was close with him, exchanging text messages with him every few minutes, she also liked one of the staff members from the Flamingo, a good-looking, muscular massage therapist. She would never act on her infatuation, though, she said. Under no circumstances was her boyfriend to find out about her fascination with him. Anyway, management did not allow fraternizing among sex workers and staff.

When I went back the following summer, Lavinia had just started to see someone new. This time, it was a man considerably older than herself, in his sixties. "He is an alpha-type man. He owns several sauna clubs," she said. They had met at the Flamingo, but he had never taken her to a room or requested sex. He just sat at the bar with her and invited her for drinks. After a few months, he asked her to join him on a trip to Spain.

A few weeks later, I saw Lavinia again. It was a hot Sunday around noon; both of us had just gotten up, and the only thing on our minds was where we could go swimming nearby. But her shift was to start soon. The dark interior of the club, still harboring the scents of bodies, cigarettes, and perfume from the previous night, seemed unreal and stale. Lavinia had something she needed to talk about. So we went to the back of the club, where no one could overhear us, and she began to tell me about her new lover and their trip to Spain. They had been lying in bed together, and she was in the mood for sex, but he said he was tired and wanted to sleep. Lavinia was visibly upset when she told me of her ordeal. She was thirty-nine years old, she said, and she still had sexual urges, but there did not seem to be any sexual excitement between them. She did not think it had to do with the fact that she worked at the club, as he owned several sauna clubs himself. He was a big-timer and planned to go into business with Hans to open a new club elsewhere. But what was she to make of a romantic relationship without sex?

Katharina: "Madams Don't Have as Much Power as a Zuhälter"

Katharina's story was different. She was a native German, like Lavinia, but was half Lavinia's age and had entered sex work only recently. I was sitting in the Flamingo's restaurant section, eating dinner, when she took a seat across the table. Trying to start up a casual conversation, I introduced myself as a researcher or, as I jokingly added, a "professional observer" writing a book about the club. She looked up, suddenly curious, and told me that she also was writing a book and already had an editor in Berlin. Her book would be something like Charlotte Roche's *Wetlands*, a phenomenally successful novel about demystifying femininity that had taken teenagers and young adults in Germany by storm. Her own book, Katharina said, would be based on her experiences but written as fiction. The editor had asked her to send him whatever she had, and so far she had sixteen chapters. If she could sell the book, she would not work at the Flamingo anymore. I had met a number of women who planned to write a book about their experiences but never one who was as matter-of-fact about it as Katharina.

Katharina was a petite blond woman. She was wearing a black bodice when I met her, the same one I saw her wear every Tuesday. It did not take long for us to get into a conversation. "Isn't it interesting that the beautiful women have a more difficult time here than others?" she asked me one day. "Men do not dare to approach me. Men can go for something better here. But instead, they go for something worse looking than they have at home." As I was trying to figure out what prompted her to make such a statement, it dawned on me that she might be talking about herself and—comparing herself to her coworkers—was trying to come up with an explanation for why she had so few customers.

So far, she had worked only at the Artemis in Berlin and at the Flamingo in Neuburg. "The Artemis, by the way, is a lot different from this club. There you have a gynecologist, and you can get treatment directly at the club," she said. "They have mandatory health checkups there every week, including a urine test and an STD swab, but here at the Flamingo, nobody knows if anybody ever sees a doctor."

Katharina was eager to tell me about herself. She had married when she was nineteen, and now, at twenty-three, was divorced with a three-year-old son. Her ex-husband had mental health issues and had to be hospitalized once in a while. He had taken care of their son in the past, but he kept asking her what she was doing and where she was going, and she got tired of it. "So I decided to let him go as my childcare option," she said.

"My family also has no idea what I am doing. They think that I have my son with me when I am working." Katharina lived over five hundred kilometers away from the club. "So whenever I come back home, I have to work hard to keep them away from him, so I can spend some time with my son by myself." Katharina received long-term unemployment money (*Hartz IV*), from which she would give €700 every month to a girlfriend to take care of her son for the ten to twelve days when she was gone to work at the clubs. "With my unemployment money, I have created a new job!" she said proudly.

Over a few weeks, Katharina and I chatted regularly. It turned out that she was intimately familiar with the subject of Zuhälter. The topic had come up often with the women at the club, who regularly pointed out colleagues who were, as some of them put it, "stupid enough" to work for them. Katharina was not perturbed at all by such disparaging comments but went straight into telling me about her own experiences. "The last time I was here, I earned nineteen hundred euros in five days. Of this, I could keep twelve hundred euros for myself," she said proudly, in spite of the fact that that was barely two-thirds of her earnings.

At the moment, she worked together with four other girls at the Flamingo as a "family." One of them was German, one was Russian, and one was a Latina. If Katharina ever had a disagreement with one of them, she would just let her Zuhälter know about it. "I never tell a girl in my family that I have a problem with her. That is the job of my Zuhälter. He needs to prevent a 'bitch war' (*Zickenkrieg*)," she explained. "And he does that very well."

I was astonished by how Katharina was talking about working for a Zuhälter. While most women at the club had spoken with contempt about such men and the women who worked for them, Katharina showed no sign of embarrassment. She told me she had met her Zuhälter on an online dating site and had no idea about it when she first went out with him. They had been dating for several months, she said, when she realized that if she did not work for him, their relationship could not last for long. "Because," Katharina explained, "when we go out together and he pays for me, he actually uses the money other women have been earning for him." Katharina's reasoning took me off guard. Not only did she speak about this logic as if it were self-evident, but she also did not signal the slightest concern about how much many of her colleagues were disturbed—if not disgusted—by Zuhälter and the women who worked for them.

I asked her how common she thought it was for girls to get into relationships with men who then turned out to be Zuhälter, a strategy that has been described as "lover-boy syndrome."[6] "Sometimes they do know it," she said, "but you can never be jealous, or you will be kicked out immediately.

You have to know how to play along and get along with the other women." Katharina's response seemed to be about the risk involved in being in a romantic relationship with a Zuhälter, while I had in mind the risk of falling in love with someone who then turned out to be a Zuhälter. Katharina added that sometimes a girl felt that her Zuhälter owed it to her to have sex with her. After all, she gave him money. But not all Zuhälter really wanted to have sexual relations with their women, she insisted: "Some [women] are so old and fat that a Zuhälter would prefer to run away instead of having sex with them." I remember thinking how strange it was that Katharina seemed to take on the perspective of her Zuhälter so effortlessly, as if she had internalized his comments or somehow been brainwashed by him.

After what seemed to be a very sexually adventurous relationship, she had gradually started to enter sex work. It started when he took her to the grand opening of one of his buddy's clubs, which turned out to be a brothel, and she discovered the thrill of having sex with other men for money.

According to Katharina, almost all the women at the Flamingo had a man in the background for whom they were working. Sometimes the Zuhälter was also their boyfriend; sometimes he was solely their manager, and there was a real boyfriend in the game as well. In terms of her service, she said, "I never offer French kissing. That is disgusting to me. You never know what a client has been licking before." And, she added, she did not like finger play either, except with a condom or a latex barrier, which guests usually brought along for themselves.

Women who had Zuhälter were in a better position at the Flamingo. What they paid their Zuhälter was really protection money. For example, if a guest acted up or got unruly or abusive, a girl could just call her Zuhälter, and he would take care of him. "How?" I asked, growing increasingly exasperated with what seemed like Katharina's boundless naivete. "Give him a knuckle sandwich? Here? With all the security around?" But Katharina was not impressed by my exasperation. "It does not necessarily have to be at the club," she responded. "A Zuhälter can just wait outside and then take care of a customer." I could not help but think how gullible Katharina sounded and wondered for how much longer I could withhold my thoughts. What proof would her Zuhälter give her that he actually had "taken care" of her customer, whatever that might entail?

I told her I was perplexed by hearing so much about Zuhälter in a place that promoted itself as model prostitution business, without connections to the underworld. So many women had told me there were Zuhälter among the guests, but I had never been able to spot one, let alone speak to one. How would I even recognize a Zuhälter? "That is easy. They look like bodybuilders. They have tattoos, shaved heads. They act in a certain way. And they have their Rolexes."

Why would Zuhälter come to a club if they had access to more sex than they could possibly want? I wanted to know. They did not come to buy sex here, she said and laughed. They came to try to recruit girls from another Zuhälter by offering them better conditions. However, that could get complicated. "If a woman wants to get out and has no debt, she can go. If she has debts, then she has to pay off her debts first. And sometimes, if a girl does not act right and brings shame on all of her family, or if she treats the other girls badly, then she can sometimes be sold for a few thousand euros to another Zuhälter." I was confused. "What do you mean?" I asked Katharina. "You can't just sell someone!" Obviously, Katharina was more concerned about the business obligations of the sex worker than the lawfulness of the Zuhälter. She looked at me, surprised about my apparent lack of understanding. "Where do you think we are here?" she asked. I pressed her: "But are you not scared about these practices and how people treat each other here?" She replied, "No. My Zuhälter is very good to me. He is treating me very well. I have to give him only a small percentage of my money. And he has done so much for me." Just the other day, she said, her car had broken down and she was about to be late for work, so he helped her find a rental car so she could make it to her shift on time. Or if he saw that she was wearing the same shoes for a month, he would give her money and tell her to buy some new ones. Unfortunately, many girls at the club did not treat Zuhälter well. "Zuhälter often have to pay three times as much as other men and get really bad service. Sometimes, the girls throw the condoms in their face. Or they tell them to 'hurry up,' or 'are you still not finished,' and rude stuff like that."

Katharina was undisturbed by my disbelief and continued to defend the position of Zuhälter. I then changed from asking about her Zuhälter to what she thought about the attitude of the club management about them; I mentioned that whenever I had asked the madams about them, I was told either how terrible they were, that there weren't any, or that management could not do anything to keep them out. "Well, it is the madams' job to keep the fighting between the girls down. But madams do not have as much power as the Zuhälter," Katharina said; the meaning of this statement would not reveal itself until later.

I asked, "So what would cause women to fight with each other? When they compete over clients?" Katharina replied, "No, that is not a big deal. Fights happen when a woman is in the room with three guys, and then again right away with another client, without taking a shower in between. That woman obviously has a problem with hygiene. If you have the same client, and on top of that, this woman shares a room with you, that means trouble. This is the kind of stuff I tell my Zuhälter. And then he takes care of it." She paused and then added, "I am often surprised how this young thirty-year-old has the tact and skill to take care of problems! How he is able to express himself! There are hardly any real blowups between us all."

Katharina looked down at her phone. She apologized. She still had some appointments outside of the club. Working only at the club was not worth it, she said. The club was elegant, but there were long periods when you just sat around and waited. But please, she said, I should not talk so loud. Otherwise she would soon be kicked out of the club. Obviously, having customers outside of the club during one's shift was not something management encouraged. Maybe as an explanation to the previous statement, she added that it was not her thing to hit on guys. She would just smile at them. Actually, she was rather shy and would talk with men only if they approached her first.

I asked Katharina whether she could put me in touch with a Zuhälter. "Yes," she said. She knew one who was pretty upfront, a really cool guy. I cautioned her that it was likely more difficult for a Zuhälter to talk to me because pimping was illegal. "No," Katharina said, "pimping is not a crime as long as you provide services." I started to wonder whether my understanding of Zuhälter and their legal definition were actually correct. "But I would never get a tattoo with the name of my Zuhälter. That is something only foreign women do, women from southern Europe," she said. "And it is always names like Ahmed or Mohammed. They usually have it tattooed on their back or on their belly. Totally stupid," she said. "With a tattoo like that, you can always be found, and you can never leave your Zuhälter." Once she knew a girl who had the name of her Zuhälter tattooed on her arm and then had it surgically removed. It had left her with a thin scar, and one day, when she was in a tanning bed, the whole scar opened up. "The blood was splattering around." Katharina laughed as she told the gruesome story, leaving me perplexed once again, this time by her apparent callousness.

We went downstairs and sat at the bar for a few more minutes. A client who had caught my attention a few days earlier because of his oversize glasses and his awkward look sat across from us. He fixated on Katharina and, after a few minutes, sat down next to her and tried to strike up a conversation. Katharina just mumbled something without as much as looking at him. He made a few more attempts at making conversation, but she paid him no more attention until he got the picture and left. I looked at her, surprised. "He was just too stupid. He has tried that a few times already and doesn't seem to get that I will never go to a room with him. He is just beyond help!"

Katharina and I had been talking for over an hour, and it was just about time for her appointment with her client at the hotel. On her way out, she would have to get past one of the tougher madams at the reception desk. I had often heard madams giving girls who tried to leave during their shifts a hard time. That night, I did not hear anything, so Katharina must have been able to leave without a problem.

A few days went by before I saw her again. I was sitting at the bar, sipping from my beer, when Katharina sat next to me, looking bemused that I drank beer. One of the madams walked by and greeted us, and Katharina told her that she thought it was great that I was there. Of course, I had been a rather attentive listener, but I couldn't help but wonder why Katharina habitually adopted her Zuhälter's perspective when responding to my questions and why she was so oblivious to many of her peers' harsh attitudes about them. I never did have the heart or the courage to confront her about it.

When I went back a few days later, Katharina sat down next to me, with the little black satchel she always carried and wearing the same black bodice she had worn every Tuesday. Picking up again my interest in meeting a Zuhälter, she said that the client she had seen me talking to the other day—the one with the conspicuous ear gauges—had in fact been a Zuhälter. She did not know him personally, but she knew of him. They would acknowledge each other but go their own ways. Her Zuhälter never came to this club. But today, another Zuhälter had been there, a bald guy with a tattoo. Katharina had actually seen me talking to him. I said he'd told me he owned a few brothels, but he would just rent them out and not work himself anymore. Katharina looked skeptical. "Well, he does not work anymore. It just means he lets the women work for him." I was surprised by her critical stance on this Zuhälter but also by my own naivete. He came at least once a month, Katharina said. Trying to improve my Zuhälter radar, I asked her about another client, a heavyset middle-aged man with combed-back black hair and tattoos. She laughed. No, that was not a Zuhälter. That was a motorcycle manufacturer, a real sweet guy. She got along with him well.

A man, well groomed, balding with white hair, approached us and asked if he could interrupt for a moment. Would Katharina have time for him later? "Yes," she said. I was surprised by how cold she was with him and how submissive he was with her. He came back a little while later, saying he would wait for her in the smoking lounge. He would just go to the sauna briefly and then take a shower. She did not need to hurry. I wondered whether he wanted to let her know that he would, in fact, be clean for her.

Katharina and I returned to our favorite topic. What did Zuhälter do in a place such as the Flamingo? I asked. "Well," she said, "they look for new girls; they try to recruit them. Sometimes they just come for fun." I looked at her, surprised. "But they don't come here to have sex with their own women, do they?" She laughed. "No, that wouldn't make any sense. The girls have to earn money." So did they come to check on them and how well they worked? I wondered.

"Are you in a relationship with your Zuhälter still?" I asked her, changing the topic to cover up my surprise about her comments. Katharina thought for a moment. "I am not sure. Maybe we have moved apart from each other and it really is already over. In the beginning, we did have a relationship. I told you I met him over the internet, on a regular dating site." I did not want to press her any further. When I had first met her the previous winter, she had just started working the sauna club circuit. Now it seemed she no longer felt entitled to make any claims about an emotional connection with him beyond a business relationship.

To cheer her up a bit, I asked about her book project. She had not had much opportunity to write, she said. Sometimes she would write something on the go, on her cell phone. She showed me a story about how she had met the perfect guy. She had been at a party with her boyfriend, so she just met him at the wrong time. "Like snow in summer. So unexpected, so beautiful, and so fleeting!" She watched carefully so that Mona, one of the madams on staff that night, would not see her with her cell phone. Mona had already caught her once and then had her do the early shift—which was not really a punishment because Katharina preferred to do the morning shift. Anyway, Mona was not a real madam; she was just working at the reception desk. She did not have any real power there. I was surprised that the staff could discipline their female guests, as they liked to call them, in this way. Weren't all the girls freelancers?

Katharina told me about a customer she'd had the night before. He had brought shoes and jeans for her to wear: "I had to ram half my fist in his ass. That was a real fetishist." But he paid her €150 for half an hour. Did she wear latex gloves? I asked. No, she said, she used a condom. The guests often brought their own toys with them. "Don't you have to check these toys? Make sure they are safe?" I asked. "I check once in a while. But the whole SM business is interesting, exciting to me. I am born for it, this role-play. My father used to be very domineering. Role-play is in my blood. My brother, who lives in Frankfurt, actually has an SM studio in his apartment." Most of the customers she received in her hotel room had these kinds of fetishes.

A few days passed before I saw Katharina again. Sitting at the bar next to me, she showed me her new blue nail polish. We chatted a bit, catching up on the things that had happened. Katharina told me about a VIP client. Flora had suggested she give him special attention. He was a high-ranking US military officer or something like that, in his fifties or sixties. She was having a pleasant conversation with him about her son when the man suddenly freaked out and slapped her in the face. She could feel his fingerprints burning on her face hours later, she said. At the time, she did not tell management anything. Because he was a VIP, she did not expect that they would do anything about it. But she did tell her Zuhälter. "He almost crushed the dude's intestines," she said. I was not sure how much I should believe her story. It reminded me of her earlier story about Zuhälter beating up customers. Again, I could not help but feel that Katharina sounded very gullible as she did not doubt in the slightest whether any of that was actually true.

Katharina would soon have another date with a client she had gotten over ads. She was now setting up appointments with escort clients herself, often while she was at the Flamingo. In the past, her Zuhälter had set up such escort dates. "Sometimes it is difficult to decide what to do," she said. "Either go with a guy at the club, who is already there, someone you can check out in person, or go to a better-paid escort date in the hotel."

Shortly before I left that night, around midnight, she was back from her hotel date and told me she would stay until 4:00 a.m., closing time, and drive home, which was a seven-hour ride. She would probably stop at a rest area to take a nap. Her back was really killing her today, she said. She had already had a few disc hernias. Her discs bulged inward, she said, not outward. That was why they were so particularly painful. Katharina looked tired and miserable.

It wasn't until a few weeks later that we saw each other again. Earlier that day, I had talked with one of the girls in Katharina's "family." They now shared a hotel room outside of the Flamingo. Katharina began to tell me the ordeal she had gone through the night I'd last seen her. It turned out that the pain in her back was not a pulled muscle or a slipped disc but kidney stones. The pain had gotten increasingly worse on her drive home, and she decided to go to the nearest hospital that Sunday morning. She had to stay for a few days before they let her go. Katharina did not mention that her Zuhälter offered any support in this ordeal.

Natasha: "Why Do You Stare at Us Like an Idiot?"

I met Natasha in December 2009, on the first day I returned to the Flamingo that winter. I was busy trying to get acquainted with some new rules, such as no more smoking at the bar, which had been condoned during my previous visits. A police officer in uniform had come into the lounge area earlier that day, an uncommon sight and one not particularly welcome by staff or clients. I was told that in the past, the club had allowed smoking and just paid the fine if they got caught, but the presence of police at the club was a more formidable threat than a fine.

Sitting at the bar, I was getting settled to watch the scene around me. Natasha walked straight up to me, without any introduction, took my hand, and, in a gesture of joint conspiracy, whispered something into my ear. I was unprepared for this unexpected intimacy but pleasantly surprised. After we exchanged a few words, Natasha suggested, "Why don't you get undressed and we have fun here together?" Flattered by her invitation, I told her I did not think I was attractive enough to work there, and I was too old for it anyway. Natasha waved off my concerns. She herself was forty-three years old, and there was a demand for more mature women like us, she said. She'd just had a guest that afternoon who was adamant that he preferred older women.

As we got into a conversation, she asked me what my role was at the club. As I was about to answer, she interrupted me and told me she would give me a miniskirt so I could start working. I was charmed by her insistence and the sense of instant familiarity but of course thought she was joking. She ignored my protests and after a while suggested we go upstairs to her room, where we could drink some wine she had bought. Then she could show me the miniskirt and shoes that she had for me.

Her bedroom had six twin beds. Next to each bed was a matching nightstand, looking like one of Ikea's lower-priced models. The black carpet, purple walls, and minimalist white Formica furniture made for a sobering ambience compared to the extravagant luxury of the public area of the club downstairs. Opposite the beds were industrial-style metal lockers—not exactly hotel furniture—for personal belongings. Natasha asked one of the girls in the room whether she could get us a couple of glasses from the kitchen. Then Natasha pulled out the two bottles she had bought at the gas station and opened them: one was a sweet spiced wine (*Glühwein*), fitting the wintery Christmas spirit, the other a red table wine. When her roommate came back with the glasses, Natasha filled them, mixing a bit from each bottle—to make it a bit sweeter, she said—and cheered. "Drinking a bit of wine first makes it easier for me to work," she said. Natasha relaxed as the alcohol began to take effect. I had looked so friendly, so inviting to her, she said, and she complimented me on my body. But Natasha's euphoria soon gave way to a darker mood. She could not sleep very well here, she said. There was just too much traffic in and out of the room, and because she went to bed early, she hardly got any sleep, as most of the girls came much later. After working at the club for three days, she was exhausted. No way could she work there any longer. I asked her about the impossibly high platform shoes that all the girls were wearing and how she managed. "You get used to it! The other day, one of the girls asked me to lend her a pair. The ankle strap on hers was broken," Natasha said. "I lent her a pair, but I really did not want to. I don't think it is sanitary to share your shoes with someone else. The girl might as well keep the shoes."

After we both had finished a few glasses of the wine mixture, I suggested we go downstairs. Natasha tried a few more times to convince me to put on the miniskirt and just try out the work. But I finally convinced her that I was better off just watching. Soliciting clients was not what I had told management I was doing. Even if I would have been curious to try, I did not want to give management any reason to become suspicious.

I suggested we check out the porno cinema. I had gone there a few times on my own but had always felt like a voyeur, watching others engaged in various forms of intercourse both onscreen and offscreen. Going there with Natasha would be a good cover. A few couples were sitting or lying on mattresses in front of the screen, absorbed with their own erotic pleasure and accompanied by the moaning from the loudspeakers. Natasha was not very interested in the film, which featured a fellatio scene, but instead begged me to let her see my breasts. I felt a bit odd and hesitated. Eventually, I reasoned, she'd had hers uncovered all night—how could I refuse to let her see mine?

A little while later, we left the cinema and sat down on a swing. It became clear how frustrated she was about her job. "All the men are assholes," she said. "After you have gone to a room with them, they often don't even bother to greet or acknowledge you again later." She had just lost all interest in sex. She had not had sex with her husband for over twelve years—he, by the way, knew where she worked. Yes, he had gotten her out of Russia and brought her to Germany, and that was good, but there was nothing between them anymore. She could not kick him out at the moment because he had problems with his family. But it had been a long time since he had brought home any money.

Then she began to tell me about one of her recent clients, who had wanted to have sex without a condom. He had rubbed his penis against her, which she thought was totally disgusting. Her health was crucial to her. She had not made a big fuss about it because he apologized in the end, but she found it nauseating. Remembering the experience, Natasha got in an increasingly bad mood. "Look at that baldhead here . . . and at that albino in the corner, or that fatso at the bar. There are just no attractive men here. Thank God I already had my first customer. At least that covers the hundred-and-fifty-euro expenses for the house." After a while, Natasha got up and excused herself. She had to go for a little "walk." For the rest of the evening, as I was talking to one of the managers, I watched Natasha making the rounds, but I could not tell how successful she was that night.

I wondered why Natasha had shown so much interest in me. Maybe she had sought me out as a sort of wing woman—I might steer men into her corner while at the same time acting as a confidante with whom she could commiserate. Maybe she saw in me a potential ally. I had reacted to Natasha's flirting with genuine sympathy, never mind that her approach to me differed little from the customer acquisition attempts she probably used with men.

The following evening, Natasha and I spent more time together. She told me that in one of the sauna clubs where she had worked, they had introduced a new rule of no longer hiring women over forty. That had been a real blow to her. She had talked with Hans Hartmann, the owner of the club, about it when she ran into him in one of his other establishments, and he had told her she was welcome to work at the Flamingo. At first, the madams there tried to send her away, which was embarrassing, but she finally convinced the main madam that she came specifically on the owner's recommendation. Only then did they let her stay.

Natasha's bad luck streak continued that night. In between doing her rounds, she looked for me and told me this had not been even as good as the day before. She had been working since 2:00 p.m. but had not yet had a single customer, and it was already 8:30 p.m. All the men here were creeps anyway, she said. "Look at them in their ridiculous red bathrobes and slippers." I began to notice negative feelings toward the men in red bathrobes myself. I told her I had considered taking a date to the Flamingo, but now I was having second thoughts. Natasha said, "Don't do it. You can do so many other things. Then he just starts to look at other women."

Natasha did not care much for the local men here and their lack of savoir vivre. At least her husband had a happy and outgoing personality; she could laugh with him. Between our chats, she made rounds looking for clients. Today she was much more depressed about her work than she had been the previous day. Yes, sometimes she would have fun having sex with a client, but that meant nothing to her.

Natasha came back again a few hours later to hang out with me and told me that my eyes looked very tired. I explained that they were always like that, no matter how much I slept. But Natasha would not keep quiet. She said I should try using some makeup so it was not so visible. I was starting to get irritated with her insistence. What business of hers was it how my eyes looked? But I tried not to pay any attention to it.

A few hours later, I went upstairs to try to take a little nap away from the smoke, the banter, and the people, as I was both tired and agitated. After a while, Natasha came upstairs as well. I was happy because I had been unable to fall asleep, kept awake by nervousness, and Natasha had quickly become a person with whom I felt I could let my guard down. She asked me how I was doing and said I did not sound too chipper. Maybe I should dye my hair. I had such a young face, but my gray hair made me look like a grandmother. I looked at her flaming-red hair, which I admired. But I told her that dyeing my hair was not something I was planning to do. Natasha was undeterred. I would look so much younger with dyed hair. I would like the results. I started to wonder why she was again so concerned about my looks. My patience was wearing thin. Finally, I blurted out, "I don't want to compete with you," and was shocked when I realized how she could take this. Natasha did stop talking about my hair.

Another time, as Natasha and I decided to sit down for dinner together, I asked her about a tall, slender brunette who had caught my eye numerous times. She always had a mysterious look in her eyes, as if in her own world. At the same time, she seemed alert and friendly any time potential clients walked by. I had watched with fascination how she approached them, looking straight into their eyes, as if she deeply cared about them. I had seen her kiss clients, closing her eyes with an expression on her face that appeared to be sheer bliss. On one occasion, she had played with a client's nipple, and he seemed to melt in her hands. Natasha knew who I was talking about; she said she was from Ukraine, that she was not stupid, and that she was doing a lot of exercise to stay in shape, but she also was so simple, so uneducated. Natasha would watch her always wolf down her food, standing up, never taking the time to sit down. She would always work stark naked because she was too stingy to buy herself a nice lingerie set. And she would do anything for a guy—suck his toes, his anus. What for, in God's name? Men did not pay more than fifty euros for half an hour anyway.

Natasha noticed a man a few feet away who was maybe in his early thirties and had been watching us. She turned to him, took his hand, and asked him whether he wanted to go up to a room with her. "Later," he said. She replied, "Why, then, do you stare at me like that? That is not very nice of you." She took his hand and tried again to coax him into going upstairs with her. He again refused. Natasha let go of his hand, and with undisguised anger, she yelled at him, "Why, then, do you stare at us like an idiot?" I did not quite understand what had made her suddenly so angry.

Natasha told me she'd had a number of weird experiences that evening. One guy she had taken upstairs to a room all of a sudden acted as if something had happened and left in a hurry. And then there was this old guy who was totally disgusting. When she was in the room with him and saw his penis, it was covered in stinky smegma. She had cursed him out and told him that he should go and wash himself.

Ariana: "This Is a Shitty Life"

I met Ariana one evening while I was still digesting an unpleasant conversation with Anton, an uninspiring client in his fifties who had tried to talk me into going out with him somewhere in town. When I asked him why he wanted to have dinner with me, a middle-aged woman, when there were so many young women around, he said he dated all kinds of women. Only if he paid for sex did he expect something special.

I was angry about his comments, but also about my reaction to them. It took a while before I noticed the three bubbly girls next to me with their red towels wrapped around them, as was mandatory in the dining area. I was curious about them, and as a pretext for a conversation, I asked whether they were speaking Turkish. It was Turkish, indeed, but they were all from Bulgaria. Perplexed, I countered that it was impossible to understand who spoke which language in the Balkans. Their cheerfulness was contagious, so I asked if they knew the film *Head On* (*Gegen die Wand*), a cult movie by German Turkish director Fatih Akin. "With Sibel Kekilli, the woman who used to be a porn actress," one of them said, beaming. Of course they knew her, and they loved her. As I was about to explain my role at the club, Ariana, as she introduced herself, waved me off. They knew about me already. They had seen me around and heard I wanted to write about the Flamingo.

Ariana and I got involved in a lively conversation, soon forgetting about the other two women at the table. I told her I had learned to love *börek*—Balkan pastries—when I visited Yugoslavia in the early '80s, but the börek sold at the Turkish fast-food restaurants in Neuburg nowadays didn't taste anything like the ones I'd had in Yugoslavia. She laughed and said she would invite me next time she made some. She knew how to make börek from scratch, not with ready-made store-bought dough. She had learned it when she was thirteen, but she had to get up every morning at six o'clock to make the dough. In fact, she used to be a börek baker of sorts, she said. But it was hard work for little pay. Time flew as Ariana and I contemplated the virtues of well-made börek.

I instantly liked Ariana. With her pitch-black hair, dark eyes, olive skin, exuberant temperament, and expressive gestures, it was hard to resist her charms. Ariana was twenty-eight years old and the oldest of the three women at the table. She had a twelve-year-old son who—she held her hand up to her head—was already her height. He lived with her mother in Bulgaria, in a town between Sofia and Varna. Every six months or so, she would fly home to see him. Ariana wanted to quit this job within a year or so and was hoping to open up a little boutique. Later she told me she had tried to get credit from a bank, but it was difficult to get money with her kind of work. The bank told her it would be easier if she had a regular job.

By the time we looked around, the other two had left. Realizing how much time had gone by, Ariana excused herself and got up. She had to "go for a walk" (*spazieren gehen*)—i.e., look for customers. I felt like a whirl-wind had come through, and I realized I had completely forgotten Anton's comments from just half an hour earlier.

Three days later, as I was chatting with several women at the reception desk, Ariana walked in from the street, wearing her regular clothes, just in time to get ready for the evening shift. Happy to see her again, I greeted her enthusiastically. But Ariana looked very tired, without the exuberance she'd had last time. Her upper lip was swollen, as if from a cold sore. Ariana told me she was not feeling well and that she had gotten hardly any sleep the last few nights.

Several days later, it was still oppressively hot and muggy at 5:30 p.m. when I made it to the club. It was the day of the long-awaited opening of the outdoors area, where clients could tan themselves in the fresh air, protected by fences from the view of outsiders and from the dreary industrial sur-roundings. Instead of making a beeline for the deck, I was happy to escape into the cool air-conditioned interior of the club.

I had been perplexed by Ariana speaking Turkish although she was Bulgarian and was wondering whether, with her black hair and dark skin, she was Roma. Not that I actually knew whether these were definite char-acteristics for Roma in Bulgaria. But it was a common rumor among the guests and staff that many of the girls from Bulgaria and Romania were Roma, although they would be unlikely to admit it.

Ariana joined me while I was standing at the bar. I don't recall any-more whether she wore anything that evening or not, as the stark effect of seeing women without any clothes had long since evaporated. Still puzzled about Ariana's ethnicity but unsure how to ask her about it, I told her of a Bulgarian friend who had adopted children from an orphanage, all of them Roma children, and how badly the kids in the orphanage had been treated. This story struck a nerve with Ariana. She'd had her son when she was six-teen and then went to work as a musician and dancer in the EU to support him. The father of her baby had never given her any money or bought the baby anything, she lamented, and the state gave her only twenty-five euros per month in child support. But her son was so big and so hungry that he would eat ten euros' worth of food in a single day. "Of course, he is spoiled," she said. "He only gets the best and only what he wants. Other kids walk around with a piece of dry bread in their hands, begging."

As long as he was small, his paternal grandmother took care of him, and Ariana always sent money to her. Then one time, when she came back to see him after three years, her son did not recognize her. That was when she decided to take him back. But his grandmother did not want to hand him over to her. "So," Ariana said, "I just took him from her. And then I let him sleep in the bed with me. The next morning, he did not want to go back. I am his mother. He knew that." Her son's father visited the baby regularly, but he never paid anything for him. "Never!" Ariana said. She tilted her head a bit to one side and thought for a moment. "Maybe I should not be too hard on him. Of course, I had a lot more money than he did, since I was working in the EU."

Then our conversation took an unexpected turn. Ariana told me she was Protestant (*evangelisch*) and would like to find a church in the area but did not know how to go about it. Back in Bulgaria, in her village, there were so many children who were Protestant, but there was no pastor for them. Ariana paused for a moment. Thinking aloud, she said, "Why am I telling you so much about myself?" Then she continued, "Annegret, I try to be friendly to everyone because God wants us to be good to other people. He will reward us for it."

Ariana said she would like to adopt a girl, but she would first have to ask her son. He would have to be okay with it. Once, when she went to an orphanage—as people in Bulgaria sometimes did to drop off donations or to take home a child for a weekend, she explained—she had seen such pretty girls there. There was "this girl with blond hair and blue eyes. So beautiful. The girl took my hand and wanted to come with me." But at that moment she was not financially able to support another child. She had sent much of her money to her mother, who had bought a house in Bulgaria, and now they were looking for something else, maybe an apartment here in town, so she could bring both of them to live with her. But at twenty-eight, Ariana said, she felt old. Much more self-confident and experienced than when she was younger, for sure, but she did not want to continue doing this job for much longer.

We continued our conversation a few days later. I had come at about eight in the evening when I ran into her. She did not feel well. Her belly hurt, she said. On top of that, she'd had root canal surgery earlier in the day. She had just decided to go to a dentist in town, and she had paid him in cash. She was sharing a room with her sister and a friend at the club, and they got along well; that was good. I told her I had called the Protestant minister in town and explained to him that she would like to find a church to join. I did not tell her that the minister had offered to visit her at home. Ariana seemed preoccupied and soon left in search of clients.

Later that evening, Ariana asked me to join her for a cigarette. We went upstairs to my favorite seat under an open window. Ariana was in a contemplative mood. She found German men were difficult where romantic relationships were concerned. She did not think they would accept her as a girlfriend if they found out what she did for a living. That was why she wanted to get out of this life. It was lonely. She liked the Americans, though; they were nice, easier going than the Germans. Her mother also had been alone for a long time. She used to be very beautiful, very educated, Ariana said, but very unhappy because her husband always ran after other women. "You know, my father was a mafiosi. He was always involved in dirty business. And he always left my mother behind by herself." Now her mother had met a nice man who lived in Greece, and they went for walks and for dinners, and when Ariana went back to Bulgaria, her mother would go and visit him. Ariana's son was getting to be an age where he was difficult at times, and her mother complained about him. Ariana had to beg her mother to hold on just a little bit longer.

Ariana looked frustrated as she gazed into the distance. She was taking care of the entire family, she said: her mother, her grandmother, even her brother, although he was just two years younger and had his own family he was supposed to take care of. He had been doing a lot of drugs and until recently had been in jail. Now, he promised her that he would change. "I don't understand why I always feel responsible for everybody in my family," she said. Her sister, Anna, who also worked at the club, was not like that. She would just say she had her own life; she did not feel responsible for their mother. I wondered how it would be for Ariana if she did not have a child.

Ariana seemed melancholic that evening. She told me how she'd once had a boyfriend she'd loved very much. He was partially Black and worked as a security guard. He was very beautiful, she said; they went out together to the movies and for walks. But then he had to go to jail because he had assaulted someone. He had been such a good person, though, Ariana said. She adored dark-skinned men, not the "real Black ones, but the dark-skinned ones."

I asked her how she got along with management. She said that since one of the girls had complained to the owner, the situation had improved a lot. She loved the boss, the owner of the club—in fact, both the boss and his manager. "Annegret, they are such good people, so good to the girls!" she said. After her complaint, he had called a meeting with all the madams. The madams knew she was not always easy to get along with, that she would fight if they treated her badly or unfairly. I could confirm that. One of the madams I had befriended had asked me repeatedly what I liked about Ariana so much, as she found her to be "one of the most chaotic, filthy, and abrasive girls."

Ariana, on the other hand, told me that many of the madams were very mean to the girls. One day, she said, she had decided to wear a sheer, lacy negligee. The madam in charge that night had not liked her outfit and said she should take it off. Ariana told her it was transparent and everything was clearly visible underneath, that she had paid a lot of money for it, and she would keep it on because she felt beautiful in it. The madam then told her she had "better not piss her off" and should do as she said. But Ariana just responded that she would tear the outfit up if she did not leave her alone.[7] Ariana explained that she had to earn money there, and she could do that only if she felt beautiful.

On another occasion, Ariana said, one of the madams had awoken her brutally at one in the afternoon. Ariana had just lain down for a few minutes. The madam stormed into her room and yelled, asking Ariana what she thought she was doing still sleeping at that time of day when she had signed up for the early shift. Another time—Ariana was now visibly agitated—she had been staying in a room with a very drunk customer until late, just before the club closed for the night. She was afraid that the client would sneak out without paying her, as the men kept their money in the lockers right next to the exit. Since she first had to return the room key to the cleaning station, she could not go downstairs with him immediately and was afraid he would slip out of the club without paying her. So she asked one of the girls from the cleaning crew to return the key for her, but the cleaning woman refused.

The more Ariana recalled such examples, the more frustrated she got. It was about ten in the evening, and dessert was about to be served, so I suggested we go down to see what it would be. In the dining area, we ran into a friendly, bald middle-aged man from Spain—a car dealer, as he introduced himself, who had just come to celebrate a deal with his customers. His boisterous spirit was contagious, and he invited us all to go to Alicante, where he had a huge beach house. Of course, this was not to be taken too literally, but it was enough to help us forget cold madams and unsympathetic staff. For me, it was soon time to catch the last train. For Ariana, this had been just the first half of the night shift.

I resumed my observation post in the club three days later. Ariana was sitting at one of the tables near the bar and waved at me. She said she'd had a night with young guys from the local soccer team who had gained an international reputation in the World Cup. It had been a whole bunch of them, and they had stayed in the VIP lounge until 7:00 a.m. "The boss gave them Viagra just shortly before the club was supposed to close! At four in the morning! Can you believe that?" Several girls had partied with them, including her sister. They switched partners again and again, and the guys went on and on and on, Ariana said with a mixture of disbelief, amusement, and exhaustion. She had just slept the last two days and would not work tonight either. She wasn't even going to wear makeup, she said.

A week later, Ariana and I got another chance to talk. I told her that some customers had told me they went to the club deliberately to look for girlfriends. Ariana's eyes widened. I would point them out to her the next time I saw one of them. We decided to assume our post under the opened window upstairs. But Ariana was in a quite different mood from the last time I had seen her. "This is a shitty life," she said. The drinking, staying awake all night, smoking—all that was wearing her out, and she needed a long time to recover. She wished she could find another job, one where she would work only four days and spend the rest of the time with her son. And she was really trying to find an apartment so she could bring her son closer to her. At that time, I was very impressed that Ariana was in a position of even thinking about buying an apartment in Neuburg, where real estate prices were extremely high, even by German standards. As a börek baker in Bulgaria, she would have barely been able to make enough to live off of, much less support her extended family and simultaneously buy a house.

Ariana leaned back, the red towel wrapped around her. She told me she had just finished reading a book about two brothers from a good family. One of them was a brutal mafioso who tortured and killed people. The other had never committed any crime, but he went to jail for many years to cover for his brother. She did not remember the author of the book or whether he was Turkish or Bulgarian. In her expressive voice, Ariana said, "I cried and cried and cried. It was so sad. I could not stop crying." And then she began to tell me about her past lover in the Netherlands. "He was a beautiful Kurd, but he was also a brutal gangster," she said. She had been working as a singer in a bar when one night, her colleagues put ecstasy in her glass without her realizing it. When it started to work, she felt as if her heart were about to jump out of her chest, and she thought she would die. The man worked as a bouncer there. And until then, she had only exchanged glances with him. But that night, he took her to his apartment and put her under a cold shower until her lips turned blue so she would come to her senses. Her heart was beating so hard, and he did this all night until she was back to normal. "Without him, I would have died for sure," she said. And from then on, they were lovers. Ariana looked off into the distance for a while before she continued her story. His mother had put a gun in his hand when he was eleven so that he knew how to use it, he had told her. He robbed people, maybe even killed people, Ariana said. But to her, he was good. He told her that she had shown him something he had never experienced before, and if he would have to die the next day, he was happy that he had met her. "I told him over and over again that he should stop his shitty life as a gangster, that he should start getting a real job. But he never listened." Eventually, he got a fake passport and went back to Turkey. After that, she never heard from him again. "Maybe he was in jail. Maybe he was dead. But it was such a happy time with him, with his beautiful eyes, his dark skin. He was so tall, so strong," Ariana reminisced. Soon after, she excused herself and got up to look for clients.

A week or so went by before our long-planned visit to a church finally materialized. It was a sunny summer Sunday morning, June 26. I had spent the night in one of the work rooms on the second floor of the Flamingo, after I put down fresh sheets. As fancy as the rooms were, they were dark and filled with the scents of spent perfume and bodies, which made it hard to fall asleep. When I got up at nine in the morning, it was too early, too hot already, and too bright after the dark club atmosphere the previous night and the few hours of sleep I'd gotten. I called Ariana's phone to wake her up. We got ourselves a coffee and something sweet at the gas station nearby, as the club did not serve breakfast until eleven. I had not brought a purse along, so I put my money in my bra. Ariana laughed hard when she saw me taking it out to pay for our coffee: "You look funny doing that! Where I am from, this is something only Gypsies do."

We left the gas station and walked toward the small town center, which consisted of a busy thoroughfare running alongside beautiful historical buildings. There was a small business district, with a few international fashion stores as well as a mix of upscale boutiques and discount stores. I steered Ariana to walk in the shade whenever possible, trying to escape the bright sunlight that was bothering my eyes. Some of the side streets were made of cobblestones and led to a pedestrian area, giving the small town a historic feel. It looked much more polished than what I remembered from riding my bike through it as a child, when this had been a dusty village of dairy and cabbage farmers, nestled between freeways and an airport. From the club in the industrial area to the town center, it was about a twenty-minute walk.

Ariana told me that her son was very sick—he had problems with asthma—and her mother had suggested she come home. She was worried about him. Then she told me about how strong her faith had been when she was young, that she had been very spiritual as a girl, that she had been able to go into a trancelike state and knew things that happened to people in their past. Ariana said she knew she had been touched by God, and her family and her community protected her and treated her as someone very special. But then, when she got older and started to hang out in discotheques, when she started to drink alcohol and got into the bad life, she lost her faith and her way. God was not with her anymore. He had taken that gift from her. She knew that the life she was living was not right.

We finally reached the church. I was not exactly sure whether it was the right one. Small as the town was, I did not think there was more than one Protestant church. As we approached the main entrance, we realized that the service had already started; in fact, it was almost over. People had just finished singing the final hymn and waited for the blessing from the pastor. Ariana and I had slipped in and stood near the entrance. To the right, I noticed posters for *Terre Des Femmes*, a traveling exhibition about human trafficking, particularly sex trafficking.

Ariana asked me what the exhibit was all about. When I explained it to her, she started to shake visibly. "Annegret," she said, "God is giving me a sign. He knows what I am doing." I was startled. I would have wanted her to see the exhibit, but I was also nervous because I had promised to meet the pastor at the other church. So we left before the parishioners were getting ready to exit.

After getting lost a few more times, we eventually found the right church. It was at the opposite end of town, in a residential area. There, the service was just about to begin. Ariana and I went in. To me, it was like traveling in time back into my childhood, to the neighboring village a few miles over where I'd had to endure endless church visits. Ariana seemed bewildered by the sterile and somber style of a Lutheran service in Germany. I could sense her disillusionment and regretted having dragged her there. After the service ended, a community gathering with coffee and cookies was held in an adjacent room, where we were supposed to meet the pastor. As Ariana and I joined the small crowd, I wondered how exactly this meeting was supposed to look. Eventually, I approached him and introduced myself as the one who had called him and spoken to him about Ariana and her desire to find a Christian community. He appeared uncomfortable, as if he had not expected someone who looked like Ariana: young, attractive, and—with her dark skin, dark eyes, and black hair—obviously different from all the other attendees at this postservice gathering. As he greeted us awkwardly, I noticed his large, dusty black shoes. It was apparent that he did not know what to do with us or what exactly we wanted from him. The conversation dried up after just a few sentences. He recommended joining a Bible study group but did not offer any more personal conversation or availability.

Ariana and I left, disappointed. We walked back. It was clear that this was not what she had expected. I felt I owed her an explanation and promised to find out about a livelier church, maybe a charismatic church in the city I had heard about. It started to dawn on me that the church she had been a member of in Bulgaria was probably the opposite of the Protestant church I had found for her. In fact, only then did I begin to understand that what she meant by *evangelisch*: not a Protestant but an evangelical church.

After we were back at the Flamingo, we split. I had to leave the club scene. Spending two days and a night there was the maximum I could handle, and I wondered how Ariana and all the others who lived there could get used to this cruel work schedule. How did they ever adjust to the irregular sleep, to the lack of privacy, to sleeping three feet apart from strangers who might decide to smoke in the bedroom any time of the day or night? I knew one could get used to a lot if there were few alternatives. But I also remembered the doctors at the health department talking about how many sex workers suffered from chronic headaches and other stress-related illnesses.

After that morning, I did not see Ariana anymore. When I went back to the club a few days later, she was gone. Neither was she there on any of the following times I went to visit. I eventually found out from her sister that she had gone back to Bulgaria because her son's asthma had gotten worse. I had her phone number and tried calling her, but I never got through. So our walk back from that church had been the last time we spent together.

Notes

1. This was a legally ambiguous practice, as advertising one's services on the website of a business would be incompatible with the status of a freelancer. Having photos of sex workers at the club theoretically could help them gain clients, but it also helped the Flamingo get internet traffic and prospective clients directed to their site. In many sauna clubs—unlike apartment brothels, where such photo profiles are essential—this remained a short-lived phenomenon. They appeared increasingly in the years after 2014 but disappeared by 2016.

2. Running into a photographer doing shoots with sex workers was not altogether unusual at the Flamingo. Like Paul, there were sundry secondary service providers—hairdressers, cosmeticians, tattoo artists, and merchants—at the club, primarily targeting sex workers. This showed not only how large and economically stratified the Flamingo was but also what a captive audience and how economically isolated sex workers were.

3. As one manuscript reviewer pointed out to me.

4. As freelancers, they technically could not be scheduled to work more than a few days in advance.

5. Condom use for all forms of sexual intercourse became mandatory with the Prostitute Protection Act of 2017. How this was going to be enforced remained unclear.

6. The so-called lover-boy syndrome is a technique by which men seduce young women to fall in love with them in order to extort sexual labor from them (Bovenkerk and Pronk 2007; Wilbrand-Donzelli, 2015). While this is a popular concept in the media, some scholars have questioned its usefulness (for example, Bovenkerk and Van San 2011).

7. This self-aggression is a form of revenge, where the target of the revenge has been rerouted from the other to the self in order to make the offender feel guilty. See, for example, Wardlow (2006) for a description of Huli women of Papua New Guinea seeking revenge by lopping off the tips of their fingers.

5

ZUHÄLTER ON THE BROTHEL FLOOR AND LABOR DISCIPLINE

"Why Doesn't Management Do Anything about Them?"

Lavinia, Katharina, Natasha, and Ariana differed in age, nationality, education, and personality. Not surprisingly, they had different life trajectories, and yet, with the exception of Natasha, their stories raised questions about the men in their lives who might have played managerial roles in their careers, variably called third parties, Zuhälter, or traffickers: Lavinia had, at some point, run a brothel with her boyfriend; Katharina proudly described her labor arrangement with her Zuhälter and how it came about; Natasha's husband left it up to her to bring home money; and Ariana might have entered sex work as an underage girl in the orbit of transnational trafficking. These similarities, if indeed they were similarities, became apparent only after I carefully reread and analyzed my field notes and conversations. Complaints about Zuhälter, however, were a constant topic at the Flamingo.

Iris, a strikingly beautiful, tall, and voluptuous woman in her mid-twenties, was the first to alert me about the presence of Zuhälter at the Flamingo. She introduced herself as a law school student who had interrupted her studies when she'd begun working at the club. Iris was not planning to do this work for much longer, she assured me. "Just until we reach the financial goals my boyfriend and I have set," she said before she excused herself to go look for customers.

A couple of hours later, Iris came back. Looking over her shoulder as if to make sure no one could hear us, she said, "There are so many Zuhälter here again tonight! . . . It is terrible to work when they are around. They spoil the work atmosphere for all of us. Why doesn't management do anything about them?" I assumed that her comment would be the beginning of future revelations, but over the next few weeks, Iris seemed to avoid my company, as if she had revealed too much about herself and wanted to put some distance between us.

Iris's complaint about Zuhälter and their upsetting presence at the Flamingo was something I heard regularly. Such comments stood in stark contrast to managers'; they insisted that in their business model, sex workers did not need to have Zuhälter and that, in fact, the Flamingo was a Zuhälter-free establishment.

Management orchestrated this public image of transparency in a number of ways. For example, they invited the entire city council to tour the facilities before the Flamingo's official grand opening, they made donations to women's shelters and children's wish foundations, they collaborated with politicians to draft new model policies for social security legislation for sex workers, and they allegedly had an in-house gynecologist so that sex workers had easy access to medical attention as well as a retirement counselor to advise their freelancer sex workers on how to save for retirement. Supposedly, the Flamingo also had a dedicated women's representative on staff, but when I asked the madam in question about this aspect of her job, she just laughed: "Is that what the owner said I was?"

As the CFO put it, their goal was to present themselves as being entirely transparent about their business practices to the public and to authorities. Their efforts seemed to pay off. Newspaper reports and magazine articles generally praised the club for its forward-looking management and social consciousness in addition to its lavish interior. Zuhälter had no place in this model of contemporary prostitution.

Zuhälter in Legal Prostitution

This chapter explores how sex workers, clients, and brothel employees felt and thought about Zuhälter on the brothel floor, where they were abundant and omnipresent according to many sex workers and clients but nonexistent according to management. On the basis of these commentaries, I trace the role Zuhälter might have played in this setup. Unfortunately, I was not able to talk to anyone who identified himself as such, which forced me to rely on secondhand accounts instead.

Zuhälter and traffickers—the two names are often used interchangeably in the media—are portrayed as victimizers and profiteers of prostitution who thrive in contexts where prostitution is illegal (e.g., Hughes 2000;

Jeffreys 2009). A major argument for the Prostitution Act of 2002, and for the legalization of prostitution anywhere, was that it would reduce the potential for crime associated with prostitution and would allow sex workers to not depend on exploitative relationships with third parties. When sex workers could seek legal recourse if they were wronged, there was no more need for Zuhälter, the argument went, and no more need for the crimes associated with the red light milieu. If that was true, what role did Zuhälter play in a context where the sale and purchase of sex was legal, where sex workers did not need them to procure clients but could recruit on their own and work in a safe environment? Where sex workers did not have to fear getting arrested and therefore would require no bail to be posted, and where they could deal with nonpaying or abusive clients directly by appealing to the law?

News reports about the rise of trafficking in German brothels had planted doubts in the public's mind about how law-abiding German brothels actually were and ignited a collective unease about the subject. However, while sex worker rights organizations have critiqued the Prostitution Laws of 2002 and its successor of 2017 for disregarding the situation of irregular migrants, migrants from countries within the European Union had the legal right to live and work in Germany and thus tended to work in more stable conditions. Rather than using the rescue narrative as an excuse to get rid of unwanted immigrants, I suggest this unease was ultimately caused by the image of Germany as the "brothel of Europe" and the collective shame that entailed.

If Zuhälter and traffickers indeed existed at the Flamingo, what was their mode of operation there? Why would management tolerate their presence? And if sex workers indeed had Zuhälter, did sex workers choose them, or did the Zuhälter somehow force them to work for them or force women into sex work altogether? If women chose to have Zuhälter, what benefits did they offer? If women were coerced, what kind of power did Zuhälter hold over them? And what role did nationality play in the relationship between Zuhälter and sex workers? The stories of Lavinia, Katharina, Ariana, and Natasha did not follow an obvious pattern: Ariana from Bulgaria and Natasha from Russia had no current affiliation with Zuhälter, while the two German women, Katharina and Lavinia, had positive opinions about them, with Katharina even openly extolling the virtues of having a Zuhälter.

Zuhälter, or pimps in English, are frequently invoked but understudied actors within scholarship and policy research on prostitution. Little is known about them particularly in legal indoor and upscale prostitution venues (Weitzer 2009; Bruckert and Parent 2018). Their ostentatious ubiquity in popular culture, particularly in gangsta rap of the 1990s, belies their elusiveness in everyday life; few scholars have been able to establish rapport with them (Katona 2017; Bruckert and Law 2013; Weinkauf 2010). Lack of direct access to these evasive actors, however, is no reason to eliminate them from the story of the Flamingo, particularly since so many sex workers, clients, and madams believed them to play a prominent role at the club.

While Iris's complaint about the presence of Zuhälter was one among many I heard, it is important to remember that they all came from people—whether sex workers, madams, brothel managers, or clients—who had a vested interest in the continued existence of legal prostitution, had firsthand experience with brothels, and mingled on the brothel floor.[1] They were not antitrafficking activists who wanted legal prostitution to be abolished or former sex workers who had exited the industry.

Of course, these actors were not closed off from the world at large, where reports about international sex trafficking in general and about Germany in particular were abundant. While clients were most aware of such reports and eager to discuss their expertise—like Henry, who explained that a man's name tattooed on a sex worker's chest was a dead giveaway, or Thomas, who pointed out Zuhälter allegedly vetting a sex worker—the vast majority of the women never referred to such debates. In fact, one of the main differences between the public outcry against traffickers and the way women at the club talked about Zuhälter was that while the former portrayed traffickers as operating through transnational organized crime syndicates, the Zuhälter described at the Flamingo seemed to operate locally, alone or in small groups, and had personal relationships with the sex workers. Where these two lines of discussion possibly merged was in the case of Eastern European migrants, for whom poverty and structural disempowerment in conjunction with transnational migration made wholesale trafficking a more likely scenario.

The State of Pimping and Trafficking Research

Trafficking has become a major discourse in research on prostitution, particularly in the United States. Wide-spanning alliances between unlikely bedfellows—from radical feminists to fundamental Christians—have made antitrafficking efforts one of the most widespread and successful human rights campaigns of nongovernmental and governmental organizations alike (Bernstein 2018). Despite an abundance of such campaigns and political rhetoric to raise public awareness about trafficking, ethnographic research on pimps and traffickers per se is limited. Empirical studies of pimps that do exist are often based on a priori assumptions, conceptualizing the relationship between sex worker and pimp as one of victim and perpetrator, thus precluding a more nuanced understanding of the relationships between sex workers and Zuhälter (Kennedy et al. 2007). Important exceptions are Marcus et al. (2014), Horning (2013), and Horning and Marcus's (2017b) study of Black pimps' relationships to sex workers in two American cities, which showed a considerable degree of agency even of minors involved in sex work, while Molland's (2011) study of prostitution in the Mekong region points out the similarities in the bad-faith rhetorical strategies used by both traffickers and the antitrafficking activists who target them.

The concept of trafficker and the conflation of trafficker and Zuhälter are relatively recent developments. Horning and Marcus argue, "Historically, pimps have not been construed as a unified group across cultures, but due to the [passage of the Trafficking's Victim Protection Act (2000), the annual Trafficking in Persons Report (since 2001) and the Palermo Protocol (2000)],[2] third parties, especially pimps are now viewed as a dangerous class on a global level" (2017a, 6). Many NGOs have emerged to increase awareness about the allegedly ever-present threat of pimps and traffickers ready to sexually enslave women and children. If pimps were minor players on the prostitution stage before the millennium, their conflation with traffickers, the portrayal of sex work as modern-day slavery, and a prolific docutainment industry have propelled the pimp onto an international stage of high visibility.

In stark contrast to such approaches, sex work activists and ethnographers who engage in firsthand participant observation have often shown that the narrative of the sexually enslaved prostitute victimized at the hands of ruthless international traffickers and pimps rarely fits the cases they describe. Critics of "the rescue narrative" and "moral panic" (Lancaster 2011; Weitzer 2006) point out that pimps often perform vital management services for sex workers, helping them to make more effective business decisions and providing emotional support (O'Connell Davidson 2005; Murphy and Venkatesh 2006); the traffickers' greatest offense is that they help to facilitate the influx of undesirable immigrants (Kempadoo, Sanghera, and

Pattanaik 2012). Nagel has also pointed out the disingenuousness of calling the antiprostitution movement "abolitionist" (2015) by uncovering the fallacies of equating the abolition of slavery with the abolition of prostitution.

Despite the ongoing debate about trafficking in German media, however, with few exceptions (Katona 2017; Löw and Ruhne 2009; Herz and Minthe 2006), there is more literature about pimps and traffickers in the form of fiction and memoir than in the form of research (e.g., Barth 2011; Feige 2004, 2013; Lemke and Marquardt 2011; Sobota 1978). Scholars studying prostitution disagree on how to assess the impact of legalization on trafficking in general: On the one hand are sociologists like Ron Weitzer (2012), who argues that legalized prostitution goes hand in hand with relatively orderly and well-regulated prostitution venues. On the other are those who argue that legal regimes of prostitution might actually increase trafficking and make it harder to combat through law enforcement (Cho, Dreher, and Neumayer 2013; Huisman and Kleemans 2014).

As in most other European countries—independent of whether prostitution is legal or not (Czarnecki et al. 2014)—pimping and trafficking in Germany are charged as criminal offenses. They are prosecuted according to §180 and §181 of the German Criminal Code, which defines "trafficking in the narrow sense" as exploitation of sex workers or the control of their labor (Herz 2006).[3] In 2005, two new paragraphs were introduced to better dovetail with the wording of the Palermo Protocol, which was adopted by the United Nations in order to provide a framework for national legislation to prosecute transnational traffickers. These new paragraphs (§232 and §233) were defined as "trafficking in the broader sense" (Herz and Minthe 2006), including exploiting someone's structural weakness (being in a foreign country, for example) and using "violence, threat, or fraud, to induce them to engage in or continue to engage in prostitution" (Czarnecki et al. 2014). German law also makes a distinction between human trafficking (*Menschenhandel*) and aggravated human trafficking (*schwerer Menschenhandel*), the latter of which applies to particularly egregious forms of exploitation. The legal definition of human trafficking in Germany does not require a crossing of national borders but also applies to domestic trafficking. In fact, between 2006 and 2013, 16 to 25 percent of all cases of documented human trafficking involved domestic victims (Bundeskriminalamt (BKA) 2013; Herz and Minthe 2006).

Criminologists Herz and Minthe differentiate between those who operate through organized crime structures and those operating individually or through a loose network. They argue that the former are "'utilizing a refined, business-like logistic, through which they can gain considerable financial and power positions'. Such criminals have managed—through corruption—to enter into various aspects of administration" (Herz and Minthe 2006, 38).[4]

Trials involving pimping and trafficking provide another source of information on the subject. One of the largest human trafficking trials in Germany in recent years involved a so-called flat-rate club (the entrance fee to the club suggested unlimited sexual services at no extra cost). The court trial revealed a tightly organized network led by two men who coordinated and directed a complex network of recruiters, drivers, financial managers, legal strawmen, and "enforcers"—sometimes fellow sex workers—involving several dozen women (*Der Spiegel* 2012; Kubitscheck 2012;). Another trafficking trial involved so-called loverboys—i.e., men who deceive young, often underage girls by winning their trust and love before they coerce them into sex work.[5] Often it is implied that loverboys are men with a migration background, and Romanian scholars working on trafficking have documented this strategy, but actual statistics are scarce. Considering the newspaper reports about trafficking in general, and trafficking of Eastern European migrants specifically, it is sobering to see that about a quarter of the women identified as trafficking victims are German[6]—a surprising number considering that almost 90 percent of women in the sex industry today are international migrants.

While such trial information provides information about traffickers' mode of operations, the judicial system operates on the basis of specific legal codes. That means prosecutors are primarily concerned with aspects of the relationship between sex worker and clients that are codified by law and can lead to convictions, thus focusing on a narrow range of behaviors that lend themselves to legal stipulations.

A particularity of German Zuhälter and traffickers seems to be their connection to specific occupational niches (doormen/bouncers in discotheques) and lifestyles (bodybuilders) and the access that these provide to the criminal aspects of the sex work industry. Closely tied to these occupational niches is the influence of biker gangs and their turf war with other organized groups over the control of prostitution venues (Herz and Minthe 2006; Schubert 2012, 2014). Schubert (2014) claimed that there is evidence of new organized street gangs consisting primarily of immigrants who escaped the brutal Yugoslav Wars in the 1990s as children and are now fashioning themselves after American gangs. However, they are merely challenging the turf of the more entrenched position of Hells Angels and similar biker gangs who have long held sway over the prostitution sector.

In the following, I describe the perceptions of Zuhälter from three different angles: sex workers, clients, and staff. The portrayal of the Flamingo as a Zuhälter-free establishment was touted only by top management and some madams. Clients and sex workers, in contrast, seemed in agreement that many sex workers had Zuhälter and that Zuhälter mingled—more or less incognito—among them as clients. What they did not agree on was whether they exerted pressure and intimidation and under what conditions sex workers worked with them.

Sex Workers about Zuhälter

As I was on my way out of the club one day, two women, close friends in their thirties, approached me together. Introducing themselves as Su and Lilly, they were determined to tell me what they thought about the Flamingo and their work. As they put it, there were women who worked with Zuhälter and those who worked without them. They had been working the sauna club circuit for several years now, traveling together regularly from one city to another. Overall, they did not mind the Flamingo, although they had their reservations about the women at the club. Su explained, "There are two types of women here, and you better not get close to women who have Zuhälter. I have never worked for one and never will. And I can't understand why anyone ever would."

Another time, when I had stayed overnight at the club and was getting up early to go home, I ran into Sabine near the communal showers on the girls' floor as she was getting ready for the early shift. The showers and dressing area were still deserted at this time on a Saturday morning. While Sabine applied her foundation, we got into a conversation during which she told me that her real job was as a salesperson in a bakery and that she worked at the club only occasionally on weekends. With no one else around, and encouraged by her talkativeness, I asked her about the rumor of Zuhälter among clients. "Oh, Zuhälter come here all the time," Sabine said matter-of-factly. "They speak to me and try to get me to work for them. They ask how many customers I have and how business is going. But that does not bother me. I always tell them that business is really slow and then they leave me alone."

Among those who initially were adamant in their disapproval of Zuhälter and the women who worked with them, there were some who would tell me eventually that they had Zuhälter in the past; some had also had intimate relationships with them. However, this had been only during their early years in sex work, when they had lacked experience and self-confidence. Nora, for example, a very slender and quiet twenty-two-year-old woman from Poland, told me that she first had worked for a Moroccan Zuhälter in a club somewhere near the border with the Netherlands. "But I never had sex with him," she said, "and once I decided to leave him, I had no problems doing so." Nora mostly kept to herself. She was not particularly close to anybody at the club and lived for her days off. Then, she would follow her favorite band and hoped to get to spend time with the bass player, whom she adored. I must have looked surprised when she told me that, as she added, "When I am not working here, I am just a regular girl. I want to have fun. I want to have a boyfriend; I want to be in love. But here, the only men interested in me are Zuhälter, with their typical Zuhälter talk, like, telling me 'I am the best guy you can get.'" Nora depicted Zuhälter as trying to manipulate sex workers into working for them by insinuating low self-esteem—a counter to the romantic flirtation Nora was seeking in a love relationship.

Jenny, a woman in her midtwenties from Hungary, shared her frustration about management letting Zuhälter come in and intimidate the women, about the naivete of clients who took her client recruitment efforts as actual interest, and about the gullibility of her coworkers who could not see that the boyfriends they bragged about saw them merely as economic assets. "All of them are working for Zuhälter," she said, exasperated. Jenny was hoping to get out of the prostitution business within a year. She was tired of the club life and blunt about her contempt for the women who had Zuhälter. However, one evening when she was at a low point because she could not save up the thousand euros it would take to move on from the club, she told me that she'd also had a Zuhälter once, while she was working in Austria. But she had left him and since then had never gotten involved with one.

Most of the women did not hold back their contempt for their colleagues who worked for Zuhälter or, worse, were "in love" with them. They belittled women who worked for Zuhälter and complained they were rude and domineering, as if they felt they could lord it over women who did not have Zuhälter. Belonging to a tightly organized group of women, like

Katharina's "family" described in chapter 4, they could flex collective muscle in a sea of individual workers in heated competition over clients. One of the top managers who had earlier insisted that the club was Zuhälter-free shared this impression later, when he told me the story of sex workers who tried to intimidate their coworkers by threatening them with their Zuhälter. "After that," he said, "we asked them to leave." Others mentioned dominant and particularly abrasive colleagues who seemed to control other women who were newcomers to prostitution and got away with it because they had Zuhälter backing them up.

Of the four women I described in the previous chapter, only Natasha did not have any connections to Zuhälter, although she had been in sex work for the longest. However, she was tired of her husband depending on her to bring home all the money: "I wonder whether my husband is turning into a sort of Zuhälter. He didn't used to be so lazy. But now, if it were not for me and what I earn at the club, we wouldn't have any money." At other moments, Natasha was grateful to him for getting her out of Russia and spoke of him as an old companion who got on her nerves but with whom she could also laugh. Tina, from Bosnia, expressed a similar worry: "My boyfriend is starting to ask me more and more for money. I wonder whether he has become a Zuhälter."

In contrast, Ariana seemed to have a history of close connections if not to Zuhälter then to criminal networks, evident in her references to her father as a mafioso and her past love of an outlaw. Ariana had described herself as well-versed in how to detect Zuhälter and keep them at bay. Her stories raised a number of questions, though. Why had she been working in the Netherlands as a sixteen-year-old? Why did she refer to herself as a musician and dancer but later described a previous work environment as a discotheque? I never had a chance to ask her, but it had crossed my mind that Ariana might have been trafficked as a minor. From what I gathered from her stories about how she'd gotten into prostitution, it seemed conceivable that it had not been entirely on her own. The love relationship she'd had with a Kurdish man who was security staff in a discotheque, a niche notorious for its connections to the milieu and Zuhälter, also seemed to point in that direction. Dina Siegel (Bovenkerk, Siegel, and Zaitch 2003; Siegel 2014) studied Turkish trafficking rings in the 1990s in the Netherlands that involved Roma women from Bulgaria; Ariana's account of being drugged in the discotheque, her ability to speak Turkish, and her Kurdish boyfriend who escaped Dutch authorities suggest parallels or at least raise questions. If not through her work experience, then through her family, Ariana had gained enough firsthand knowledge to devise a strategy to stay aloof from Zuhälter and their attempts to recruit her. This was particularly evident when she told me the story of her visit to the discotheque in Neuburg and her caution about not going home with anyone there lest she wanted to be claimed as belonging to a Zuhälter.

When our conversation turned to Zuhälter, Ariana became very serious: "I have nothing against Zuhälter. If they want to have sex, I go to the room with them and treat them well. Not all girls treat the Zuhälter well here. I give them good service. But if they ask me to work for them," she added animatedly, "I will give them such an earful. I will cry and get so emotional that they don't want to have anything to do with me." Throughout our many conversations, I had no doubt that Ariana was in charge of her earnings and that she was a critical source of support for her family in Bulgaria, as described in the previous chapter.

Despite her apparent financial independence, Ariana was often unhappy, depressed about her life, which did not seem to go anywhere, and frustrated that since she was working at the club, she never met a nice man who would want her as a girlfriend or partner. Only once did I see her really happy and carefree, after she had gone out on a Monday night, the day many sex workers took off. She had gone with her friends to a discotheque that was rumored to be a gathering place for Zuhälter. "Ah, Annegret," she said, "there were so many beautiful people. I danced so much. I had so much fun." When I asked her whether she had gone home with someone— as she lived in a room with other sex workers, taking someone home with her was not an option—she said, "No, you cannot do that there. If you do that, then the guy thinks automatically that he is your Zuhälter." Ariana, fully aware of the ulterior motives of her suitors at the bar, nevertheless seemed thrilled to flirt outside of the commodified flirting through which she earned a living.

Lavinia described the relationship with her former boyfriend—the joint owner of their brothel—in positive terms. Was he a Zuhälter? Lavinia did not describe him as such but instead went on to defend the honor of Zuhälter in general. Lavinia's proximity to the upper management of the brothel industry opened venues for her, not only in regard to clients but also for her romantic interests. Her story paralleled that of a number of madams and midlevel managers at the Flamingo who had friendly relationships with senior Zuhälter (*Alt-Luden*) who were retired but still well-known in

Neuburg's red light milieu. Several of the madams at the Flamingo had been in romantic and working relationships with them in the past. And in one case, when I relayed greetings between them, it looked like they were clearly mutually appreciative of each other. Another madam was still in a relationship with a legendary Zuhälter from the 1970s and '80s who, one of the managers indicated, now played an advisory role at the club. One senior police officer who had spent most of his career in vice suspected these madams' intimate associations with former Zuhälter granted them high ranking and well-paid positions at the club.

If most women disapproved of Zuhälter and the women working for them, Katharina was the exception. She made no secret of her affiliation with a Zuhälter. Instead, she spoke about him freely and unapologetically, and at least initially she was proud that she had to give him only 10 percent of her earnings. In turn he took care of her in terms of clothes, transportation, and other work logistics; recruited clients for her; and claimed to "put them in their place, if needed." A year later, though, their romantic relationship had morphed into a mere a business relationship. He had become her manager and boss; he also demanded that her relationships with the other three women in her "family," described elsewhere as a family pimping arrangement (Weinkauf 2010), would be arbitrated through him. Though she didn't state specifically the percentage of her earnings she gave him, it seemed to be much more than the 10 percent he had asked her for initially, and he ceased to support her the way he used to. When I last saw Katharina, after her kidney stone ordeal at the hospital, she did not mention any support from him.

On several occasions, Katharina's statements were perplexing to me—for example, when she explained why she had started working for her boyfriend and that "every penny he spent on me was actually other women's money," so she could not in good conscience want him to spend money on her, and it was only fair to him and the other women that she worked too; when she explained why sex workers had to pay off their debts to their Zuhälter when they wanted to leave them; and when she explained why she had fewer clients, despite being more attractive than her colleagues. Katharina seemed to have utterly internalized her Zuhälter's rationale when she spoke about the obligations a sex worker had to her Zuhälter.

Katharina was also surprisingly matter-of-fact when she explained to me the rules of working for a Zuhälter and the means by which he disciplined his girls, including "selling them" to another Zuhälter for a couple thousand euros. I was disarmed by her apparent attachment to me but also alienated, as so many of Katharina's statements sounded as if she was replaying snippets of conversations she'd had with her Zuhälter, internalizing his voice, including its gendered position.

At the same time, Katharina did not fit the stereotypical image of a trafficking victim. She did not hesitate to reject clients—I saw this firsthand—and did so without any apparent repercussions from management. She enjoyed playing the dominant role with her BDSM clients. She also never gave any indication that her Zuhälter had forced her to get into prostitution. Rather the opposite—she had described her initiation into sex work as a celebratory moment when she was discovered as "a natural-born whore," which she regarded as an epiphany about her true self. Her rationale for sharing her earnings with her Zuhälter as payment for his services—such as managing her ads for escort services, helping her out with renting a car, or allegedly putting unruly clients in their place—was entirely plausible to Katharina, who also seemed to accept the transformation of their love relationship into a Zuhälter-prostitute relationship without resistance. And yet Katharina's story also fit the playbook of a girl falling for the stereotypical loverboy who seduced young women, pretending to fall in love with them, then coerced them into prostitution in order to remain in a relationship with him. But Katharina was not a teenage girl who was economically destitute and disconnected from familiar support networks, nor was she in a foreign country where she did not speak the language, although she was working many hours away from home. Katharina was an adult woman with an intact family and social network, native language skills, and access to institutional resources such as childcare, unemployment benefits, and health insurance. Prostitution for Katharina was a sexual thrill, at least initially, a means to afford a more upscale lifestyle and independence, and the opportunity to get to know influential people.

In conclusion, then, the women cited here had few doubts that Zuhälter were a feature of the industry they worked in, and for some, Zuhälter were an integral part of their work at the Flamingo. How they thought about Zuhälter, however, varied widely. The overwhelming majority complained about Zuhälter or thought of them as a nuisance to put up with, quite different from the image circulating in the media of Zuhälter as all-powerful criminals forcing women into sexual labor through intimidation and coercion. With the exception of Katharina and maybe Lavinia, the women I spoke with at the club insisted that they did not work for Zuhälter, although some of them admitted they'd had Zuhälter in the past. Even in these cases, they considered Zuhälter more like legitimate business or intimate partners from whom they managed to get away. The fact that many had developed a repertoire of phrases and tricks to stave off Zuhälter attempts to recruit them supports this impression.

Clients about Zuhälter

Many clients were convinced that a majority of the girls at the club were working for Zuhälter. Henry, the client who gave me the introductory tour of the Flamingo, told me frankly that in his opinion, almost all of the girls at the club had one. Pointing to one of the girls who had just stood beside us, he asked me, "Have you seen that 'Ibrahim' tattoo that she had on her chest? Why would anyone want the name of a boyfriend tattooed on their chest? These are all women working for Zuhälter. The tattoo shows everyone that they are his property. And with such a tattoo, they can never really escape their Zuhälter either. As long as they have that tattoo, he can find them, even if they change their names and the city they work in." While Henry was certainly not immune to the violence and emotional suffering of women who worked for traffickers and an astute and critical observer of business practices at the club, he also seemed to want to create an image of himself as being in the know about things in the sex industry.

Some clients were indeed apt observers of the interactions at the club, as I witnessed one evening when talking with Thomas, a guest, and Nina and Sara, two young women from Romania. A boyish and pleasant middle-aged man from Frankfurt who insisted he was happily married, Thomas assured me that although he was there with his business clients, he would never purchase sex himself. While we were going back and forth about whether it was more benevolent to the sex workers for him to purchase sex or not, Nina was called over by a group of three young men with clean-shaven heads, nicely trimmed beards, and buff, tattooed bodies. One of them had, from across the bar, asked me earlier what I was doing at the Flamingo and whether I was not a little too old to work there—an uncharacteristically frank and provocative question from a guest. Now, watching him with his buddies, seemingly negotiating with Nina, Thomas said, "See these guys? They want to try her out. See how good she is in bed. And then they make her work for one of them." I looked at him, surprised that Thomas thought these three men were Zuhälter. While there was no way to prove whether his assessment was accurate, at least their looks were very much in line with what Katharina had described as the telltale signs of Zuhälter at work.

Another potential interaction between sex workers and Zuhälter was illustrated one evening when I spent some time with a client watching the couple across from us. Olaf was a lanky and awkward but friendly young man who had just recently finished his apprenticeship in carpentry. He had come all the way from Leipzig and was happy to have found in me someone to socialize with at the club. Olaf and I had been talking about the financial sacrifices he'd had to make to come to the club. "I either come here for a night or spend a week in the Canary Islands, with my airline discounts. The expense is the same." Meanwhile, Ramona, a very attractive woman from somewhere in Eastern Europe, sat down ten feet away from us, next to a tall, middle-aged client, and began to flirt with him. As the two sat right across from us, it was hard not to pay attention to them. It was already midnight after what had been a slow day. I had watched Ramona walking around for hours looking for customers, but without success. Now, she finally seemed successful. Soon the two of them started to hold hands and kiss each other. As midnight passed, and another half hour went by, Olaf and I watched the growing intimacy between the two of them, wondering when they would finally go upstairs. Getting impatient, Olaf said, "Only jerks act like that. You are supposed to let a girl know when you don't want to have sex with her, or when you can't have any more sex, so she can look for someone else." Fifteen minutes later, Ramona got up and came back with a *Piccolo*, a small quarter-liter bottle of champagne from the bar, for which she would get €25 commission. Ramona drank the champagne while the intimacies continued until suddenly, in what seemed a desperate act, she went up to one of the stages to perform a pole dance—for which she would also get a small compensation from the club—and then returned to her prospective client. Another forty-five minutes later, after more caressing and French kissing, the man got up and disappeared, leaving an utterly distraught Ramona behind. All the while, a few men with tattoos, shaved heads, and bodybuilder physiques had been observing her from the bar. A few minutes after the man left Ramona, she went and talked with them. "See what is happening?" Olaf asked. "At first they observe her, making sure she keeps looking for clients. And now they are giving her a pep talk. I bet they are Zuhälter." I had no proof that these were indeed Zuhälter watching over a sex worker and consoling her in the end. But several of the women that night had made comments about this and similar scenes, complaining that management did not restrict entrance to Zuhälter, who were keeping an eye on the girls while they were working.

How management responded to clients who were too explicit about their suspicions concerning Zuhälter is illustrated in the case of Freddy. He had VIP status at the club because he spent a lot of money there. In fact, he was rumored to have astronomical monthly bills for drinks alone. Freddy, a very wealthy widower, had become a celebrity in the club and among the girls because he treated everyone, especially the girls, very generously. When it became known to management that he had criticized some of the women for letting themselves be used by Zuhälter, he was barred from the club. Flora, the madam who related that story to me, said, "We have not had forced prostitution for a very long time. What he said was totally untrue. There are no Zuhälter here. We can't have someone instigating the girls against management that way. That is why he is no longer welcome here."

While all these clients were convinced that they knew how Zuhälter operated and which of the girls worked with one, none of them had any firsthand experience. This was different for Alwin, a well-built but not burly forty-something-year-old. "I have to skip dinner once a week to not get fat," he told me. Alwin did not share the other clients' critical views of Zuhälter: "You cannot lump them all together. Not all of them are abusive or exploiting the girls." He explained that he had worked as a bouncer in numerous nightclubs, a job niche that was often controlled by more or less organized "groups" and easily segued into lucrative business ventures within the red light industry: as Zuhälter, discotheque owners, or even brothel managers. Actually, he said, "Girls want a strong guy. They like bodybuilder types. That means he can protect them. He can fight other guys. And they profit from his prestige." Prestige, as others, particularly old-timers, had commented, was one of the biggest benefits of having a Zuhälter. Sex workers could capitalize on Zuhälter's prestige in terms of social access to select groups and lifestyles. And as the hairdresser in the RLD had told me, some women would deliberately turn men into Zuhälter and outfit them so that they could play the part.

Being a bouncer was a very desirable job, Alwin explained. Not because of the money you could earn—the going rate was just about €50 for an evening—but because it put you in a position of power over who could get into a club. And you got in touch with a very wide circle of people. The male customers in discotheques would try to be on your good side, and the girls admired you if you looked strong and could be tough. At some point in our conversation, Alwin suddenly looked at me with suspicion. "Why do you actually ask me all these things about Zuhälter?" he asked, as if he was suddenly wondering whether he had revealed too much and incriminated himself. After reassuring him that all this information was confidential and that he was entirely free to stop talking to me, he relaxed. During the rest of the evening, Alwin told me that he had been in jail once for an assault charge, while he was a bouncer. Then he was about to stand trial in a second assault case—he had gotten into a kind of "road rage," as he described it, after chasing someone down. To avoid prison, he left for Thailand. "To Thailand?" I asked. "There are a lot of German sex tourists there. Did you have a brothel there?" Alwin just laughed, without being explicit. "You gotta know how to treat the girls. You gotta give them what they need." He had only recently returned to Germany after the statute of limitation for his conviction had expired.

Although Alwin had been a bouncer and maybe a Zuhälter or brothel owner at some point, he did not have the typical look of a bodybuilder. Anton was a different story. Anton was a very close friend of Hellmut, a regular visitor at the Flamingo, to whom I had become a sort of confidante. Anton had a Herculean body and was ready to go home when I asked Hellmut to introduce me to him. As suggested by his enormous arms, the size of tree trunks, Anton had been a professional bodybuilder and even won a number of titles. "No bodybuilder can get those muscles without steroids. Everyone does it," he said. Awed by his proportions, I could not help but ask him about the connection between bodybuilders, bouncers, and Zuhälter. Anton too had worked as a bouncer and still did occasionally, "but just for fun." He turned out to be an astute observer of people and their behaviors. "So," I asked, "besides the size, how do you actually recognize a Zuhälter?" He replied, "You just need to watch them. Zuhälter are the only men here who are more interested in other men than in the women. Zuhälter watch the men. They make gestures to the girls when they think they should work on a particular guy. You recognize them by these gestures alone."

Orhan was another client who spoke from an insider perspective. A Turkish German man in his late thirties, Orhan had come to the Flamingo to celebrate a business deal with two of his partners. Stocky and muscular, he also had worked as a bouncer. He confirmed Anton's comments about the widespread use of steroids among bodybuilders. Orhan was well informed about biker gangs and their turf wars with each other. Turning his head toward the security guard at the club's entrance, he said, "See this guy? He is a big shot in an influential biker gang. He was in jail for pimping and assault. . . . If I were you, I would not stay at the club much longer. Don't underestimate them." I took his warning as a kind of bluster, trying to impress me with his alleged insider knowledge. But for a number of reasons, chief among them my growing questions about and understanding of the role of the Zuhälter at the club, I was to fall out of favor with management. That winter's visit turned out to be my last season at the Flamingo.

Employees about Zuhälter

I had noticed the tattoo on the security guard's forearm and was told it was the logo of a well-known biker gang consisting of rather nationalist-minded German men. My attempts to engage him in a conversation were unsuccessful. However, the police officer in charge of the Flamingo confirmed Orhan's statement that this security guard had a criminal conviction for pimping and assault. One of the bartenders, a German guy in his fifties, had the same tattoo and was more forthcoming. As I sat down with him on his break, I pointed to his forearm. He spelled out the acronym and what it stood for—the biker gang. In his younger days, he said, he had been a Zuhälter in Frankfurt, where he used to "put four women on the street" (*aufstellen*) in a lucrative area. Back in the day, he and "his women" had spent half a million DM—equivalent to €250,000—in a year for cocaine alone. This was the third time someone affiliated with prostitution had measured their former success in the amount of cocaine consumed. But those had been different times, he said. Back then, the women liked their jobs, and they all enjoyed their lives together. Nowadays it all had changed. While his insistence about the good old times with his alleged sex workers was believable, it was surprising that a club that insisted on being transparent and that wanted to avoid involvement in the criminal underworld would hire staff with obvious biker tattoos and a history of pimping.

A conversation with Thorsten, one of the midlevel managers, shed light on the club's peculiar strategy of having members of this biker gang in high-visibility staff positions. Thorsten had just recently started to work in the brothel industry after a successful career in music entertainment. As we sat in the VIP lounge early one afternoon, I asked him, "Why is the club so vehement about wanting to shed the seedy red light milieu image but then hires members of a biker club for their staff?" He replied, "You need to have protection, especially in this kind of club. If not, someone will try to force you into paying protection money. One way to deal with this is to hire an experienced security manager, another to have high ranking members of the ruling biker gang as employee. That is the best protection against a takeover."

While biker gangs engaging in hostile takeovers, extortions, and attacks on competitors' brothels with stink bombs were not uncommon in the red light industry, trafficking charges against them were less common, despite their proclaimed or actual personal histories as Zuhälter. After several months at the club, and prompted by the frequent comments about Zuhälter from sex workers and clients, I raised the topic with one of the top managers. He insisted that Zuhälter were the "lowest of the lowest . . . the most abysmal of human types" and that the Flamingo's business model made Zuhälter no longer necessary. After months of me pestering him about this issue, however, he said, "We don't know whether someone who comes through the door is a Zuhälter or not. And even if we did, we cannot discriminate against clients on the basis of such preconceived notions." This, of course, was at odds with the concept of security staff at the entrance and the bouncer's image as someone who would remove a client or block him from entering if needed. As I had seen, denying a client entry—for example, because he was too drunk—was something that madams routinely could decide on their own (with security personnel in close reach).

That the club was a Zuhälter-free establishment was also the line of the top-ranking madams. Flora, who had told me about the VIP client who was no longer allowed on the premises after he "scolded" sex workers for having Zuhälter, talked about the old days of prostitution with a degree of nostalgia. "Back in my days, being a Zuhälter meant you had status, you were somebody. I knew many Zuhälter back then. Some of them were real celebrities. But nowadays, there are no Zuhälter anymore. All the girls work for themselves."

Not all the madams at the Flamingo felt so sanguine about Zuhälter. Brigitte, one of the madams who had lived at the club for prolonged periods of time, had a different opinion. Like Flora, Brigitte was an old-timer: "In the last twenty-five years that I have been working in this industry, I have never had so much to do with Zuhälter as here," she confided in me one night. "Ninety percent of the girls here have Zuhälter, if not more. I hear them arguing every night with their Zuhälter on the phone and see them cry. And it is not only the women from Eastern Europe who have Zuhälter. Ulla is a case in point. This girl takes home five to six hundred euros every night. She has paid for three different luxury cars for her Zuhälter. And she does not even have a driver's license. And then, on her one day off, she often comes back already in the afternoon, ready to work again. What kind of life is that? Do you think anyone would do that without being forced?" Ulla was one of the 30 percent of German women at the club, showing that despite the prominent role of Romanian and Bulgarian women at the Flamingo, it was by no means only women from Eastern Europe who allegedly worked for Zuhälter.

Brigitte's condemning remark about the industry, described at the beginning of chapter 4, illustrated the dilemma she faced as a madam who empathized with the girls but was also charged with managing them. As she explained another time: "Almost all of them hate this job." Comparing sex work in the club today to her days as a sex worker, she continued: "We worked half of the month and took the other half off. Here, I see a lot of girls who work nonstop. They do not have a life outside the brothel. So many just have Zuhälter to whom they give their money. This is all very sad! But then, so many girls here are so simple, so chaotic. This morning, not a single girl was ready by noon. I was about to flip out." I asked, "But wait, if they are self-employed freelancers, how can they actually be forced to be up at a certain time? Aren't they technically just guests like the men, and pay entrance fees, just like them?" "Yes, exactly!" Brigitte exclaimed in frustration. "This is exactly my point. And if I yell at them for not being here, then I am guilty of 'pimping,' or of 'incitement to prostitution.'"

Brigitte's dilemma was the Achilles' heel of labor management at the sauna club. To avoid charges of procuring, pandering, or pimping as well as official employment obligations, the Flamingo, like other sauna clubs, hired sex workers as freelancers. As the web page reminded prospective visitors, by charging the women the same fee for using the facilities—"just like our male guests"—they further signaled to clients as well as service providers that they had no formal employment relationship. Thus, the transactions between a sex worker and her client were exclusively between the two of them. Club management was therefore not to be held accountable for her services. However, for the business to run smoothly, the club needed to have a minimum number of women sign up for a particular shift and be available to customers during that shift. While the former was difficult, the latter meant that madams had to regularly corral the sex workers into the contact area of the club so they could be visible and accessible to customers or get them out of bed early in order to have girls present for the morning shift.

Now it became clear how the presence of Zuhälter and their ability to act as enforcers of labor discipline among sex workers could actually be very convenient to the club in the way my observation with Olaf had suggested.

Zuhälter and Labor Management

The snippets and stories about Zuhälter at the Flamingo were bewildering and confusing. One way to make sense of them was to recognize the Zuhälter as a category of actors defined by their relationships to female sex workers and their joint financial interests. A romantic or erotic component was not critical and often only of transient significance. The diverse references to Zuhälter suggested that there were different kinds of relationships and tasks performed: from romantic or managerial, working individually or in families, to managing a business together.

Some women expressed the fear of an intimate partner turning into a Zuhälter after their husbands shifted the financial responsibility for their joint households onto the shoulders of the sex workers alone, as Natasha had complained and Bettina from the Night Owl before her.

Another type of Zuhälter emerged in the stories of Lavinia and the staff at the Flamingo: the madams, the security guards, and the bartenders. These predominantly German Zuhälter, now in their fifties, sixties, and seventies, were for the most part no longer active but rather a leftover from the '80s and '90s, the golden years when prostitution was a different kind of business altogether: when money was good, cocaine was the hallmark of conspicuous consumption, and as Flora put it, a Zuhälter was a man of character and prestige. I had in fact met Flora's old Zuhälter several times in a bar in downtown Neuburg and had heard him talk about her on a number of occasions as an old and dear friend.

Some of these accounts resemble the sex worker–Zuhälter relationships Katona (2017) described for Romanian and Hungarian Roma engaged in street prostitution in Berlin, where Zuhälter acted as brokers during women's early sex work careers, when they tended to be socially isolated and unfamiliar with the working environment and the legal conditions. While such economic arrangements could turn into love relationships— which, Katona (2017) showed, are often initiated by women and provide more security for them—women often left such arrangements behind once they became familiar with the sex market and the working conditions in Germany. Such a situation was reflected in the stories of Eastern European sex workers described above. They were in their twenties but not novices in the industry. They had a repertoire of behaviors to deflect the recruitment attempts of Zuhälter, they were aware of their romantic overtures, and they were determined not to enter into relationships with Zuhälter again.

Then there were women like Katharina, born and raised in Germany, who eventually worked for a Zuhälter (in Katharina's case, her former boyfriend) as part of a tightly organized group, a "family" structure also seen in street-involved sex work in the United States (Weinkauf 2010). Such an arrangement conferred some bargaining advantages to the women working as a unit when they worked at the club. Other women complained about the dominant or rash behavior of sex workers who worked for Zuhälter, which could have been due to the greater power positions such "families" could wield.

Following the accounts of the many others cited here, however, there seemed to be a contradiction: while many stated that a majority of sex workers at the Flamingo were associated with Zuhälter, there were as many who vehemently denied having any affiliations with Zuhälter and the sex workers who associated with them. Two explanations are conceivable here. In one, the sex workers who did have Zuhälter did not confide in me—a quite likely scenario, as contact with an outsider might make themselves and their Zuhälter more vulnerable. In the other, sex workers denied that they were in relationships with Zuhälter because it was so stigmatized in this context. Yet another option was that sex workers whom others described as having Zuhälter did not themselves regard these men as Zuhälter. As Katona (2017, 51) has stated, "Narratives are told with certain purposes; they are always defined by the current needs of the person how he or she aims to represent himself or herself." However, that does not mean that every utterance is a staged act, an attempt to consciously manipulate the audience. Iris's concern at the beginning about Zuhälter spoiling "the work atmosphere for all of us" makes me wonder about her statement a few minutes later, when she told me she wanted to remain in sex work only until she and her boyfriend had reached their financial goals. If Iris's relationship with her boyfriend were to falter, and their financial assets were left in disarray, would she wonder whether he had been her Zuhälter all along?

If the previous was an attempt to interpret the varieties of relationships between sex workers and Zuhälter as they emerged from the narratives of different actors, another story about the role Zuhälter played in labor management emerged quite clearly, particularly when it came to labor discipline.

As Katharina stated, "Zuhälter have more power than madams." They can therefore more effectively enforce labor discipline than madams.

Judging by the observations and statements described here, it was evident that there were Zuhälter among the clients. Many more sex workers suspected others were working for Zuhälter than actually stated they had Zuhälter themselves. Only one woman, Katharina, revealed that she was currently working for a Zuhälter as part of a "family." The public disavowal of Zuhälter and those who worked for them was ubiquitous, although some women, like Lavinia and Ariana, did not share the general notion that such colleagues and their Zuhälter were dangerous or intimidating. Others raised the question of whether their own intimate partners were turning into Zuhälter, literally or figuratively. What were described as Zuhälter might have been quite different manifestations of third parties.

Clients' statements were equally suggestive, whether they spoke from the vantage point of clients observing suspected Zuhälter at work or of bouncers and bodybuilders involved in the industry themselves, as in the cases of Alwin and Anton.

Why management emphasized that they were Zuhälter-free is easy to understand. As a new establishment with a novel business concept and high investment, presenting themselves as providing a new model for law-abiding prostitution was important. After all, pimping and trafficking were defined as criminal activities in Germany, and allegations of this kind could quickly risk their considerable investment. While the Prostitution Act of 2002 had given brothel owners greater legal protection from charges of trafficking and pimping, the specter of criminal charges remained. This was evident in the allegations against the club at the beginning of my research, which might well have been the reason why I was granted access to do fieldwork there in the first place.

So why, then, was the Flamingo not more vigilant about Zuhälter coming in as clients, and why did they hire employees with personal histories, legal records of pimping, or links to organizations notorious for pimping and trafficking (Herz 2006; Herz and Minthe 2006; Schubert 2012)? Thorsten's answer about having such employees on staff as deterrence for competitors seems plausible, although it also raises the question of why such employees would not want to use their expertise to ply their trade at the Flamingo. In a similar vein, why did the PR manager admit he had links to old-time Zuhälter—referring to himself as merely their apprentice—if not to convey that he recognized the managerial know-how of these entrepreneurs of a bygone era and considered them critical allies of the club?

There were clearly two incompatible stories being told by management. Zuhälter attempting to recruit sex workers would not be of interest to the club. As long as the Flamingo had enough women on the floor during their open hours, there seemed no obvious reason why management would tolerate the presence of Zuhälter. More important from the business perspective was that there were enough women to sign up for a shift and that they made themselves available and remained visible to customers during their shift, as the more sex workers there were, the happier the clients were and vice versa—the fewer women working the floor, the more clients would complain or, worse, stay away. Whether women were available to customers during their shift was not something management had actual control over, as the Prostitution Act of 2002 spelled out that employers had limited rights to issue directives (*eingeschränktes Weisungsrecht*), meaning they could not tell any employee to have sex or how to have sex with a client, as this would go against her right to sexual self-determination, anchored in the civil law. In the absence of a formal employment relationship—sex workers all worked independently as freelancers—there was even less of a basis to enforce any form of discipline. Sex workers who wanted to leave early could technically do so, without a madam giving them a hard time. Taking a break during their work shift presented a similar situation. As sex workers were freelancers who paid an entrance fee just like the male guests, a madam would have little formal power to force her to keep working until her shift was finished. Madams were there to enforce rules that they legally had no right to do so, as indicated in Brigitte's exasperated comment about having to de facto do the work of a Zuhälter. Similarly, when women preferred to spend time in each other's company rather than making themselves available to clients or straight-out rejected clients for whatever reason, management had no official recourse to force them to remain on the floor or to take on clients. Zuhälter who mingled among clients, however, were in a position to keep sex workers on their toes (at least those who were working for them): by observing them, pointing out available customers (as Anton suggested), and consoling them (in the case of Ramona and Thomas), thus making sure that sex workers remained available to customers. Even if it was not their own Zuhälter, Katharina's assessment that there were several of her Zuhälter's buddies on the floor seemed to imply that it was to control the women, which raised the specter of clandestine quality control and labor intimidation. This would explain Iris's complaint that Zuhälter on the brothel floor were spoiling the work atmosphere for all of them.

Most telling, finally, was Katharina's statement that Zuhälter were more powerful than madams, who had the task of managing the girls and facilitating their relationships with clients: to make sure women were getting up in time for their shifts and remaining on-site and available to customers during their shifts and to ensure that conflicts between women were settled. But madams had only limited means to accomplish this—one reason why conflicts between madams and sex workers routinely ran high. Here, Zuhälter performed a vital function in terms of assuring labor discipline of sex workers that madams couldn't, as it was incompatible with the limited directives in prostitution and sex workers' status as freelancers or guests. One answer to the broader question of why there were Zuhälter at the Flamingo, then, is that they provided a discipline regime that brothels and their legal staff were unable to. That Zuhälter could be involved in providing large-scale brothels with sex workers has been alleged in mega brothels elsewhere, although there were no explicit indications that this might have been happening at the Flamingo too.

Notes

1. I use the concept of a brothel floor here to emphasize the parallels of the sauna club to other settings of shop floor cultures in which people make a living; see, for example, Willis (1981).

2. This antitrafficking legislation was initiated by the United States through the Trafficking Victims Protection Act (TVPA) and the Trafficking in Persons (TIP) Report. The Palermo Protocol was adopted by the United Nations in 2001 to provide a more uniform terminology that would allow different national legislation to pass laws with which to prosecute international traffickers. In Germany, two new paragraphs (232 and 233) were introduced and added to the already existing laws against trafficking and pimping.

3. Paragraph 181 of the German Criminal Code (*Strafgesetzbuch*) defines *pimping* as "economically exploiting another person who is engaging in sex work" (StGB Paragraph 181a, [1]) or "controlling or directing a person's sex work, or preventing a person from leaving prostitution," a condition that also applies to spouses (181a [2]). Exploitation here is understood as someone extracting more than 50 percent of a sex worker's earnings. In cases where the victim is underage (below eighteen), inducement to prostitution alone, even without direct financial exploitation, is punishable by law (180), as is the exploitation of a person in a prostitution venue in which she or he is held personally or financially dependent (180a, 1), or by offering underage persons an apartment or a commercial venue to engage in sex work (Strafgesetzbuch, http://dejure.org/gesetze/StGB/232.html).

4. "*Nach Erkenntnissen der Untersuchung unterscheidet sich organisierte Kriminalität von traditioneller (Banden-)Kriminalität vor allem durch eine spezielle Logistik. In allen*

untersuchten Deliktsbereichen würden "komplexe Tätergruppen mit Hilfe einer ausgefeilten Logistik geschäftsähnlich agieren und dadurch erhebliche Finanz- und Machtpositionen erreichen. Den Tätern sei es gelungen, mit Hilfe von Korruption in einzelne Bereiche der Verwaltung einzudringen. Neben streng hierarchischen Organisationen würden insbesondere im Bereich deutscher Zuhältergruppen lockere Straftäterverflechtungen existieren" (Herz and Minthe 2006, 38).

    5. *Frankfurter Allgemeine* (FAZ) 2015; Schubert 2012, 2014.

    6. Bundeskriminalamt (BKA) 2017.

6

PRESTIGE, BELONGING, AND COERCION

The Gift in Sex for Sale

Prostitution between Gift and Commodity

If Zuhälter and their presence at the Flamingo seemed to be on everybody's mind, the gift and its spirit—in the form of loyalty, trust, and generosity—seemed to be worn on everybody's sleeve: when employees swore loyalty to the club owner and insisted that the Flamingo was their family and Hans Hartmann their savior; when clients extolled the virtues of their friendships with sex workers and their admiration for the house and owner; or when clients celebrated with their guests by spending lavish sums of money on drinks. Unlike the Zuhälter, who were inextricably linked with prostitution, the gift seemed utterly out of place in an establishment that for many represented the quintessence of the market and everything that turned bad once commercialized. As I show in this chapter, as much as the Zuhälter was the covert actor that could enforce labor discipline, the gift was the overt force that held the Flamingo together, and as much as the Zuhälter challenged the notion of the Flamingo as a crime-free economic establishment, the workings of the gift challenged the notion of the brothel as a place devoid of deeper forms of attachment.

While the slogan "sex work is work like any other" has been the rallying cry for sex worker rights advocates to have their work legalized or, better, decriminalized, anthropologists and sociologists who study prostitution have often used the frame of economic analysis and labor to understand commercial sex: to counter the claim of prostitution as a form of sexual exploitation (e.g., Bernstein 2010; Brents and Jackson 2013; Hoang 2015), to counter the claim of pimps as purely exploitative (e.g., Horning 2013), or to counter the claim of sex workers as destitute and disempowered, with no agency (e.g., Brennan 2004; Kelly 2008). What these scholars have in common is the idea that prostitution and its role in modern society cannot be understood as an archaic leftover or an isolated economic endeavor but that it is linked to the wider economy.

Yet in this seemingly monolithic conceptualization of prostitution through the lens of the market and labor, there are also significant countercurrents that illustrate how sex for sale often does not consist of a one-time market transaction—bounded and without future commitment—alone. Instead, sexual commerce is often embedded in social relationships with far-reaching ramifications and long-lasting human bonds: in Takeyama's (2016) analysis of male host clubs and their female clients in Japan, in Dewey and St. Germanin's (2016) research of street-involved women with social workers and police, in Mitchell's (2015) examination of the love relationships in Brazil's transnational gay sauna clubs, or in Padilla's (2007) analysis of transnational family relations between American sex tourists and their Dominican lovers. Foregrounded in these studies is not the economic transaction but the strength of intimate and emotional connections that seem to be diametrically opposed to conventional notions of brothels as places where men seek no-strings-attached sex and as sites of commodified intimacy incompatible with human emotions and attachment. Zelizer (2005) has aptly called such juxtapositions the "separate and hostile worlds" argument, where the intimate and the economic are thought of as antithetical to each other despite the fact, as Zelizer (2005) shows, so many aspects of our lives connect intimacy and economy. In this chapter, then, I focus on the affective and enduring dimensions of relationships between various actors in prostitution and the lasting bonds they form between them. What I show is that notwithstanding the fact that these relationships are taking place within the domain of commerce, they follow a logic of the gift. They are based on the exchange of presents over time and the obligations, attachments, and relationships these exchanges foster. Such relationships take place between sex workers and clients but also between clients and the house/manager and between employees and owner. However, such gift exchanges are not only cementing relationships of warm and fuzzy feelings. Instead, I show how the concept of gift exchange also explains the dark side of the gift: the possibility for manipulation, the trap of loyalty and indebtedness, and the potential for coercion.

The hallmark of gift exchanges are open-ended relationships. According to Mauss (1990), gift exchanges entail three obligations: to give a gift, to accept the gift, and to return the gift. Participants in a gift exchange engage in relationships with ongoing obligations based on moral economies. Giving a gift puts the giver in a morally superior status vis-à-vis the recipient and vice versa. Only after returning the gift over time—and possibly a more valuable one—does the original recipient assume the higher moral status. Through such a back-and-forth of gift and countergift and the dynamic relations of indebtedness and moral superiority it produces, the two parties are bound together in an ongoing exchange. The epitome of the gift constitutes the potlatch (Mauss 1990), named after the extravagant feasts celebrated by the late nineteenth-century Kwakiutl of the Pacific Northwest. In this clan-wide festive celebration, a chief acquires prestige, status, or titles through his competitive display of "sumptuary" and "usurious" generosity in competition with another chief (Mauss 1990, 95).[1]

Maussian scholars have often treated the gift economy as radically opposed to and incompatible with a market economy. Hart and James (2014, 5) write, "Anglophone anthropologists in the last three decades have built up a discourse of gift versus market (commodity), which opposes them as economic principles and often contrasts them as representing a gap between the West and the rest of the world." As these authors and others (Deflem 2003; Sansi 2014) show, there is a growing consensus that both kinds of economies occur simultaneously and often in articulation with each other. To complicate matters, "in any given situation, there are likely to be completely different principles [of economic relations] that could be brought to bear" (Graeber 2011, 89–90). Understanding which kind of economic exchange and underlying moral obligation is at work and how they are articulated is the task to embark on here and provides a key to the kinds of relationships at play.

Examining gift exchange in prostitution, then, raises questions about its relationship to the market economy and about the social meaning of sexual commerce and its significance in creating ongoing relationships rather than clearly delimited, bounded transactions implicit in statements such as Charlie Sheen's: "We pay them to leave." Focusing on relationships between sex worker and client, between client and house, and between management and staff, this chapter asks: in which ways are actors engaged in a gift exchange, what kinds of relationships do these gift exchanges generate, and how is such a gift linked to the market exchange? In the relationships between sex workers and clients, I show that clients provide gifts above and beyond the sexual purchase to deliberately initiate or maintain long-term relationships. In the relationship between client and house, I show how hosting can be seen as a form of potlatch. In hosting, clients engage in a triangular gift exchange where sharing expensive drinks with others becomes a means to acquire prestige vis-à-vis the invited guests as well as the house. In the relationship between management and employees, I show how the owner's demonstrations of generosity toward his staff facilitate loyalty but also coercion. Finally, this chapter raises the question of what role such a gift economy plays in the context of legalized prostitution, where service providers, consumers, and entrepreneurs can conduct their business without fear of legal persecution. Viewing these relationships through the lens of the gift economy reveals a web of shared vulnerabilities that ties actors together in multiple ways; this will be further developed in the last chapter, which explores the relationships clients develop with each other, thus expanding the reach of prostitution culture into society beyond the brothel.

Client and Sex Worker: Men in Search of a Care Object

The notion of brothels as serving men who seek sex with no strings attached was represented in a popular news magazine's story about the Flamingo. A client who was interviewed at the club was quoted as saying he had been getting tired of women chasing him after a one-night stand. That was why he started with "pay sex," as he called it. Prostitution allowed him to have sex for a set amount of money and time, without expectations of future commitment.

This client, as it turned out, was Richard, to whom the manager introduced me on my first visit to the Flamingo. Richard soon volunteered the reasons why he had become an avid pay sex fan, but his rationale was different from the one quoted in the article. He explained that while there might have been the occasional one-night stand chasing him, it was the difficulty of finding a compatible partner who would accept him and his three small children after his wife died. Instead of crisscrossing the country to find a partner tolerant of his children, the brothel and the relationships he managed to develop there made him feel at home, connected, while also getting his sexual needs taken care of.

Richard maintained close and affectionate ties to a number of sex workers, one of whom I came to know more closely. Besides being one of her regulars, she told me, he often invited her for lunch in town, and they became friends, although not erotic ones, as it was clear to him that she

192 | *Legalized Prostitution in Germany*

had a boyfriend. Richard helped her out financially a number of times, and although he had a reputation of being stingy with his own children, he was always generous with her and a reliable and caring friend.

Heiner, another regular at the club, had also given up seeking romantic partners the old-fashioned way. "Look at me," he said. "Who do you think wants a guy like me, so short and overweight?" However, he was thoughtful and compassionate, and I came to value his friendship highly. Heiner had thought a great deal about his relationship to prostitution and to the girls he would pay to have sex with him. He did not pursue romance with any of the women he had befriended. But this did not diminish his desire for authentic friendships, which he would go to great lengths to establish and nurture. Heiner was known among sex workers as polite, reliable, and generous. He explained that when he got together with a "girl" in a sauna club, his first goal was to make her feel good: he would always offer massages and oral sex first, before he allowed her to take care of him.

Heiner was also generous outside the bedroom. He regularly provided refuge for sex workers he had befriended when they were down on their luck, when they had not earned anything in a while, or when they needed a safe place to stay. One summer, I was trying to set up a meeting with him as we had done over the previous few years, but he was practically unavailable. He had spent most of his free time visiting a sex worker who was in jail and charged with trafficking, after she had refused to testify against her trafficker in a high-profile lawsuit. Heiner, astute in legal matters and a tenacious autodidact, not only provided emotional support but also helped her navigate the difficult legal and cultural terrain. Heiner would race down the autobahn on a five-hour trip just to visit her for several hours in jail. He did so numerous times and often took off extra time from work to visit her. When I asked him why he did it, he said he would do that for any friend.

Hellmut was another example of this kind of client. A youngish-looking forty-year-old, blond, well built, and always bringing his own bathrobe to the club, he in no way fit the stereotype of a man unable to find sexual partners. He had met his previous girlfriend in a sauna club and saw brothels as a place to search for potential girlfriends. At the club, he wanted not only to get off but to provide sexual stimulation too. The first evening we talked, he had just broken up with his girlfriend. He came to the club then almost every night and confessed he had fallen in love with one of the women there. Hellmut was proud of being able to give girls a record number of orgasms, but he could not understand why he would fall in love with the one woman he was unable to give any at all. Over several weeks, he brought her presents and consoled her over the death of her grandmother, and eventually they were planning a trip together. After numerous delays, however, she eventually told him that she was not interested in him and never had been.

Hellmut's self-presentation as a generous client and friend was particularly striking but not uncommon, and I wondered whether it was more performative than authentic. But it was proven to be the latter. In a long conversation with Hellmut and his best friend, a man with a Herculean body, the conversation turned to their etiquette with sex workers in the bedroom. The two friends could not disagree more. While Hellmut insisted how important it was for him to be "giving" during his purchased time, his friend blandly stated that if he paid a girl, he had no problem in letting her do the work and really was not all that interested in whether she had any fun herself. Hellmut appeared visibly disturbed by his friend's revelation and, blushing, was too stunned to provide a coherent defense. Hellmut struggled to understand him while also defending his own generosity, which all of a sudden might have seemed naive.

The most striking example of generosity, however, might have been Werner, whose wife had died of cancer several years earlier. Werner was in his midfifties and one of the most frequent customers of the Flamingo. Werner's reputation was legendary among the sex workers. He was known to invite them to his mansion just to be able to cook for them the most extravagant dinners and breakfasts and treat them like queens. His recipes were sought after among the madams. Werner's reputation was that he had never expected sex from the girls he invited to his house; in fact, as one of the madams told me, he was never known to have had sex with any woman of the club.

Richard, Hellmut, Heiner, and Werner were representatives of a type of "pay sex" practitioner who approached sex workers not as service providers from whom they could get the most "bang for the buck" but as fellow humans with whom they also pursued lasting connections. These men went to great lengths to foster relationships, showering the women with sexual pleasure, individual attention, and presents and offering places to stay, help with legal matters, and numerous other material and immaterial gifts. Sometimes these relationships were erotic in nature, but many times they were just friendships. The men engaging in these relationships were deliberate in their choice of sauna clubs as the place and environment where they were looking for women with whom to form such attachments. Rather than seeking sex objects to be used and then discarded, with no further strings attached, they sought "care objects" with whom they could establish affectionate relationships.

With the exception of Heiner, who seemed to be deliberately looking for a girlfriend in the brothel, most of these men were not seeking exclusive sexual relationships with the sex workers. It might be noted that all four were in their forties and fifties and were not married or in ongoing relationships with women outside the brothel. This meant they had more resources in terms of money, time, and affection and maybe a stronger need for intimacy and belonging.

Clients with such generosity and desire to engage in and maintain affective relationships might not be the norm. Married men, in contrast, were more likely to describe their interest in terms of a market logic. Who better than a sex worker to fill sexual needs and desires unmet by their beloveds, wives, or partners? Unlike a romantic partner, a sex worker would never come after them in jealousy, demanding love, thereby jeopardizing their marriage. For them, the sexual adventure was bound in time and expenditure and left no outstanding balances to settle. In their reasoning, sex with sex workers was not actually cheating because it did not involve any emotional attachment.

The care client was not unfamiliar to those working in the industry. While management encouraged such relationships insofar as they ensured regular customers, there were widespread notions among clients, sex workers, and brothel managers alike that if such affectionate relationships turned into love relationships, they would end badly. Members of a local pay sex forum reminded each other regularly to never confuse sex for pay with the real thing. Sex workers, in turn, while eager to recruit regulars, often despised and ridiculed men who brought them chocolates, lingerie, or other presents. Heiner once found out that one of the women he had befriended in the Flamingo had been making fun of him behind his back about his gullibility. Sex workers often resented the inherent obligations that both gift-giving regulars and clients infatuated with them expected, which could sometimes have fatal consequences for either the client or the sex worker, as in the case related to me by a retired sex worker about a frustrated suitor who had fallen in love with her and set himself on fire in front of her apartment because she had not returned his feelings. Another example of the immense risk that overgenerous and infatuated clients can pose to sex workers will be discussed in the next chapter.

Sex workers used a derogatory expression—*love clown* (*Liebeskasper*)—for men who fell in love with them. They often ridiculed them and sometimes joked about the silliness of the gifts their clients showered on them. Yet love affairs and nonerotic friendships were not uncommon. Many sex workers, especially the younger women I talked to, hoped to one day find a romantic partner among their clients. Others were happy to find real friends whom they could trust and on whom they could rely for help. The fact that they were working long stints in places isolated from the rest of the world, with often tense and competitive relations with coworkers and far away from their families and friends, made it very important to have friends among customers.

Management tolerated friendships among clients and sex workers as long as they remained on neutral ground but warned sex workers about erotic relationships with their clients. As one of the madams informed a group of sex workers during a meeting, "Only a real whore will give it up for free," and "no man that you encounter here will ever forget where he has met you." Of course, any sex act taking place between a sex worker and a potential client outside of the club meant an economic loss for the house and was therefore likely to be vilified by management.

Analyzing these clients' relationships with sex workers through the lens of the gift economy suggests that the gifts they provided—the massages and orgasms, the material comforts, the dinners, the loans, or the legal support—were means to continue and extend relationships that had begun with a sexual purchase. Never did clients say anything about a return gift of equal kind. Instead, the return gift seemed to be the continued engagement, sometimes leading to encounters outside of the club—although not necessarily to sexual relationships. For some men, giving gifts might have been a means to soften the harshness of the sexual transaction, reminiscent of the hetaeras in ancient Greece, who received gifts rather than payments to differentiate them from ordinary prostitutes (McClure 2014). With other men, it seemed to derive from a genuine desire to give something of value or to make the other party happy. Sex workers themselves did not always welcome such gifts and sometimes even resented the implied expectations. At the same time, though, working at the club often meant that they had to provide intimacies and emotional labor for free in order to recruit clients. In this back and forth of free labor on one hand and client gifts on the other, and despite the explicit warning against becoming a love clown, a surprising number of clients insisted that they had meaningful friendships with sex workers. Whether these men felt that their payment for sexual intimacy was insufficient and left them with a moral debt to pay off—hence they were morally inferior debtors—or whether they wanted to continue an ongoing cycle of engagement with the sex worker remains unclear. But independent of whether the gift was a means to balance out a debt or to forge a new relationship, the gifts they offered and the relationships that were established through these gifts made the Flamingo a place crisscrossed with affective ties, a place to experience social intimacy and connectedness, and thus a challenge to the notion of prostitution as a marketplace solely for commitment-free sexual exchanges. Instead, for these men, it was a place where they sought and maintained lasting and meaningful relationships.

Guest and House: Hosting

If gift exchanges create relationships over time through a dynamic imbalance of indebtedness between giver and receiver (or creditor and debtor), potlatches create systems of hierarchies through staged and competitive generosity in the presence of an audience (Mauss 1990; Graeber 2001). In the institution of potlatches in the Pacific Northwest, which Mauss used as the prototype for prestige-generating agonistic gift exchanges in general, chiefs tried to outspend each other in lavish festivities to acquire honor and prestige while clan members were hosted generously through entertainment, food, and gifts.

Hosting at the Flamingo can be compared to the institution of the potlatch. Hosting is the practice of clients buying expensive alcoholic beverages to share with others: sex workers, friends, colleagues, and employees of the house. Like a potlatch, hosting is a particularly ostentatious performance of gift exchange, "the object being to foster friendly feelings" between the participating partners (Radcliff Brown 1906, 83, cited in Mauss 1990, 19), and it often takes place with a sizable audience in a lavish and festive setting involving both trust and debt (Graeber 2001). First and foremost, however, both are status-generating performances that incorporate competitive gift exchange, sometimes to the point of outright material destruction. As Mauss observed, "This act of 'service' on the part of the chief takes on an extremely marked agonistic character. It is essentially usurious and sumptuary. It is a struggle between nobles to establish a hierarchy amongst themselves from which their clan will benefit at a later date" (Mauss 1990, 6). Comparing hosting at the Flamingo to a potlatch, however, raises a number of questions: Who was the competitor with whom the client-host competed? What was the relationship of the client-host to the guests with whom he shared the drinks (sex worker, friends, fellow clients, employees)? And if potlatch is a status- and prestige-generating mechanism, what does this status consist of, and who bestows it?

Hosting practices take place in a variety of commercial sex settings, from outdated hostess bars in Neuburg's red light district to the fancy FKK sauna clubs in its periphery or lavish karaoke bars in Asia (Allison 1994; Hoang 2011; Parreñas 2011; Takeyama 2016; Zheng 2009). While Allison's (1994) ethnography of Japanese karaoke bars in the 1980s has shown how deeply imbricated such clubs were with business culture and the performance of the corporate masculinity of "sarariman," Zheng (2009) has shown how such bars operate within the status culture of businessmen and political functionaries in China. Hoang (2015) describes how in Vietnam, hosting takes on global dimensions, as hostess or karaoke bars become the stage for high-stakes status performance between wealthy Vietnamese and international businessmen where finance and investment transactions are brokered. In such hostess bars, *hosting* refers to the social and erotic services hostesses provide to a client and his guests and for which clients are paying them, indirectly, via the house. While the original host might differ in the two cases—the hostess in Asia versus the client host in Germany—a client's conspicuous consumption vis-à-vis his guests and the house is the same. An important difference between hosting in Germany and hosting in the Asian contexts mentioned above is that erotic entertainment is much less institutionalized in the former's business culture than in Asian countries. Newspaper reports of excessive spending bills on corporate accounts in sex work venues prove the existence of such practices in Germany, but they are considered inappropriate at best and illegal at worst, and thus newsworthy scandals in the first place.[2]

As in a potlatch, I argue, the host's display of generosity toward his guests provides a stage on which he can perform largesse and acquire prestige: for the duration of the bottle of expensive liquor being emptied, the host is the center of attention, which can be considered a rather instant "return gift." However, as I show, it is the status a hosting customer acquires over time that earns him prestige at the club in the form of VIP status and privileges. The higher the spending, the more informal these privileges are and the closer the relationship of the guest to the house and the owner. The most visible manifestation of VIP status is the privilege to wear street clothes rather than the mandatory house-owned bathrobe and slippers. A client's growing VIP status and greater status proximity to the house and owner, however, often comes with a growing sense of entitlement and "taking stock" of the house and a competition with its authority. Thus, it was not uncommon for the house to eventually suspend the VIP status of a client or suspend the client from the house altogether for overstepping his boundaries. At the lower end of the honor/VIP spectrum, there were other means by which the house limited undue demands for status recognition from guests.

A Bachelor Party for the Ladies?

One form of hosting is illustrated in the case of Sadan and Ejder, two young Kurdish men. Sadan had attracted my attention because of his boisterous behavior and bodybuilder appearance. I was curious about this tattooed young man with a shaved head who fit the stereotypical image of a Zuhälter I had learned about through conversations at the club. He shared an over-size three-liter bottle of Moët & Chandon with his friends, and before long, he asked me to join them. I just had to get a champagne glass from the bar. I happily accepted, but not without also feeling a bit sheepish for having to get my own glass. When I came back, he poured me a generous portion and introduced himself and his friend Ejder, who was about to get married. Sitting next to Sadan was Juttka from Hungary, with Amina from Morocco and Svetlana from Bulgaria sitting between him and Ejder. Sadan laughed out loud when I asked him whether he was a Zuhälter. We soon engaged in a lively conversation about all of us being immigrants, albeit from different countries. In the course of our conversation, Sadan called Rosie—one of the older madams at the club—to join us. Sadan was leaning against Juttka, who was lying behind him on the couch, her legs wrapped around his waist, as he absentmindedly caressed her thighs. Before long, another three-liter bottle of Moët & Chandon, at a cost of €900, arrived in a bucket of ice. Sadan visibly enjoyed my expression of disbelief while Rosie, the madam, seemed unfazed by this astounding degree of consumption. I asked Sadan how he could afford to go through almost €2,000 in the span of an hour, young as he was. Sadan just shrugged. He had a number of businesses, he said.

The party ended abruptly. Before the bottle was finished, Sadan and Ejder disappeared, leaving behind three baffled women whom I had as-sumed were their friends. I had never noticed Sadan and Ejder before at the club. Sadan's striking display of generosity and conspicuous consumption in this spontaneous if brief bachelor party could lead one to wonder whether it was part of their Kurdish cultural heritage to spend lavish sums on wedding-related expenses, although this kind of bachelor party was rather informal. Judging by Sadan's evasive answer about his source of income, his apparent familiarity with and ease around the three women, and his invitation to Rosie, who seemed not the least bit surprised by it, I could not shake the suspicion that Sadan was in fact a Zuhälter, and the impromptu hosting of his friend's bachelor party was also a convenient occasion to give a demonstration of his largesse.

The Fallen VIP

Freddy represented a different kind of hosting. I introduced him earlier as the VIP who had become a persona non grata when he started to talk with sex workers about Zuhälter, which had become untenable for management. Freddy's example shows how hosting is a means to acquire prestige vis-à-vis the house but also how that prestige is tenuous and can be rescinded whenever the house decides. I met Freddy one Friday evening at the bar, where he was standing with Cecilia, one of the older German sex workers, who was drinking champagne with him. As Cecilia and Freddy carried on some lighthearted banter, she waved me over, requested a glass for me, and poured me champagne. Freddy was already staggering and leaning in on me at times, obviously quite tipsy. While he listened half-heartedly to Cecilia flirtatiously asserting that he was her true love, he told me he had not slept in several days. I was intrigued by the degree of intimacy between them, as if they were a seasoned couple who treated me like an old friend. When Freddy stepped away for a moment, Cecilia told me that she had been throwing up all morning from drinking so much liquor the previous night, but it was easier to earn money that way than by having sex, and I should help her by drinking as much as I could so he would buy a new bottle.

Judging by the fact that Freddy wore street clothes rather than the mandatory bathrobe, it was clear he was a guest who enjoyed special VIP privileges. Only the club owner, the managers, and employees were allowed to wear clothes. The madams greeted him as an insider, and the bartender did not seem the least bit bothered by his increasing drunkenness. Freddy, in fact, was rumored to have monthly bills at the club for drinks alone to the tune of an astonishing €150,000.[3]

When I returned the next year, however, Freddy had fallen out of favor with the club. Rosie, one of the lower ranking madams, explained: "Freddy made such a scene that the boss kicked him out. He left a lot of money here, yes. But he also got all kinds of privileges, such as free entry, for example, and other things you get with VIP status. And then he started talking bad about the club. He literally interrogated the girls and then scolded them when they had a Zuhälter and turned them against each other. That is why he is no longer welcome here." When I asked her what she thought the reason for all this was, she said, "A craving for prestige" (*Geltungssucht*).

Before our conversation had turned to Freddy, Rosie was telling me that she really did not want to drink any more alcohol, not tonight and not ever. Several women had told me stories about Rosie drinking too much, at one point even falling off her stool while she was gambling at a slot machine. As we talked about Freddy, I noticed that Rosie was in eye contact with a young, broad-shouldered, and very buff man who sat at the bar. At some point, he asked her whether she wanted to drink something. "You know what I want," she answered. He ordered her a piccolo, and our conversation ended abruptly.

The case of Freddy illustrated the long-term buildup of prestige that he had achieved over his months of heavy patronage and liquor expenses and the very public privileges he was given as a result of that prestige. Freddy could enjoy the club as an extension of his living room and the staff and admiring fellow clients as an intimate and admiring social circle. At the same time, this example showed the limits management put on this attempt to gain prestige and growing influence and how easily the privileges tied to his VIP prestige could be suspended. The role of Rosie, the madam who was providing the details about Freddy's excommunication, provides yet another example on how hosting—in this case, the hosting of a madam by a likely Zuhälter—is the prime tool by which influence is planted and favors are won at the club.

Limiting Performances and Suspending Prestige

Another example of how hosting behavior and the prestige it generated was controlled by the house was illustrated in the following encounter I had one night at the Flamingo. I noticed a cluster of five or six women standing next to me around a client and realized they were all sharing a bottle of champagne. The client, noticing me watching them, began to lean on me and whispered something into my ear. It was obvious that he greatly cherished this moment of having the attention of everyone he had invited to drink with him—all the women would get a percentage of the bottles he purchased for them, and thus they were obliged to stick around. However, it was also apparent that they were not enjoying his company. The second bottle of champagne was nearly half empty, and the client was leaning on me again, and some women seemed to be looking for escape routes. When I looked at the counter where the bottle had just stood, it was gone. The client started to complain, asking what had happened to it. The bartender just shrugged, telling him that they had finished it, not particularly concerned that this sounded like the lie it was. Although the client was drunk, he seemed to have noticed that was not true and started to protest, but the bartender ignored him. Meanwhile, the cluster of women around him was dissolving rapidly. Without anybody else left, he started to whisper in my ear, asking me what I was planning to do after the club closed. But only a few seconds later, the burly, bald, heavily tattooed security guard who had been watching us all the while walked casually toward him and told him it was time to go home. The client took the hint and disappeared into the changing room without further objection.

The whole purpose of a client inviting others to drink with him became apparent in this particular instance: spending money on overpriced drinks and inviting others, in this case sex workers, provided the client with an opportunity to make himself the center of attention, as others "owed" him courtesy for the duration of the drinks. But as in the previous case, this status display was limited to what the house allowed; in this case, taking away a half-empty bottle was one way for the house to eliminate unwanted behavior and retain control over a customer's attempts to gain status.

Hosting as Potlatch

Hosting is a practice deeply embedded in the market transactions orchestrated by the brothel and crucial to its financial bottom line. Yet the meaning of hosting, the expenditure it entails, and the purpose it serves cannot be understood within the frame of a market transaction alone. If the generous gifts a client provided to a sex worker led to affective relationships beyond the time of the purchase and the confines of the brothel, generous hosting functioned like potlatches, as means to acquire prestige in the context of lavish celebrations and competitive generosity.

At the basis of these examples of hosting was an economy of the gift—the invitation to drink expensive liquor and, for those invited to drink, the obligation to provide attention. At the same time, hosting gave the client the opportunity to acquire prestige in the form of VIP privileges, a publicly recognized status. Clients in house-owned bathrobes and slippers had limited possibilities to display status and prestige via indicators such as watches, clothes, shoes, or cars. The champagne menu, listing items costing up to €3,000, offered a degree of ostentatious spending that consumption of sexual services—with their fixed prices, private nature, and finite consumption potential—could not. In fact, the Flamingo was certainly not the club with the most expensive champagne selection, as sauna clubs elsewhere offered bottles up to €18,000, a staggering price for short-term entertainment.[4] The VIP facilities of the club—a VIP lounge, a VIP garage, and a VIP entrance—and the permission to wear street clothes emphasized this distinction. At the same time, while lavish spending was a prerequisite for VIP status, it was not clear exactly how one acquired that status, although it was clear when someone did.

While the house sold the champagne to be shared—the item of lavish spending that marked the host's generosity and through which he laid his claim to prestige—it also bestowed VIP privileges on the highest spender, and thus the host was trying to compete against the house. Hosting, then, was a potlatch, staged within the confines of a capitalistic market transaction that tapped into a moral economy of the gift as a means to reap an economic profit. It did so by enticing clients to compete in a status and prestige system generated at the club's discretion and on its behalf. But prestige gained through hosting always entailed the risk of losing it on a whim, or as Mauss states about the potlatch, it is a status that can be lost as suddenly as status is lost "in war, by gambling, or in running and boxing" (Mauss 1990, 36). And as in a potlatch, where a chief could maintain his privileged position only as long as he kept on giving, a client could maintain his VIP status only if he kept on hosting. Moreover, at the moment when a client began to challenge the authority of the house, prestige in the form of VIP status was easily withdrawn.

At this point, Graeber's (2011, 2014) concept of debt offers another insight into the moral economy of the gift. Rather than assuming reciprocity as the ultimate logic on which moral economies are based, Graeber (2011, 2014) argues that there are in fact three kinds of logic inherent in economic transactions: baseline communism, exchange, and hierarchy. While baseline communism is the mark of economies of great need and dependence where all parties are tied together in a web of outstanding debts that cannot or should not ever be leveled, hierarchies are the result of economic relations between unequals, where the debt can never be repaid. As Graeber argues, only "exchange allows us to cancel out our debts." And only "exchange gives us a way to call it even, hence, to end the relationship" or to choose to continue the dynamic imbalance of indebtedness that characterizes the gift (Graeber 2014, 71).

In Graeber's reanalysis of the potlatch (2001), the gifts that guests receive at a potlatch do not necessitate a return gift. "Insofar as anything even remotely like 'repayment' was involved, it was not in the object given (a mere 'trifle'), but in the act of recognition giving it entailed" (209). Similarly, one could argue that the guests a host treated to drinks were not required to provide an equivalent return gift but provided the trifle of being audience for the performance, of providing recognition; their presence validated the status of the host by paying him respect and attention, and they disseminated stories of his generosity. "Ultimately everything goes back to theater, to what one can put over on a (demanding but appreciative) public" (203). Moreover, as Graeber states, sharing is about pleasure. "[S]hared conviviality could be seen as a communistic base on top of which everything else is constructed" as "the most pleasurable activities almost always involve sharing something: music, food, liquor, drugs, gossip, drama, beds" (2011, 99). Liquor amplifies the character of shared conviviality, as it heightens the mood, lowers inhibitions, and intensifies a sense of community. Shared liquor erases barriers between people and ties them together through yet another web of shared vulnerabilities. In this regard, the gift that the host provided to his guests in the form of champagne could be seen as a gift of shared conviviality, a gift that fell under baseline communism, where no particular material return gift was expected.

But while shared champagne generated a sense of togetherness, the prestige acquired through hosting was ultimately based on and affirming the hierarchy of the house. If the relationship between a host and his guests could be considered a relationship among equals—or the attempt to create an image of a relationship among equals—the other is based on a hierarchical relationship among unequals. House and client will never be equal, hence there is no expectation of reciprocity. As Graeber writes, "Hierarchy works rather by the logic of precedent" (2014, 73). In that regard, the status of the house/owner remained absolute, and a client could maintain elevated status only through continued spending. The spending became a tribute required to maintain VIP status without providing a guarantee that it would. Such an absolute authority of the house and, by extension, the owner vis-à-vis the hosting client is captured in the term *Bordellkönig* (brothel king), prominent in the news and tabloid press where owners of luxury brothels are frequently featured.[5] Furthermore, even if both parties "assume they are operating by a shared code . . . they are unlikely to [equally] calculate the quality or quantity" (Graeber 2014, 73) of their mutual obligations. In the case here, only the hosting client could be held materially and quantifiably accountable for the bottles of champagne he purchased and consumed, while the house/*Bordellkönig*'s bestowing of VIP privileges was neither quantifiable nor contractually guaranteed. The parties involved were as unequal as the "gifts" exchanged between them were incommensurable. But vying for prestige with the house through hosting provided the client the opportunity to get into the orbit of the house and its prestige.

Employees and Owner: Prestige, Credit, and Indebtedness

If clients used gifts to establish ongoing relationships with sex workers and hosting to gain prestige from the house, the owner's legendary generosity toward his employees showed yet another facet of the gift: to many of his employees, Hans Hartmann had become a personal savior, a relationship that would also become a means to extort unquestioning loyalty from them. As a number of employees told me, Hans Hartmann had grown up in the streets. A promising sports career had ended prematurely after he was convicted of robbery, for which he spent many years in jail. After his release, he managed to achieve enormous success as a business tycoon through a series of different ventures, first in real estate and later in the sex and gambling industry.

Belonging

Despite his astonishing business success, Hans Hartmann presented himself as approachable, caring, and personable. He often went to the Flamingo in the evening and on weekends, apparently just to have a good time. After I earned his trust, I was eventually awed by his generosity and the almost unlimited access he granted me for my research, including permission to stay overnight without paying anything for entrance, food, or the bed I slept in. As I left the Flamingo at the end of the summer to return to the United States, I asked him whether I could come back the following winter. Hans Hartmann emphatically responded, "You are one of us now. Come back any time you want, for however long you want."

Earlier that summer, I had met another sauna club owner at the Flamingo. His name had appeared regularly in the newspaper, and he worked hard to cultivate an image of outrageous public notoriety. Hans had taken it on himself to introduce me to him. With his boyish physique, faded black T-shirt, and unassuming appearance, I had a hard time reconciling this live image with the image I had of him from the news. As neither he nor I were particularly interested in conversing with each other, I soon left him at the bar to catch a breath of fresh air outside. As I walked past the reception area, Hans followed me, tapped me on the shoulder, and said, "This guy is a pretty big name in the industry. I can get you a connection to him if you want to interview him." Although I was not really sure why I should be speaking to him, I felt extremely elated to receive such personal attention, marveling at what an excellent fieldworker I had become for gaining the trust and rapport of such an influential actor in this milieu.

Hans Hartmann's employees praised him as generous and understanding, noting that he had rescued them from precarious legal or financial predicaments and offered them jobs and even a safe and pleasant place to live within the sauna club premises. This was the story of Thorsten, one of the club's three managers, who had made a phenomenal career in the music industry, working with the music icons of my adolescence. Due to fiscal negligence, Thorsten explained, he had fallen on hard times and was charged with tax evasion. As a result, he lost almost everything he had ever owned. On top of that, he was on the verge of a heart attack and no longer able to maintain the lifestyle of a music manager, with nights on the road, heavy drinking, and constant high stress levels. That was when Hans Hartmann contacted him and offered him a job, although he had never worked in the red light industry. To learn the ropes of this trade, Hans Hartmann granted him a three-month on-the-job training opportunity where he got acquainted with similar clubs all over Germany.

Brigitte's case was in some ways similar. She had lost her job as a madam in a well-established apartment brothel when her boss was charged with tax fraud and was forced to close down the business. Brigitte herself was also charged with tax evasion and had to pay penalties and back taxes. She was jobless, moneyless, and homeless, with a huge bill to pay off, when Hans

Hartmann offered her a well-paid job as madam and a place to stay at the Fla-mingo. On top of that, he helped her save her beloved Toyota RAV and a valu-able collection of paintings from being seized by the Internal Revenue Service.

Personality Cult

Sex workers who had come to know Hans Hartmann personally often lined up to shake his hand and receive his customary peck on the cheek when he showed up at the club on the weekends. They turned to Hans Hartmann when they had problems with customers for being disrespectful, refusing to pay, or becoming physically abusive. I watched him many times listen-ing empathically, providing advice, and promising solutions. Natasha, the Russian woman described in chapter 4, was saved by Hans after madams turned her down because of her age. Also, customers—whether business-men, lawyers, or retirees—who managed to meet Hans Hartmann spoke fondly of him, with a glint in their eyes, honored that he would indulge them with a personal conversation and feeling they had an actual relationship with him.

Hans Hartmann's financial adviser, a former CEO of a large credit card corporation, told me that he was often horrified by the manner in which Hans managed the business. "Sometimes I am thinking he is running the club more like a charity than a for-profit business," he pondered one eve-ning. But this adviser, who was at the same time a major financial investor in the Flamingo, also described both of them as "an unbelievably talented management team," each bringing his own extraordinary expertise to the business. He never forgot to emphasize the intense trust relationship he had with Hans. "He and I and our families are extremely close. If something should happen to me, I know he would look out for my family. And I would do the same for him," he told me one evening. "There is no one I trust as much as I trust him."

Hans Hartmann's kindness and the loyalty it engendered in his employ-ees was apparent all down the ranks. The new receptionist at the entrance could barely contain her excitement when she explained to me how happy she was to work at the Flamingo and how she could not wait to give up her job as a nurse at an intensive care unit. She was an attractive forty-something woman with chiseled arms and an immaculate appearance. Her happiness was contagious, and every time she came to work, she made sure to give the security guard and her coworkers big hugs, radiating a sense of happiness. Here at the club, she said, she felt at home; she had a family, even more so than at her actual home, as she confided in me a number of times. I left the Flamingo that summer. When I went back the following winter, however, she was gone. My questions about her elicited only a laconic answer: she had not fit with the house and needed to be let go.

Not all of this admiration was entirely spontaneous. In fact, some of this adoration for Hans Hartmann seemed to be a personality cult that was the product of a deliberate staging. I realized that one day, as I managed to listen in on a team session in the girls' lounge led by Hedda, the main—and the most feared—madam. As it turned out, there had been serious tensions between clients and sex workers and between sex workers and madams. With the girls sitting crouched on the floor in front of her, Hedda introduced the session in a grave voice: "As you all know, Hans is not able to come to the club these days and help you and watch out for you and be available to you, as he usually does. In fact, we had to force him to stay home and take care of himself. You should know, Hans Hartmann is so worried about you, and about your well-being, that he became sick." Hedda's portrayal of Hans Hartmann as a highly sensitive and caring boss seemed convincing enough for at least some of the young women, who started to express emphatically their concerns about him. I had doubts that anything Hedda said about her boss's concern for the girls had anything to do with reality. She was a shrewd madam, with an ice-cold expression on her face that went well with her former occupation as a dominatrix.

Banishment

Eventually, I experienced how it felt to be ousted from this cocoon of comfort and familiarity. While my self-confidence had swelled dramatically by feeling completely accepted by Hans and welcome at the club, it was brutally crushed the following season, when I went back to resume my research at the Flamingo. I had called ahead to announce my imminent arrival, something I had thought was going to be a mere formality, as usual, but instead I was met with evasive answers from various managers and receptionists. Eventually, I managed to talk to Hans himself, who reluctantly agreed to let me come the following day. I wondered whether I was still "one of them"; his hesitation made me more than a little nervous.

When I arrived at the club, I was greeted with an icy welcome. Gone was the casual banter with the ladies at the reception desk. Brigitte, the madam I had befriended during my previous visits, stood at the desk and looked at me with apprehension. Instead of hugging me, as she had done in the past, she made a comment about my wet coat making a mess on the floor, as if to publicly disavow any connection she had with me in front of Hedda, the top madam, whom I had long suspected of being hostile toward me.

I swallowed my pride and embarrassment and began with my routine of locking up my backpack in the locker room and changing into something more comfortable to wear for the rest of the evening. Brigitte later took me upstairs and showed me my bed in an empty six-bed dorm room, where I could sleep and have the room to myself, as business shortly before the Christmas break was slow and few girls were working. Brigitte seemed to be trying somewhat to make up for the harsh reception she had served me earlier.

After a few sluggish days on-site, I was told one evening that one of the managers wanted to see me the next morning at eleven. This was not a good sign. I had always instinctively avoided him because he seemed dismissive or inscrutable. When we met, he told me that I would not be welcome at the pre-Christmas party the following day. Suddenly, my mouth became all dry. I asked what, who, and why, and whether I would be able to come back another time. I could come back, but only for a few days, not for as many days as I had in the past, and only after clearing it with him first. And, by the way, where was that report about the club that I had more or less promised to write?

Upset and ashamed, I walked upstairs to collect my things. As I left the room, I decided to stop to see Brigitte, who had a private room on the same floor as the girls. She had just gone upstairs to get some rest. Brigitte had been my friend and anchor at the club. She had told me about her life before she'd begun working at the club, about her family, and often how she hated this work. I genuinely liked her and was still reeling from the icy reception she had served me earlier in front of her boss. Maybe behind closed doors, she would speak to me. And she did. With a grave expression, she told me that in the last few months, several of the employees had been cut off. Christa, another madam who had just started to work there the previous season, was let go from one moment to the next without any explanation. Hans Hartmann had assured her that her job was safe one day, but she was fired by the manager the next day. After that, no one dared to talk to her anymore or even mention her name. It dawned on me then that Brigitte might fear for her job as well, as Hans Hartmann had saved her from a financial abyss. I asked Brigitte how Hans could be so friendly to me, and the next thing I knew, I had become a persona non grata. Brigitte said that was exactly his style. He himself would never tell anybody anything bad; he left it up to the manager to do the dirty job for him.

The banishment from the Flamingo was a hard pill to swallow. I tried to figure out what I had done wrong. I was not convinced by the manager's explanation that clients had complained about me; most of them appeared to thoroughly enjoy the opportunity to talk with me about themselves and their experiences. I suspected it had to do with my increasingly blunt questions about Zuhälter and my growing understanding of their symbiotic role at the club.

While Hans Hartmann had gained a reputation as a savior through his generosity toward his employees, it was also generosity that kept them morally indebted to and financially dependent on him. As a result, employees tended to speak very highly of him and showed fierce loyalty. The ugly underside of this loyalty, however, became apparent when an employee was let go, and former colleagues cut any ties to them, presumably out of fear of being fired themselves. Considering how highly many of his employees spoke about him and about their sense of belonging to the "family" of the Flamingo, such layoffs were not rejections confined to work performance but a banishment from an intimate group with whom they had lived and worked in proximity and for extended periods of time. On the other hand, the generosity Hans Hartmann provided his employees also ensured a sense of fierce loyalty. In a way, Hans had become like a godfather in the Mafia: fiercely supportive as long as one fit in and was loyal, but always with the imminent threat to be cut loose at the drop of a hat.

While this might have been one of the more extreme forms of owner-employee relations in a sauna club, a certain amount of family-like ties were built into such relationships in other brothels as well. One reason for the effectiveness of this form of management style might lie in the fact that employees and sex workers often lived and worked together in close quarters, with little or no distance to their place of employment and few opportunities to maintain social networks beyond the sauna club. Not only sex workers complained about social isolation but also employees in higher positions, who found the nonstop sauna club party atmosphere stifling. Financial hardship, as experienced by several of the employees in this sauna club, was likely to exacerbate this dynamic.

Conclusion

Applying the Maussian lens of a gift economy to exchanges and relationships between actors at the Flamingo challenges the concept of prostitution as a market for no-strings-attached sex where the purchase of sex as a market transaction liberated sex from the shackles of romantic expectations or commitment. Instead, I have shown how this new business concept was imbricated with a moral economy of the gift that tied actors together in a web of relationships. Gift economies are relationship economies, and the product of a gift economy is primarily the relationship forged through a dynamic imbalance of indebtedness. Exploring gift economies in prostitution therefore forces us to focus on the gifts given, on the relationships actors form with each other, and on the affect and social bonds that such relationships generate.

But gift economies are not taking place instead of or displacing market transactions. Rather, as this study of the dyads between clients and sex workers, guests and house, and employees and owner has shown, the gift economies at work were deeply intertwined with market economies and benefited the club's financial bottom line. In fact, the types of gift economies presented here were closely linked to the way the sauna club brothel and its income-generating strategies were orchestrated.

The gift exchanges and resulting friendships between clients and sex workers unfolded in an environment designed to facilitate extended social interactions between the two parties. The club provided spaces and opportunities for socializing before and after sexual services. Freelancing sex workers, who spent a significant amount of their time and labor on unpaid client recruitment and after-purchase care, had an incentive to turn their clients into regulars in order to develop a more reliable and predictable pool of customers. Clients who became familiar with the kinds of relationships offered by the sauna club setting appreciated the opportunity to socialize with sex workers at length, which was not available in most other prostitution settings. With its diverse entertainment features, and by utilizing the free recruitment labor of sex workers as an attraction of the sauna club business model, the club helped clients to develop relationships with sex workers that extended beyond the sexual purchase and sometimes beyond the confines of the club. The spontaneous gift economy unfolding between sex workers and clients at the club was encouraged by both the way the business was organized and the unpaid recruitment and post-labor socializing exacted from sex workers. Such gift exchanges also signal the importance of attachment and relationship for a segment of clients, if not for the sex workers. Rather than a purchase bounded in time and affect, as Bernstein (2007) described for upscale escort service workers in San Francisco, the gifts provided by clients at the Flamingo led to open-ended relationships. Some clients would doubtless look for sex objects and no-strings-attached experiences, but the ones described here can be better described as looking for care objects with strings attached.

The gift relationships established through hosting—between host and guest and between host and house/owner—were an even more deliberate business strategy of the Flamingo. But the logic of this expense to a sauna club client cannot be captured through the logic of the marketplace alone. Rather, like in the potlatch, hosting provided a network of relationships that fed into and generated prestige. This happened in the form of VIP status, whereby the competition occurred between client and house. Invited guests were mere recipients of the gifts of generosity and, most significantly, an audience that granted space for and witness to a host's splendor. The institution of hosting brought clients closer to the orbit of the house and its gravitational center, the owner or "brothel king," while at the same time celebrating conviviality with their guests with whom they shared the drinks.

The relationship between employees and house illustrated yet a third example in which market exchanges were overlaid through gift exchanges. The personality cult around Hans Hartmann was built on his legendary generosity toward sex workers, madams, and staff alike. While it created fierce loyalty among staff and a profound sense of family, it was also an effective means to coerce compliance, as banishment was always only an arm's length away.

Notes

1. Mauss writes, "The purely sumptuary form of consumption (which is almost always exaggerated and often purely destructive), in which considerable amounts of goods that have taken a long time to amass are suddenly given away or even destroyed, particularly in the case of the potlatch, . . . give such institutions the appearance of representing purely lavish expenditure and childish prodigality" (1990, 95).

2. Spiegel Online 2016; Stern.de 2012.

3. A retired police chief offered an insight when I mentioned this story. He was aware of the local history and knew that Freddy's family used to be farmers. At the turn of the millennium, a commercial mega enterprise was trying to buy up most of the fertile farmland,

and a fierce local protest ensued in the community, trying to stop this development. Despite his neighbors' and the town's protesting, Martin sold his land and became a millionaire overnight. In the eyes of the police chief, what Martin was doing with his exorbitant bills at the club was "spending guilt money." The police chief likened it to criminals engaging in hasty spending sprees, not only because the money was hard to channel into more sustaining endeavors but also as a way to assuage their conscience. In Freddy's case, his expenses at the club also afforded him VIP status and a community of instant friends.

4. As reported in Schulte (2007) and the *Handelszeitung* (2012). Such prices seem high for Germany but not so much for Japan or Vietnam, where visiting hostess bars is an institution deeply embedded in company culture and finance relationships (e.g., Allison 1994; Hoang 2015).

5. M. Böhm 2017; R. Böhm 2018; *Radio Zwickau* 2011.

7

SEX CLIENTS

At the Club, on the Forum, and at the Pub

A Stammtisch Visit

It was still hot on that Friday evening in July when Harald and Marianne picked me up to go to the Stammtisch.[1] Harald had chosen a restaurant facing a picturesque lake. It would be the first time the members of Harald's client forum would meet face-to-face. Harald arrived in his spacious Mercedes station wagon. His girlfriend, Marianne, was sitting next to him, cradling her Chihuahua in her lap. We continued our conversation from the day before about Ronaldo, a client who had been accused on the forum of pulling off his condom during sex, which was a serious offense for which he could face assault charges. Ronaldo had vehemently denied all wrongdoing and threatened to file slander charges against the forum.

Harald had nervously anticipated this first gathering. He was not sure whether Ronaldo would show up and if so, whether the situation would escalate. He had wavered on whether to make the location public. Fortunately, Harald's fears proved unfounded. When we arrived, everyone seemed to be in good spirits, and Ronaldo was nowhere in sight. Harald had not expected that so many people would show up. Of the forty or so guests, most were middle-aged men, some wearing wedding bands. Several of them were employed in the IT sector, and many had master's or other advanced university degrees. Most of them came from the region, although some had driven four or more hours to get there. Among the guests were also five women, who introduced themselves as brothel entrepreneurs, sexual service providers, and old friends of some regulars and Harald.

As we entered the room Harald had reserved in the back of the restaurant, I made sure to get a seat next to him and Marianne. I felt a bit silly sticking so close but soon got involved in a conversation with the man seated next to me. He looked like he was in his sixties and introduced himself only as Lenny48, his username on the forum. Looking at me, in my A-line brown skirt and grey T-shirt, he asked, "Does your job start with p-s?" "You mean a psychologist?" I answered. "Or a social worker, or a theologian," he offered. Sexy as I was dressed—at least for my taste—I was taken aback by this statement. "I can tell that you are not from the scene," he added. After I had introduced myself and my study, he abruptly volunteered, "I have been doing pay sex since 2005, for five years and two months." I looked at him, surprised. "That sounds like a . . . confession?" I asked. With a stern face, he responded, "You have to be careful not to get too involved with this." "Because of . . . the money?" I asked. "That is just one reason. There are other risks that come with pay sex. Some of us get way too deep into it."

"Like Netherworld," someone from across the table chimed in. He was one of the three forum administrators, as he introduced himself later. A man in his fifties, he had overheard our conversation. "Netherworld is the kind of guy who would kill himself if he were to be kicked out of the forum." Knucklehead—as the forum administrator introduced himself—explained how Netherworld had fallen on hard times. When he was forced into early retirement, he started to deliver pizzas six days a week and spent most of his rapidly dwindling resources on pay sex. Administrators had threatened to kick him out of the forum after he had become increasingly provocative in his comments. Knucklehead continued, "Netherworld is the prime example of a guy for whom the forum became way too important."

Field notes, July 20, 2010

In the first chapter, "Sex in Public," I showed how pervasive sexual representations were in public, ripe with explicit advertisement and suggestive slogans but also with a vibrant counterculture where conventional gender taboos were challenged, patriarchal privileges castigated, and sexism and misogyny the target of explicit protests. Here, I return to the wider ramifications of prostitution on society through clients' relationships with each other—at the Flamingo, online, and at their regular gatherings—and what such relationships say about the larger society.

With its legalized purchase and sale of sex, liberal approach to sexuality, low-cost sexual services, and reputation as an advanced social democracy where women enjoy a considerable degree of equality, Germany promises to be an ideal playground for sex clients. Society's tolerance for prostitution is expressed in the terms commonly used to describe it. For example, *Freier*, an archaic expression for *suitor*, lacks the pejorative connotations of the term *John*, used in journalistic writing (e.g., Malarek 2011) or sociological and criminological studies (Blevins and Holt 2009; Elias 1998; Stalans and Finn 2016) in the Anglophone world. Considering this apparent tolerance for sex and sexual commerce, how do sex clients assess their own participation in the industry, how do they relate to their peers, and what role do online client communities and their regular meetings at the Stammtisch play in their lives?

The field notes excerpt above, taken during the first of what was to become a biannual gathering, reveals a number of themes in the lives of these men, from policing each other and socializing with each other to confessing their dependency on sexual commerce—all themes covered in the first fifteen minutes of conversation at the forum. This chapter, then, focuses on the relationships men have with other sex clients and how they share their activities, negotiate their positions, and, in the process, form an intimate community with their peers. I show that the forum provided these men a refuge where they could share their adventures in pay sex with like-minded men and experience a sense of community. Notwithstanding the apparent tolerance toward prostitution in society at large, there was a pervasive disapproval of men who paid for sex, even among those working in this industry. The forum, then, provided an escape from the social stigma associated with being someone who purchased sex. But as these men gained a sense of sociability and shared community, they also became increasingly vulnerable and dependent on each other. In fact, the greater their intimacy with this community became, the more their risk of isolation from society at large grew.

If recent sociological studies of sex clients have countered their portrayal as objectifying women with an exploration of the range of emotional attachment clients have to service providers, few such studies have looked at clients' relationships with other men. Those that did disproportionately focused on hostess bars in Japan (Allison 1994; Parreñas 2011), China (Zheng 2009), or Vietnam (Hoang 2015), where male socializing through commercial eroticism is an essential component of business masculinity (Allison 1994; Zheng 2009). The Flamingo, and other sauna clubs like it, deliberately presented itself as a site of male socializing, and some men did go there to celebrate business deals or to bring new clients or business partners in order to develop trust relationships. However, such practices were not comparable to the institutionalized performance of business masculinity ethnographers have described in Asian host clubs. In fact, when such practices were reported in the newspapers in Germany, they caused a scandal. This was the case in 2016, for example, when two managers of the insurance company Hamburg-Mannheimer organized a party with twenty sex workers, or in the case of Volkswagen's CEO Peter Hartz, who offered both managers and union members free trips to sex orgies in Hungarian spas, complete with escort services.[2]

While different actors at the Flamingo engaged in a gift exchange to forge relationships with each other and to offset the commercial character of the market exchanges in which they participated, I argue here that clients also used gift exchanges with other clients through the sharing of intimate information and in order to cultivate a sense of community with their peers on the forum. The strength of this community was directly related to the degree of stigma associated with pay sex, and following Zelizer's (2005) concept of intimacy, the more they shared intimate and potentially discriminating revelations about themselves in the anonymity of the forum, the greater this sense of community became. The intimate bonds that were forged in the forum, however, came at the cost of a greater sense of alienation from society at large, thus creating a vicious cycle and for some a degree of dependency from which they found it difficult to extricate themselves.

Tracing the self-presentations of men and their interactions in these three contexts, I show how clients established a sense of community in three dimensions: first, a consumer community that helped them to collectively bargain in the sexual marketplace; second, an intimate community that provided them with social support and instructions on how to be a successful client; and third, a moral community where they actively negotiated ethical positions and behaviors.

Ambivalence at the Sauna Club: Insecurity, Shame, and Guilt

Sauna clubs were the preferred brothel type for many of the men at the Stammtisch. While one exuberant client described the Flamingo as "heaven on earth," visiting a sauna club brothel could also present hurdles and pitfalls to clients. For example, when women were taking the lead in their sexual pursuit and some men felt the need to protect themselves or miss out on the excitement of the chase. Martin, a middle-aged entrepreneur, stated that after going to the club and experiencing sex workers chasing him, he understood why women got cranky when constantly approached by men in clubs and bars.

Besides being able to put up with being pursued by women, a client also had to be able to stomach rejection. It was not uncommon for sex workers at the Flamingo to send clients away or to tell them to wait until an undetermined later time. On one particularly busy day at another club, I had watched how difficult it was for some men to find available women, so much so that they began forming a cluster around the women's showers out of desperation, hoping to find one before she was snapped up by others. Watching this scene, a middle-aged client voiced his frustrations to me but also his disgust for his fellow clients: "I did not realize that you had to know how to flirt here in order to get a girl. But watching the guys trying to catch a girl by hanging around outside their showers and grabbing one as soon as she comes out is just embarrassing."

The courting ritual between client and sex worker was a public affair, conducted in plain sight of others: women and men, sex workers and clients, and madams and bartenders. Although the women's flirtatious invitations— from inviting looks to courteous introductions, and from casual brushing against a client to directly touching his genitals—outweighed their rejections, a client could never be sure that the woman he set his eyes on would actually go to a room with him. The barely concealed triumphant smile that I often observed on men—and sometimes on women—when they walked up the stairs to the rooms where they would have sex suggested that there might have been a degree of uncertainty and thus a feeling of conquest on either side that added spice to the transaction.

Independent of how authentic this courting game was, men reminded each other regularly on the forum that they should not mistake the flirting in clubs for an actual dating ritual and that the women at the club had sex with them only because they got paid for it. In fact, online and offline, many pay sex clients were acutely aware of the stigma attached to men who visited prostitutes. After all, in the eyes of many, having to pay for sex was not a sign of masculine prowess. Yet, few were aware of the degree to which those profiting most from prostitution—the sauna club entrepreneurs and their employees—often despised sex clients and scoffed at what they described as their demonstrations of masculine impotence.

This was the subject of a conversation I had one night with the financial comptroller of the club. Wearing a casual off-white linen suit and leaning his arms on the bar, he explained, "My job is to lure in the largest number of clients by providing them with top facilities, so that I can make maximum profit. But this here has nothing to do with eroticism. Really, I loathe these men who come here to buy sex. I would never tell them that to their faces, of course, but what a sign of ineptness [*Armutszeugnis*] is it for a man to have to purchase sex. It is like a safari hunter who has no clue about hunting but is going on a trophy hunt. The only chance that he can make a kill is if an animal is put right under his nose." He underscored his contempt for sex clients, who constituted the largest source of revenue for the club, by telling me about his own "hunting skills" in gaining the attention of a beauty pageant winner at a bar, who would later become his wife.

The bartender attending to us shared this disdain for clients. A shrewd, middle-aged man with a bald head and a friendly twinkle in his eyes, he once had owned a successful Italian restaurant before he'd lost it to an expensive cocaine habit, he had told me earlier. Pouring me a glass of wine while eyeing the men at the end of the counter, he casually commented, "These men are idiots. Never in my life did I pay for sex. What kind of loser do you have to be to go to a brothel to pick up women and pay for sex?"

Some clients were aware of this contempt. Richard, introduced to me by club management as a client who understood the industry really well, and who was also a regular contributor to the client forum, told me about the infamous owner of another sauna club in the area: "So this guy calls us—his clients—douchebags and says that we should just be happy that he provides us with a constant supply of fresh meat for fucking."

Another source of ambivalence club visitors expressed was a sense of shame for going to sauna clubs. Thus, it was not uncommon for clients to express doubts about whether the girls working at the club did so of their own volition and whether they liked what they were doing. An attractive middle-aged man who described himself as a public relations consultant told me in a moment of self-doubt, "I don't think that the women here enjoy what they are doing." Some clients began talking about their daughters who were the same age as many of the women at the club. A middle-aged man of Turkish descent, who described himself as having a business employing fifty workers, told me proudly that his daughter had won a scholarship for a prestigious business school. Then he reflected for a moment and, with a voice filled with self-doubt, said, "It is sad what the girls are doing here. I would be horrified if I would find out my own daughter would be working here." His comment could have easily come across as callous and cold, as compartmentalizing women between those who were respectable and in need of protection and those excluded from this concern. But that would not be honest to the situation. Rather, it sounded like a sudden realization, an admission of guilt, which he allowed me to witness.

Some men openly talked about the risks they took in regard to their marriages, like the pleasant retiree who described himself as happily married: "If my wife caught me, she would divorce me immediately." Others had actually experienced their family's contempt after they discovered their pay sex hobby. This was the case of a man in his fifties who described himself as a neurologist in a nearby university town. "When my mother found out where I spent my money, she disowned me," he said. To reduce the risk of being discovered or seen by family or friends, some clients went to sauna clubs several hundred miles away from home.

The sauna club, then, was not a haven of unfettered male privilege but a site that posed a series of challenges. Sex workers at the club helped to buttress clients' masculinity in a way similar to the Filipina hostesses Parreñas (2011) studied in Japanese hostess bars, whose job was to make men feel desired. But clients at the Flamingo and other clubs also had to stomach rejections from sex workers, competition with other men, and contempt from staff and those who profited the most from the men who patronized the clubs: their owners. Being a client at a sauna club was not considered a feat of masculine accomplishment by society at large. Rather than enjoying the sexual benefits of what the Australian scholar of masculinity Raewyn Connell has described as "the patriarchal dividend" (2005, 41) and sex work abolitionists have called the hallmark of patriarchal exploitation (Farley et al. 2015; Hughes 1999), the sauna club was an ambivalent space: supremely titillating but also humiliating, thus contributing to the readiness, if not the need, for some clients to seek consolation with peers in the anonymity of a forum.

If sauna clubs were a titillating environment that provided intense erotic experiences but also social challenges, the forum was a stage on which men could relive their experiences and share them with a generally sympathetic community of like-minded peers. The tense competition some clients felt in the face-to-face interaction with other men at the sauna club gave way to amicable companionship when pay sex practitioners conversed in the anonymity of the forum. There, in the company of their peers, men could either share their experiences and show off bravado and virility or reveal their insecurities.

A Consumer Community: Market
Information and Purchasing Power

Sex client forums attract men who are curious about or already active in commercial sex. They provide information on brothels and their locations but also have a social function. Comparing itself to the renowned institution Stiftung Warentest (Consumer Reports), the NR9[3] was a forum focusing on the larger Neuburg region and described itself as providing "impartial and objective information" to help the buyer make the best decision. In this regard, the forum functioned as a consumer community that provided crucial information about the market as well as about what to do and not to do in different settings.

To provide authentic and individual user reports, the NR9 forum encouraged its users to post about their experiences with commercial service providers, or CSPs, as sex workers were respectfully called. Generally, the format of such reports differs from forum to forum: some feature fixed evaluation criteria while others encourage free-form, detail-oriented prose. The British client forum punternet.com, for example, uses a set number of criteria—such as money for time spent, services purchased, and ranked performances (Sanders 2008)—while others, like the *Roemerforum*[4] in Germany, use a more individualized and free-form report where detailed, vivid, and salacious descriptions are encouraged, with no formal structure and only a few set criteria, such as "repeat factor" (*Wiederholungsfaktor*) and attractiveness (*Optik Fick*). By comparison, the NR9 definitely encouraged more creative client reports. One of the larger forums of its kind in Germany, it listed about fifty thousand users and an overall volume of seven hundred thousand postings. According to these numbers, the NR9, which focused on service provider locations only within the region, was comparable in size to punternet.com,[5] which covers the entire UK plus Ireland. While this provides a comparative framework to gauge the size of the forum, it possibly also speaks to the popularity of such client forums in Germany.

The NR9, which had been in existence since the early 2000s, was the brainchild of Harald, the webmaster who invited me to the Stammtisch. Harald was proud of this forum and called it his "baby." He had invested considerable effort over the years to develop it, which demanded a good handle not only on clients and their online interactions but also on service providers and the legal ramifications and liabilities that came with such a platform. Harald continued to play a central role in the forum, although he also had a number of administrators and moderators to help him with the daily tasks of managing the platform.

To inspire men to post reports about their experiences and to increase traffic to the site, the NR9 offered monthly sweepstakes where members posting the most evocative reports could win prizes, consisting of free entry to sauna clubs or sexual services ranging from €30 to €150. Although the NR9's primary intention was to facilitate the exchange of client experiences and to do this for free, it also generated revenue for Harald, who charged a fee based on clicks for brothel advertisements on the site. In turn, the NR9 offered providers the opportunity to post information for free about specials, planned events, or sex worker availability. Sex workers and brothel operators were encouraged to participate in forum discussions, which sometimes led to lively and informative exchanges, such as the growing demand for girlfriend sex and to what extent that was compatible with safe-sex practices, discussed earlier. The internet traffic generated through the clients' reports and their readers attracted a convenient and targeted audience for these services and the paid advertisement. In addition, the forum was also used by nonprofit and nongovernmental services who offered critical information about health and legal issues.

Although users did not have to be registered in order to read, write, or post new threads, registered members enjoyed greater access to forum content than guests. A VIP area on the forum, which could be accessed only by members with specific privileges, rewarded frequent contributors with special insider information—for example, where and when Stammtisch meetings were going to be held and what would happen or had happened there. With growing seniority, registered users acquired considerable freedom to create individualized online identities, and many were quite creative in coming up with clever and raunchy usernames, campy bylines, and salacious avatars. Each member's name was automatically outfitted with individual statistics, including the date of becoming a member, number of reports posted, and thank-you nods received. To advance in the forum's hierarchy from freshman to senior status, users had to regularly post reports about their sexual experiences with sex workers.

As a consumer community that provided users the benefit of detailed information about service providers and establishments, the NR9 forum and others like it also contributed to power imbalances between sex workers and clients that might have played a role in the declining value and increasing demands on sexual services that has become the hallmark of legalized prostitution in Germany, as explored in chapter 3. The Prostitution Act of 2002, and the greater protection it offered to entrepreneurs, helped to make prostitution a more transparent market, with a greater flow of information on both the supply and the demand side. Sex work providers' and prostitution venues' greater freedom to advertise helped clients to find relevant information and therefore to have more purchasing power. Since that time, the internet has grown significantly, not only in advertisement for erotic and sexual businesses and services but generally in unleashing possibilities of information exchange about sexuality (Jacobs 2007). In this context, client forums in their function as consumer reports about the performance of sex workers contribute substantially to this explosion of market information for clients (Cunningham and Kendall 2016) but without giving sex workers themselves comparable access to information about demand or quality of the buyer.

Many sex workers and brothel entrepreneurs I spoke with therefore saw such forums as a mixed blessing at best. While good reports were a boon to the business, bad reports could damage the reputation of a sex worker and the establishment, with few means to openly challenge a false report or accusation without jeopardizing future business. On the other hand, service providers and their managers, and anyone else with a stake in the industry, could easily use the forum to discredit their competition or make advertisement for themselves by posting fake reports: either exceedingly positive ones about themselves and their services or negative ones about their competition.

This constituted a challenge of authenticity for the forum and the reports posted there. To counteract such misuse and to maintain credibility among users, the forum posted explicit rules and enforced them publicly. More behind-the-scenes policing occurred through vigilant checking for "double nicks"—i.e., members who were posting under two different usernames, which seemed the preferred way to discredit sex workers and establishments. Administrators were able to do so by comparing IP addresses as well as other data provided in the registration process. Alerting a user and the public about posting under a double nick was therefore a warning that the webmaster or administrators could use to discipline members and increase the trustworthiness of the reports and the trust of forum users.

At times, the client forums and the anonymity they provided became arenas for trade wars, which forum administrators tried hard to avoid. A brothel owner or manager might leave a negative report on a forum to discredit a competitor's establishment. On the other hand, disgruntled customers, not satisfied with the sexual services they expected, had an easy outlet for their frustration with potentially damaging consequences for the service provider. In one case a madam related to me that a sex worker decided to provide service for a client despite the fact that he had a genital infection, under the condition of using a condom for both oral and vaginal sex. The customer agreed but later berated the sex worker for not following through with the customary condom-free oral sex and for providing a substandard service overall. The sex worker had few means to tell her side of the story without revealing the health status of her client.

The PR manager at the Flamingo could barely hold back his contempt for "forum types," as he called them. In the process of negotiating services and prices with the girls, some clients would casually mention that they wrote in forums, knowing full well that this would put pressure on the women. Such a comment then could easily turn into extortion, pressuring a sex worker to go against her own rules in order to avoid potentially negative repercussions. Some employees of the sauna club who had more casual contact with the clients had developed an outright dislike for forum members and what they perceived as their often overbearing conduct, particularly when such men came in groups. Another manager described them as usually "unattractive men," "short" with "big bellies" and often "physically disfigured," who deliberately tried to coerce sex workers by telling them they would write about their services in a forum.

Sex workers at the Flamingo and other sauna clubs tended to be much less able to participate as equal partners on this platform. While the forum invited sex workers to participate, it was not suited to create a community of sex workers comparable to that of clients, as the former were tied up for long periods of time with client recruitment and were unable to be online. Many sex workers also did not have the technological resources or language skills to respond to such reports effectively, even though in theory they had equal access to post on client forums. Sex workers were thus at a disadvantage vis-à-vis clients.[6]

In this regard, then, the client forum as a consumer community was a powerful player in the market, disproportionately empowering men in their ability to negotiate prices and services. Clients could negotiate with sex workers by referring to services and prices reported by others or make up such "facts" and coerce sex workers to comply or otherwise threaten to blackmail them on the forum. As one madam stated, back in the old days, customers would never have dared to make the demands they were making today because they knew that Zuhälter would make sure to put them in their place.

Thus, the NR9 forum was a means that unilaterally empowered clients to negotiate prices and services. Prospective clients got valuable information on being a sex client and on sex workers available but also on which kind of services they offered, how they delivered them, and at what prices. Not surprisingly, sex workers and sauna club managers therefore often had less than favorable opinions about such forums and the men who wrote on them.[7] Most sex workers with whom I discussed this issue said they categorically avoided looking at forum reviews, as they found it too painful to read the negative comments, even if most comments were positive. In economic terms, forums provide clients with an information advantage that directly gives them leverage in their negotiation power.

A Social Community: Confessions, Dependency, and Feeling Rules

In contrast to the advantages clients gained through greater access to information, one of the major challenges of being a pay sex client derived from the notion that a man who has to pay for sex is not really a man at all, a sentiment also reported in research on prostitution in the United States (Blevins and Holt 2009) and Britain (Sanders 2008). As I showed above, this attitude was common among sauna club employees and generally widespread in Germany (Gerheim 2011; Grenz 2007). Yet—or rather because of this—some men formed intense relationships with others on the forum. And while many described mainly the performance of sex workers, some also included information about themselves and their social, physical, or sexual shortcomings, such as premature ejaculation or erectile dysfunction. The pay sex forum thus was a place where clients divulged intimate information about themselves, a place for confessions and consolation, and, for some, a place for important social connections.

Some men at the Flamingo expressed their doubts about the social ramifications of being sex clients. Early one evening on a weekday, Mario, a short and slender man in his fifties, sat next to me at the bar in a white bathrobe he apparently had brought from home. He introduced himself as a psychologist living in a town an hour away, who came once a month for relaxation. As our conversation turned to the social risks of prostitution, he cautioned, "Pay sex has an addictive potential. But no doctor or patient would ever call it that."[8]

His concern was echoed in the confessionary tone in which some of the forum members had introduced themselves to me at the Stammtisch. Lenny48, the man described in the opening vignette, had presented himself as practicing pay sex "for five years and two months." His precise recounting of the time when he'd started suggested there was a clear before and after, a conversion of sorts, and a radical life change that pay sex had ushered in for him. Other men had used similar phrases when they'd described their entry into the world of pay sex, and sometimes they couched it in regard to their marriage or divorce.

Michael, a forty-seven-year-old IT specialist whom I had met at the Stammtisch, described the beginning of his pay sex career[9] with reference to what he called his "pay sex awakening." During an interview we had set up after the Stammtisch meeting, Michael told me that it had been twelve years earlier, at the age of thirty-five. By that time, he had been married for six years. "But when I began a new relationship, I stopped with pay sex," he said. Surprised by what sounded like yet another confession, I asked Michael what he thought about the statement of becoming addicted to prostitution and the forum, as the psychologist described earlier. Michael responded, "People spend an insane amount of money on pay sex. Some men on the forum appear out of nowhere in a splash, and then disappear equally fast again. Everyone needs to know when to pull the plug." For Michael, the risk of pay sex was both the financial drain and the emotional vacuum it left: "You ask yourself, Should I go to the club? Your account says no. Even if it is not exactly wasting money. But the emptiness afterwards is there, and it's real." Michael went on to describe how one day in 2008, he suddenly realized that he had spent ten thousand euros of his savings on pay sex in one year alone. "It is the spontaneous desire. You go there, have great sex. But you are left feeling unsatisfied. The feeling of being close to someone . . . you get to feel that only in a relationship. Pay sex is a brief kick, and afterwards there is a huge hole." While Michael's description of the void after pay sex could sound like a description for a drug high or other addictive behavior, it also fits the description of someone abandoned by their lover and pining for them.

Michael was thoroughly steeped in the culture of the forum, in which he had participated for almost a decade. He had taken on an active role first as moderator and later as administrator, which kept him busy about two hours every day, sifting through threads and sorting them or watching out for postings that didn't stay on target. "Pay sex is a demi-world [*Halbwelt*]," Michael said pensively. "You can talk about it only in the club or the forum. It is a closed world, cut off from the world at large. You are always an outsider to the milieu itself. Within the brothel, there seems to be a degree of normality. You have contact with other clients, with the girls, with the madams. The sauna club offers you a complete experience. It's not just a kiss and a hello with the madam, as in apartment brothels. In the club you can spend time and enjoy yourself and socialize with others in a carefree way. But none of this carries over into the real world." In fact, Michael said, he had confided to only two of his friends—the most open-minded ones—about his experience with prostitution. And, he cautioned, you had to be careful not to fall in love with sex workers. "Falling in love is very easy for me, but I am cured now!" he said. "I have learned the hard way that girls who work in the clubs usually have some sort of psychological issues that make them not fit for a relationship." This comment struck me as peculiarly harsh. He generally came across as sensitive, self-reflective, compassionate, and highly educated. Did he not see how condemning this statement was? I soon would learn, however, how little Michael was able to follow his own advice.

The risks associated with pay sex that the three men had described then involved a number of facets: the risk of losing control financially (spending more than they could afford); the risk of losing control emotionally (falling in love); and the risk of getting involved in a stigmatized activity that threatened social isolation. Last but not least, there was the risk of a growing emotional dependency on fellow pay sex clients, as was the case with Netherworld's mental breakdown after he was blocked from the forum, a subject of discussion during the first Stammtisch.

If Netherworld might have suffered from more serious mental health issues, social isolation, or both, the problems of dependency and risk were a frequent topic online.[10] In his farewell note, one NR9 user urged his fellow members, "It is time to pull the plug. Those who—like myself—want to leave the sweet poison of pay sex and clubs behind them and can imagine a similar strategy to get out, please send me a private message." His post received fifty-six responses and a surprising twelve thousand hits. Such farewell notices, it turned out, were a common feature on the forum. For example, Munchkin wrote in his farewell post, "Thank you for the good and meaningful friendships and contacts with other three-legged creatures whom I came to know through my time at the clubs. Pay sex is a world unto itself. Rarely ever have I met people from so many different walks of life with whom I had such open and interesting conversations as I did in the pay sex world. After all, when we [men] are without clothes, we are equal. Thanks also to my forum colleagues, with whom I often had fun and with whom I had deep conversations about important topics."

Users also shared with each other what they perceived to be the negative effects associated with pay sex. One thread, entitled "Pay sex, a closed community?," asked fellow members whether they were still able to maintain normal and healthy connections to the world beyond the club. Another asked, "Do you still meet women outside of pay sex?," pondering whether pay sex users' sense of their own attractiveness had become so inflated that they found themselves no longer attracted to the "average" women outside of the pay sex world who would be interested in dating them. Yet another user asked, "One year of pay sex, and now what?" He wondered about the purpose and the cost of pay sex in the long run. He received sixty-four responses from fellow forum members and three thousand five hundred hits on his post. Finally, one user asked about "wear and tear" (*Abnutzungserscheinungen*) in pay sex, in the sense of having lost interest in sex after sleeping with so many different and beautiful women. This post received eighty-six responses and eight thousand hits from users.

The most striking example of a discussion about the addictive aspects of prostitution was initiated by one of the administrators, the very well-respected Knucklehead, when he posted a long and eloquent statement under the thread "Ways out of pay sex." His post struck a chord with a sizable segment of the forum, evident in the over one hundred responses and sixteen thousand hits it received within just the first two weeks. In this thread, Knucklehead posted a call for help for a member who requested to remain anonymous, even with his username in the NR9 community. Knucklehead described a man in his late thirties who had been in pay sex for ten years, who had no social contacts outside of family and work and no leisure activities or friends. His only contact was with others in the pay sex community, and his only leisure pursuit was pay sex. All of his income had been going toward prostitution, and with no more savings and growing debt, he was close to financial ruin. He had made numerous attempts to get out of pay sex, but all had failed. He tried to go cold turkey, stopping his pay sex activities from one day to the next and breaking off all contact with other clients. He unregistered from all pay-sex-related online activities. He joined a self-help group, sought professional help, tried to find alternative leisure activities, and pursued financial counseling, all without success. In the end, he tried to at least limit his pay sex activities and forced himself into a public coming out, so as to be reminded by outsiders regularly about his promise to leave pay sex behind. While it had aspects of what some would call sex addiction—the relentless pursuit of sexual satisfaction with no regard for the high social and financial costs associated with it—what this client stressed here was the dependency on the milieu altogether, not only the sex per se but also the intimacy with fellow clients.

Many of the men who answered identified themselves as having been or still being in similar situations. Several recounted their own more or less successful attempts at dealing with the hazards of pay sex or their attempts to leave it behind. Like the anonymous client whose case Knucklehead presented, there were others who regarded the forum itself as a crucial element of the pay sex dependency spiral and therefore paradoxically advised their colleague to avoid the forum as well. To them, participation in the forum was part of a vicious cycle of addiction, alienation, and social isolation. Johann, one of the first to respond to Knucklehead, stated, "I would start with getting out of any [pay sex] forum. I believe they are more of a problem than the brothel visits themselves. And then, go only to brothels where you don't know anyone and don't maintain any communication with other pay sex fellows."

A few suggested gaining control by focusing on his finances—for example by cutting all credit cards, requesting his bank not give him overdraft privileges, and setting strict budget limits for himself that would force him to ask a friend for money if he wanted to go to a brothel. Others explained how changed life circumstances had helped them to get out of the dangerous rut of pay sex. Sex Lover wrote, "In the past, I had to constantly watch myself to keep my expenses for pay sex within certain limits. Then my life took a drastic turn. Today, I couldn't care less. I don't feel the need to spend money on prostitution. I feel liberated and also younger."

The confessions and dependency clients voiced in the context of the forum and its Stammtisch were certainly only two topics in their exchanges with each other, but they show that the forum functioned as an intimate community that provided a social support network, where men confided in each other and could count on a sympathetic ear and maybe a helpful response, but sometimes also biting critique. The intimacy reflected in these kinds of exchanges were fueled in part by a shared perception of their hobby as a risky or even shameful one, about which they could hardly be proud, but one that they all participated in.

In a study of online forums in the United States, Blevins and Holt (2009) argue that members of sex client forums belong to a deviant subculture that structures its members' attitudes about experience, commodification, and sexuality. In contrast, the sex clients described here identified themselves not as part of the red light subculture, in which they were merely sojourners, and not as a subculture in opposition to the culture at large. Rather, they were a community that sought acceptance rather than demarcation. They presented themselves as a community that strove to uphold binding moral codes in regard to each other as well as the women whose services they purchased, and even more so to prove society's contempt for sex clients wrong. The forum was a space where clients sought and received advice, reassurance, and, although anonymous, a means to represent themselves to a wider public. As I will show below, the forum also was a domain where they could demonstrate their own proficiency and acquire distinction and social capital (Bourdieu 1990). As such, their community was not limited to sharing sexual experiences in sauna clubs and brothels but extended into the realm of expertise about the sex industry more generally as well as their ability to show empathy toward other forum members and sex workers.[11]

Becoming a Love Clown

One of the most widely acknowledged risks pay sex clients warned each other about was that of becoming a love clown (*Liebeskasper*). Whereas being a client entailed widespread disapproval from society at large, being a love clown entailed disapproval from the brothel community and fellow clients. Forum members constantly reminded each other not to become the kind of client who would fall in love with a CSP who did not share his feelings. While the understanding was that this was dangerous for men, at least in regard to their psyche and their wallets, it was also dangerous for women, who sometimes became the victims of such one-sided infatuation when it turned to stalking or worse. Even outside the NR9 forum, *love clown* is a well-known concept among German sex clients, as a number of books dedicated to domestic (Remiess 2009) and international sex tourists (Schelm 2013) show.

Sex workers used the term *love clown* often in a pejorative way for someone who was emotionally immature or needy; they were also aware that they were toeing a fine line between making a client a regular and having him fall head over heels in love, where attempts at "rescuing" the sex worker could be one of the more benign complications. Several knew of such stories firsthand, and some had known women who were murdered by clients who claimed to love them. But love clowns could also be regarded as risks to themselves, as I will show later. For forum members, learning how to distance themselves from what Alexander Remiess (2009)—himself a forum member—has called "purchased illusions" and learning to see their trysts as mere sexual services rather than genuine love was crucial in becoming a successful pay sex client.[12]

However, clients did fall in love with the women from whom they bought sexual services, and although they knew that they would likely be pitied if not ridiculed, many felt compelled to reveal their infatuations to their peers on the forum. In a way, becoming a love clown had elements of a rite of initiation into the forum, as if enduring this painful experience once was an inoculation against it in the future. But it also happened to seasoned clients. Of all people, Harald, the webmaster of the NR9 forum himself, blatantly defied this rule. His girlfriend of a year, Marianne, was a woman twenty years his junior whom he had met at a sauna club. Luckily, the infatuation was mutual, and they began a romantic relationship. Harald was perfectly aware that he was in violation of his own forum's philosophy and that in the eyes of his members, he was a fool engaged in a relationship that was destined to fail. After a year or so, Harald and Marianne's relationship did break apart. However, it was not because it was incompatible with her job as a sex worker but because she had fallen in love with someone else—someone she eventually married and had a child with after she got out of sex work altogether.

An even more striking example of the difficulty of aligning one's own emotions with the rules of how to be a successful pay sex client was provided by Michael, the forum administrator described above. While Michael had told me earlier that he had learned never to fall in love again with a sex worker, he seemed to have forgotten this lesson when I met him several years later at Club Ecstasy, another upscale sauna club where I conducted follow-up research. It was a hot Sunday afternoon in June when we ran into each other. I was genuinely happy to see Michael again. He told me he had driven three hours to the club to meet his favorite, Janina. Unfortunately for Michael, Janina had not made any time for him. After spending the afternoon and better part of the evening waiting for her, Michael left shortly before closing time at midnight. He had not had sex with anyone else and did not want to, he assured me. I saw Michael again the following Tuesday.

He was hoping that this time—a much less busy day at the club—Janina would be available. However, at nine in the evening, she was still busy with other clients. As Michael was about to leave, he explained, "Well, in a way it is like in a real relationship. You can't expect that your partner always wants the same thing you want and wants it at the same time as you." I doubt that Michael at that moment was aware of the meaning he had assigned to his relationship to Janina, how he deluded himself in thinking of being in a relationship with her—quite the opposite of his earlier statement that relationships with sex workers would be an absolute no-go for him.

The love clown syndrome, as forum members described it, can be explained as a type of *feeling rule*—a term coined by the sociologist Arlie Hochschild (1983) in her analysis of flight attendants performing emotional labor for passengers. Rather than pretending to feel emotional concern for passengers, as the flight attendants did, pay sex clients had to pretend to be emotionally detached from sex workers, even if they did feel attached. The forum instructed its members on how to manage their emotions in order to become successful clients. The risks of becoming emotionally attached to sex workers are substantial, not only for the client but also for the sex worker, and thus constitute a threat to all clients. It is therefore also a protection of clients' shared interests while at the same time reducing what could otherwise be perceived as competition. However, although the forum officially condemned love clowns collectively, many members did provide supportive ears for what seemed to be a predictable stage in the career of a sex client. In some sense, then, the forum's rules not to get attached emotionally to sex workers invited the transfer of a member's emotional attachment from sex workers to the community of fellow clients and thus added another layer of intimacy between clients.

Clients' experiences of guilt and dependency constituted the darker side of their pay sex hobby. The forum provided a supportive social community where men could exchange their experiences and reflect on their behavior without the social condemnation from society at large. The forum thus played the role of intimate support network; it also bore the potential for dependency and a growing spiral of isolation from the larger society. Another dimension of this community, then, consisted in the emotional support and feeling rules it provided to the sex client community. Here, the intimate dimension of the client community became amplified as members offered warnings about and consolations for the emotional trials and tribulations of men who became love clowns.

Mark Neal (2016) has made a similar observation about feeling rules among sex clients in regard to the role of morality in the study of international sex clients in Thailand. Neal describes the means by which clients and sex workers attempt to neutralize societal stigma attached to their involvement in prostitution. In contrast to sex clients in Germany, Neal shows that German sex tourists in Thailand emphasized their emotional attachment to their favorites in their online interactions with other tourists as a means to offset the stigma of being what Neal has coined—a "dirty customer" (132).[13] While clients in both countries used a deliberate moral discourse, the contours of this discourse were rather opposite: extolling the virtues of emotional attachment in Thailand but warning against it in Germany. The striking difference in the feeling rules for sex clients suggests that the particular moral codes by which sex clients abide are dependent on the cultural context in which commercial sex is embedded.

A Moral Community: Establishing and Policing Moral Boundaries

Sex client forums differ in tone and substance. Michael, one of the NR9 moderators mentioned earlier, described it the following way: "Forums are like a congregation, and the administrator is like their pastor: it is the pastor who sets the tone for the type of congregation that he is ministering to." As stated in the forum rules on the website for the NR9, membership was based on the acceptance of and adherence to the rules and the agreement to not write messages and posts that were "obscene, vulgar, racist, disgusting, threatening, or violating any laws."[14] It was the task of the webmaster, the administrators, and the moderators to enforce these rules. They vetted new users for authenticity, scoured the reports for "fake" posts, reorganized threads, and corrected misconceptions where appropriate. They also assumed a disciplinarian role, publicly admonishing misbehavior and sending undesirable postings to the so-called troll meadow, which—equivalent to a pillory—functioned as a site for public ridicule. But this was merely the extrinsic structure and formal hierarchy of NR9. The forum also gave rise to an intrinsic hierarchy that emerged among members through the threads and discussions that took place there.

If the comparison to a religious congregation seems like hyperbole, the forum had other similarities to faith-based communities. Some members assumed a confessionary tone by introducing themselves with reference to when they first became involved in pay sex, as if there were a clear before and after, not unlike a spiritual conversion. Other similarities existed in the charity aspect of the forum, as in the case of a young sex worker who had died from leukemia; the administrator set up a space for condolences and commemoration and a donation account for an animal shelter, as she had asked for in her will.

The contours of the NR9 forum as a moral community became most visible in a violent assault one day in August, when a client killed a sex worker, with whom he had been infatuated, in front of a sauna club and then killed himself. The emerging news of this murder-suicide was followed closely on the forum. It soon became clear that the assailant had been a regular on the forum who, over several weeks, had posted intimate details about his obsession with Marie, the woman he ended up killing. The forum members' gradual realization that the murderer had been one of their own caused a profound sense of shock, disbelief, and self-doubt. Johnny, the assailant, had not regarded himself as a love clown but as someone emotionally abused by a sex worker whom he did not regard as just his favorite but his lover.

The proof of her emotional attachment to him, he had argued in his posts, was the fact that she had sex with him without a condom and the time they spent together outside the club. In the responses to his post, several forum members had warned him that he had gotten far too deep into this, that his infatuation with her was turning pathological, and that he needed to seek professional help. Some now wondered whether their responses had in some way encouraged him or whether the forum itself—by providing him with a platform for venting his frustrations and feeding his obsessions—had allowed him, if not encouraged him, to reach this point.

Following the example of her coworkers, who had started a collection for Marie's family back in Bulgaria, the webmaster set up an account for anonymous online donations. Posting a eulogy for Marie and a call for solidarity with her family, he announced the account on the forum. The discussion that followed illustrated how members identified themselves as a community and how they advocated, challenged, and forged moral positions. Their comments appealed to a collective sense of empathy and humanity but also raised questions about guilt, complicity, and responsibility of the client community in general and of the NR9 forum in particular. This illustrated a community that was actively negotiating a code of ethics by which to abide in pay sex and with the women from whom they bought sexual services.

Opening the thread, Joystick wrote:

The loss of a loved one cannot be undone with financial help. Maybe the family of the victim does not even need any financial help. When CSPs[15] return to their home country, their families get an idea what the ladies are doing in Germany. Often they don't mind it all that much, as long as they can profit themselves. If one considers that the murder victim generated 50,000 € in one year from her murderer alone, she is likely to have earned significantly beyond 200,000 € in one year. When a CSP recognizes that a client is pathologically in love with her and tries to book more and more dates with her, a lot of them will reject such easily earned money, because they are afraid about what might happen down the line.

Joystick did not receive a single thank-you nod for his post; he received instant condemnation from other forum members instead. Special Juice, a well-respected member with senior status, sharply criticized Joystick for implying that the victim was partially to blame for her death and appealed to a sense of moral obligation and of doing the right thing, particularly as members of a misrepresented and stigmatized community. Special Juice wrote:

I am disgusted by your suggestion that the murdered CSP carries any responsibility for her demise. We forum members know nothing. We only have his postings, but we don't know either of them. Therefore, we are not in a position to cast a guilty, or partial guilty verdict or to throw stones. . . . It is also not our job to speculate. This is about how we as forum members deal with this situation. It is about us, as forum members and clients to make a statement: That we are not the jerk-off blokes some try to cast us as. I will make a donation because it is the right thing to do. And it is not going to be a symbolic contribution only. I hope the administrators are censoring further obnoxious speculations of this kind.

Special Juice received over twenty virtual thank-you nods from fellow members instantly. Another senior member, Netherworld, agreed with him. He wrote, "The forum proved itself to be a real community in an exemplary way. The support for the family cannot bring back the girl, but at least it can ease the financial difficulties for the family after her death. Your [Joystick's] post is in contradiction to everything I am holding dear: the regard for a fellow human and decency, rather than looking at others as objects or— excuse me—a piece of meat to fuck. I did not know the girl, but her death touches me deeply. Netherworld, who thanks all those who still retain a shred of decency."

Within just a few hours, the condemnation of Joystick's post generated more than seventy endorsements. But Joystick, who had not usually made comments of this nature, soon came back to defend himself against the charge of blaming the victim. Backtracking from his original focus on the partial responsibility of the victim, he now directed attention to the family of the assailant as another unacknowledged victim: "Would I, as a family member, want to accept the donations from clubs and clients? If somebody really wants to donate, then also to the family of the murderer. They must not be blamed for their father's sins. Or, do those wanting to make a donation have a bad conscience because they are themselves whoremongers [*Hurenböcke*]?"

Joystick here tried to gain the moral upper hand by pointing to the innocent and not yet acknowledged victims of the perpetrator: his wife and children. What proved to be more relevant to those responding to his post was not the tragedy of the assailant's own family but Joystick's insinuation that the donations were guilt money that sex clients gave to pay off their own complicity in the murder. The attempt to shame his fellow members and the community of sex clients in general, however, did little to defuse the anger against him. Instead, Special Juice's and Netherworld's calls for setting an example that showed sex clients were caring human beings was picked up by Unicorn when he reiterated the importance of showing the victim's family that forum members—and potential clients of the victim— cared about her. He wrote: "[Our contributions show her family that she was] a human, a colleague, a friend to us. But especially, she was not treated by clients as a fucking machine, used by disgusting johns, but as a human. Humans, who see much more in her than only a CSP."

In his appeal to show Marie's humanity, Unicorn made an illustrative slippage between the humanity of the sex worker and the humanity of the clients. By the end of the post, it was the clients who were human while the victim was referred to merely as more than "only a CSP."

In a somewhat priestly tone, Sammy thanked the others for their critique of Joystick and the collective empathy that they expressed for the victim. Asking Joystick to reconsider his statement, he opened a door for him back into the community:

> Reconsider your perspective, Joystick. I consider myself a part of this community, which helps me to live and share my encounters with others in the pay sex world. We are all shocked, speechless beyond comprehension. This man, one of us . . . a murderer? He received thank you nods from us. He received encouragement for his contributions. Including me. Guilt!!! This drama has stuck with me for weeks. And not only me. Why? Because . . . the situation was also a bit influenced . . . by the forum, as we let him go berserk. We don't see inside a human. But we can show compassion. Symbolically and otherwise.

Odysseus, responding to Joystick's earlier post that Marie was herself in part responsible for her demise, tried to provide an explanation for the rationale that guides sex workers in general: "If a prostitute tries to recruit a client as a regular, she will act in her own self-interest. She will do what the client expects her to do. She will say what the client wants to hear. If a whoremonger cannot recognize the flattery, then he has already entered an escalating spiral. . . . The frightening thing about this crime is that both were normal people. He was not a career criminal, and she was not a sex worker with the reputation of a trick [*Abzockhure*]."[16]

In this post, Odysseus invokes the contours of a moral community that includes both respectable clients, who are themselves responsible for not taking flattery for reality, as well as respectable sex workers, who do not intentionally rip off (*abzocken*) their customers who are infatuated with them. Unicorn picks up another dimension of this moral one-upmanship. Rejecting the suggestion that it was love that drove Johnny to kill Marie, he wrote, "This has nothing to do with love. Just with egotistical possession. He thought he could purchase her with €. In his reports you can see his egotism. He complains about her not wanting to have sex with him during the two days he took care of her after her surgery."

Sammy revisits the moral argument about donations for Marie's family as guilt money raised by Joystick earlier:

> Does the family really need the money? Or is that also a speculation? Are we sure that the donations are used in the intended way, considering that there is no upper limit? Do all of you know the family so well that you know that without your help, they would run into significant financial problems? I recently read an article by a professor about the psychology of donations: that it provides more satisfaction for the giver, who is primarily acting in his own self-interest and not concerned with whether the recipient really needs it. Even in a community of solidarity, one should remain sober and unemotional, tolerant to different positions and also question one's own motives.

Amid questions about whether Marie's family would find donations from clients acceptable and appropriate, for how long they should be paid, and to whom, Sammy again raised the issue of guilt money, suggesting that the donations were more about the satisfaction they provided for the giver than for those receiving the donation. One could ask whether Sammy's appeal to unemotional rationality here was a response to the forum exerting moral pressure on clients and a resentment against the implied notion of members' shared guilt and complicity in the murder.[17]

Most members who engaged in this discussion—about twenty-five were actively posting comments and at least as many participated silently through thank-you nods—showed deep compassion for the victim and her family. Several argued that it was their obligation as clients and forum members to show the family that they cared for Marie, although the desire to use the opportunity to present themselves as sex clients in a positive light seemed equally important, at least for some.

The moral community of the forum and its members was invoked here a number of times: in the donations to be collected from clients, as an obligation of their community, and as a demonstration of solidarity and respect for the victim and her family. The discussions were based on who could claim the moral high ground. Almost as prominent, however, was the seeming desire of its members to present themselves to the family of the victim, and thus to society at large, as morally upstanding humans—as men who regarded sex workers as fellow humans who deserved their respect, just as they themselves were humans and not just wankers (*Wichsbrüder*) hoping to be respected. The use of the term *whoremonger* (*Hurenbock*) by Joystick as well as a few others threatened the notion of a moral community, as did the suggestion that the forum itself had been to some extent complicit in the murder, an issue vehemently rejected by others.

For Harald, the forum webmaster, setting up a donation account for Marie underscored the notion of the forum as a community. The debate that ensued about it signaled the members' concern for doing the right thing but also raised broader questions about the ethical implications of practicing pay sex and participating in the forum. The suggestion of donations as guilt money and the reference to themselves as whoremongers and wankers suggest pervasive self-doubt and internalized stigma that seemed to be driving sex clients to the forum in the first place. The spirit of moral one-upmanship—a characteristic mode of interaction on the forum in this context—was a means to perform ethical behavior and thus establish one's investment in the moral fabric of this community.

Community Entanglements

Stigma, Intimacy, and Vulnerability

Considering Germany's legalization of and long history of relative tolerance toward prostitution, one might expect that sex clients there would be relatively unencumbered about their involvement in commercial sex.

238 | *Legalized Prostitution in Germany*

What these clients' stories have shown, however, is the opposite. Instead of enjoying their privileges and feeling carefree about their adventures in pay sex, there was the paradox that sex clients were often hyperaware of the stigma associated with their role in prostitution, even if they called it their *pay sex hobby*. They felt the need to be secretive about it or else suffer the consequences if exposed. In such a situation, companionship, exchange, and trust with other like-minded people became important dimensions of community.

The relationship between stigma and intimacy is critical here, as each begets the other: being a sex client is what Goffman called a "behavioral stigma" that can be hidden from the public (1963b), but it bears a secret that constantly risks exposure; the sociologist Viviana Zelizer (2005), in her book *The Purchase of Intimacy*, defines intimacy as the information one has about another person that, were it made public, could lead to that person's damage. How did clients manage this intimacy and the associated risk of vulnerability? Zelizer provides key insights into intimacy and its relationship to trust, a crucial aspect of intimate relations: "Intimate relations depend on . . . knowledge received, and attention provided. . . . Intimate social relations thus . . . depend on trust" (14–15). Trust demands that such information and attention are shared, even in risky situations. But trust can also be betrayed when information is made available to others that "would damage the second person's social standing" (14–15). This aptly expresses the relationships among the core group of clients on the forum: networks were maintained through the sharing of intimate information and trust that the anonymity of the members would be protected from the public at large. Such trust relations became turbocharged when members of the forum decided to form a Stammtisch, replacing online anonymity with face-to-face interaction and thus making themselves vulnerable to breaches of confidentiality by others at the Stammtisch, who now could potentially trace their identities and harm their reputations. That was the reason why most of the visitors at the Stammtisch introduced themselves only by their forum names.

Clients and administrators together established and negotiated norms, with the admin—not unlike ministers of a faith-based community—clarifying the rules of the community and enforcing them. These norms were not static but had to be maintained and renegotiated through the flow of communication between users and moderators, as the discussion about the donations illustrated.

Pointing to the meaning of community going back to the Latin *munis*, meaning *labor, gift,* or *sacrifice,* McGinnis writes in his book on bioregionalism and the meaning of community: "At [the etymological roots of community] is the idea of an exchange of services—out of duty, it may be, but also pointing to another dimension of the idea, freely, even affectionately, as a gift, or even a sacrifice. A community, then, is the assemblage of individuals to whom one is bound by this kind of relationship—one defined, we might even say constituted, by mutual obligation and by an exchange of gifts" (2005, 213). Of course, such a service or gift is what Mauss (1990) has described as the "prestations" or "total services"[18] that sustain communal relationships.

Sharing their sexual experiences with pay sex peers on the forum thus can be seen as a service or gift that clients provided to each other. These intimate accounts functioned like sacrifices required for men to become members of this community and advance in its social hierarchy (i.e., gaining senior status). At the same time, however, such revelations would increase their vulnerabilities if they were made public. While the anonymity of the forum and the built-in seniority structure encouraged members to share and even overshare to increase their status on the forum, such gifts enticed others to reciprocate with counter gifts of similar revelations, thus strengthening the trust network. However, it did so by also increasing one's vulnerabilities.

The stories and exchanges, then, that men shared on the forum can be compared to such a service—or, in Mauss's term, prestation—to each other and were the gifts required to create intimacy and confidentiality. They were the glue for the community but also produced vulnerabilities that could be exploited and liabilities that could be claimed by others. In the absence of other guarantors of trust, demanding high moral standards, in regard to each other as well as in regard to their relationships with sex workers, was a means by which community members also tried to protect themselves.

Subculture and Moral Community

If communities, at their most basic level, define an in-group against an out-group (Morris 1996), members of a moral community hold their in-group accountable for their actions and moral behavior and are concerned that their actions do not violate group norms or harm group members (Morris

1996). Those who do harm in-group members are sanctioned through a series of disciplinary measures that can lead to expulsion from the group. In contrast, subcultures, according to Hebdige (1991), are characterized by members of a recognizable group of people who define themselves in opposition to the values of the dominant culture. Subcultures do not eschew moral obligations from their members, but their emphasis is on their opposition to society at large. While the client community in the NR9 forum did share some aspects of subcultures—for example, "a unique language or argot" (Blevins and Holt 2009, 621) that has been described as a characteristics of Johns' subculture (2009)—their self-understanding revolved around proving to each other that they were not all that different from men who did not purchase sex. Rather than demarcating themselves from society at large and proving the dominant culture wrong, the sex clients I described wanted to prove that they had a moral compass equally as strong as those who did not purchase sex and condemned their behavior.

Conceiving of clients as a community, and a moral community rather than a deviant subculture, therefore privileges a different set of questions. Instead of asking how they oppose the dominant culture, the question is how they establish such a moral community and how they maintain a binding code of morality. To hold together a moral community requires networks, norms, and trust (Eriksen 2016). How did these come to bear on the intimate relationships among sex clients?

The comfort provided by the forum community and the depth of relationships it generated for some often came at the expense of an ever-deeper enmeshment with the world of prostitution and an accelerated cycle of escape from their regular lives. Seen in this light, the stigma associated with going to brothels and purchasing sex was directly linked to their search for intimacy with other clients on the forum. In addition, one could question to what extent the forum sanctions against becoming a love clown and the emotional safeguarding that this entailed vis-á-vis sex workers were not, in part, responsible for the strong attachment some clients felt toward each other. For some, such attachment consisted of dependency on the forum, from which they found it difficult to distance themselves. As these men enjoyed the thrills of commercial sex, they feared the stigma from the outside world. As they came to enjoy the community of their peers more and more and advanced in their pay sex client careers and forum seniority, the growing fear of public condemnation by society at large produced a heightened sense of moral accountability to the forum and its members.

This active negotiation of moral standards and boundaries seemed to be built into the fabric of the relationships between pay sex clients, aided by the intimacy of their reports and posts exchanged. At the moment of threatening moral collapse, when forum members realized that one of their peers had become a murderer, they struggled with their client identity and the moral fabric that they thought they had cultivated. The tone of the exchange and the moral one-upmanship they engaged in when they realized the forum's implications in the crime illustrated a moral community actively negotiating and forging their position.

Sex Clients and the Postindustrial Sexual Ethic

Why does prostitution remain such a stigmatized arena for social interaction? I now return to the larger questions about what the culture of intimacy between sex clients reveals about sexuality, relationships, and gender, or, in more general terms, what Bernstein (2007) has called the sexual ethics of the postindustrial society. What is the role of sexuality available in the marketplace when the pursuit of sexual fulfillment has become decoupled from reproduction, marriage, and relationships? Considering the high number of migrant sex workers from poor countries in Eastern Europe, there certainly was no economic equality between service provider and buyer in the way a vision of postindustrial recreational sex suggests. An awareness of such unequal economic power relations between buyer and purchaser might well add to the fact that purchasing sex remains a highly stigmatized activity in Germany, even though prostitution is legal.

I offer three considerations for this paradox: First, where prostitution is legal, it becomes more acceptable in public and more visible in the media, as shown in the first chapter. Such heightened visibility is making a growing number of men curious about the idea of purchasing sex. Second, as the greater visibility of sex has made commercial sex more acceptable and accessible, it has also made clients' participation in it more visible. This has enhanced the possibilities for a client to be detected and publicly exposed. Third, while the subject of prostitution becomes more openly discussed in the media, it also becomes publicly criticized from a broad range of ideological positions, including the question of how sex for purchase is compatible with progressive concepts of gender equity and sexual self-determination. Such a public discourse might constitute a powerful mechanism of social control and produce formidable obstacles for embracing the identity of the sex client.

Rather than choosing one of these factors over another, it might be more realistic to assume that all three of these conditions are at work. This complicates the notion of a postindustrial sexual ethic in states where prostitution is legal, as the clients' search for commodified intimacy, authentic but bounded, also entails the risk of stigma and other risks not previously acknowledged, such as emotional entanglements with sex workers, financial instability, and social isolation. Last but not least, there is the risk of dependency on virtual and actual client communities. Outside of sauna clubs that encourage male socializing, sex client forums provide a space where intimate experiences in the realm of commercial sex can be exchanged. Where else would men who purchase sex find the space to communicate with each other?

Notes

1. *Stammtisch*, literally, means a table in a restaurant where an informal group of people meet regularly.
2. Deutsche Welle 2007; Spiegel Online, 2016.
3. NR9 is a pseudonym used to protect forum users and managers.
4. See the client forum http://www.roemerforum.com/.
5. In comparison, punternet.com, which has operated for about the same amount of time as NR9, also cites seven hundred thousand postings total but lists reports of different regions all over the UK and Ireland.
6. The Austrian forum sexworker.at was created deliberately to counterbalance this prominence of client forums. It has a much larger geographic focus—sex workers in German-speaking countries—and does not provide an adequate counterweight to the prominence of the regional client forums.
7. The women who ran mostly smaller prostitution venues, such as apartment brothels, were even closer to such client reports; some regularly sat down with sex workers and discussed client reports about them. Having a small number of sex workers at their brothels and maintaining personalized client relations made them more concerned about such reports. For one madam who operated and owned a brothel apartment, the online reports were yet another dimension that allowed her to optimize the service. Together with the sex workers, she would read the reports about them and then discuss strategies to improve.
8. Sex addiction is a widely recognized concept in the United States. At the time of this writing, however, it was not included in the diagnostic manual of psychological diseases. Similarly, in Germany, it is not recognized as a psychological disorder. Unlike in the United States, there seems to be significantly less public conversation about the concept in Germany.
9. Horswill and Weitzer (2018) have developed the concept of a sex client career in their insightful exploration of how sex clients learn critical information about entering the pay sex identity. While *career* is an emic term in some sex client communities in Germany (see Gerheim 2011), I propose to use it here in the sense of Goffman's (1959) concept of the moral career of the mental patient: as a socialization into a pay-sex client identity constructed or experienced as deviant, with a distinct pre-client, client, and sometimes post-client phase.
10. Number of Posts on NR9 Client Forum about Pay Sex and Forum Dependency:

TABLE 7.1 Comparison of responses and hits in regard to key posts on the NR9 forum. Retrieved from their website, December 6, 2015.

Title of Post	Responses	Days Thread Was Open	Hits
"Paths out of Pay Sex"	123	135	16,000
"Last Trip to Club X"	56	300	12,000
"Wear and Tear"	86	N/A	8,000
"Pay Sex Addiction"	95	95	5,000
"One Year of Pay Sex, Now What?"	64	300	3,500
"Pay Sex—Closed Community?"	5	2	857

11. In his study of sex clients in Germany, Udo Gerheim (2011) describes a client who compares the addictive element of pay sex to other addictions, insofar as it requires a constant increase in "dosage" to attain the same initial effect. Summarizing his experience with fellow clients on an online platform, this customer explained, "At the end of the career [of a sex client] is always the fucking without a condom. . . . The dosage is constantly increased" (Gerheim 2011, 265, my translation).

12. See, for example, Milrod and Weitzer 2012.

13. Neal's (2006) concept of the "dirty customer" (132) emphasizes that it is not only the sex worker who is battling with the stigma of her profession but also her clients. "Customers engaging with such [sex] work can thus arguably be characterized as 'dirty customers'— consumers of dirty work, who are also physically, socially, or morally tainted by their engagement with it" (132).

14. To preserve the confidentiality of the members on the forum, the name of the forum is a pseudonym, and no link is provided.

15. CSP stands for *commercial service providers* or *commercial sex providers*, as mentioned earlier.

16. *Abzockhure* has a decidedly negative connotation, meaning a sex worker who has managed to coax out an unreasonable amount of pay for her services.

17. The discussion took another turn when the questions of liability and victim restitution were raised. One client explained that according to German law, the family of the victim would have the right to sue for victim restitution. Restitution, however, would come out of the estate of the murderer, which in this case would be what he had left to his family, leading to the paradoxical situation that the family of the perpetrator would be victimized twice. However, if the sex workers were employees rather than freelancers, one would assume that victim restitution (*Opferentschädigung*) would presumably come out of the pocket of the employer. The question of liability on behalf of the club where the victim worked—as the ones who benefitted the most from her labor—remains unstated.

18. "Prestations" is the term Mauss used to describe the complex exchange of gifts. W. D. Hall, the translator of the 1990 edition of Mauss (1990), writes in the editorial note, "The French terms 'prestations' and 'contre-prestations' have no direct English equivalents. They represent, in the context in which they are used by Mauss, respectively the actual act of exchange of gifts and rendering of services, and the reciprocating or return of these gifts and services. Normally they have been referred to in the translation for brevity's sake, as 'total services' and 'total counterservices'" (Mauss 1990, xii).

CONCLUSION

"SO ARE YOU GOING TO TRY IT OUT tonight?" Brigitte wanted to know one evening, after we had dinner together at the Flamingo's restaurant. "Try out what?" I asked, although I had a good idea what she had in mind.

"Try to get some clients of your own. If you want to know what sex work really is all about, don't you think you should try it out yourself, at least once?"

"I am trying to understand not only the women selling sex but the whole culture of selling and buying, including the clients and the management," I responded, well aware that this was a meek response.

Brigitte's suggestion was flattering. After all, I was surrounded by stunning women in their prime, and I was significantly older than most, so it seemed presumptuous to even attempt to compete in this arena. But the thought of how it would be to work there had crossed my mind. Many of the clients I had talked to over the course of my research were attractive men, of all age ranges and from a variety of ethnic and educational backgrounds, and it was not uncommon that I would find myself in animated conversation with them. Some clients seemed genuinely concerned about my well-being, since I was resigned to merely watch. Gerhard, a middle-aged client from Switzerland who had just ecstatically waxed about the club and the good times he'd had there, offered to take me to a room: "Wouldn't you like to go upstairs? We could have some fun too. You don't have to just come here and work and observe. Why don't you join the partying?"

Fun or not, sometimes I asked myself whether in fact I did not owe it to the women who had shared so much about their lives with me. It most likely would have created a deeper understanding of the nature of the work and a closer connection to them—for example, to Natasha, who begged me to work with her, even offering to lend me her platform shoes. Of course, since I was interested not only in sex workers but in the club culture as a whole, Brigitte could also have suggested I try out how it felt to be a client, although female clients were an unheard-of option. What ultimately prevented me from giving in to my curiosity was not a sense of impropriety or moral concern, and it was not because I thought offering sexual services in a sauna club was particularly degrading or humiliating. Among a number of reasons why I did not follow Brigitte's suggestion was the question of whether doing so would make me vulnerable to extortion by the club management.

Brigitte's invitation was a stark contrast to her stated misgivings about prostitution described earlier, when she criticized the photographer and me for having too idealized a vision of the industry. Good-natured and easy-going, Brigitte seemed at peace with her work and the path in life she had chosen. When she asked me to try out the trade, I had a sense that we were both fond of each other, making me doubt that her question came with ill intentions, although she might have wanted to test how deep my idealization of the industry actually went. Brigitte's apparent contradictions about prostitution and her role in it, however, hinted at the ambiguities at least some insiders felt about the industry and this labor. This, then, is a befitting way to end this book. In addition to showing Brigitte's and my own ambivalence in regard to sex work, it also illustrates the role of stigma associated with this labor and the social vulnerability it entailed. My own fear of becoming susceptible to extortion also suggested that at least for me, sex work was not "a job like any other." My fear had less to do with losing credibility as a researcher and more to do with the fact that it would give management a means to coerce me into silence—which, of course, could be a threat only if I were worried about reputational damage.

The fear of becoming vulnerable illustrates both my own sense of stigma associated with the work as well as the relative impermeability of what has been aptly called the milieu. Not that it was impossible to get out of the industry, but as long as one was in it, revealing one's involvement was likely to be met with negative repercussions, as I had heard numerous times from my research participants. This was the case for sex workers and madams but to some extent also for clients, many of whom hid their involvement in prostitution from close friends and relatives.

The Uses of Ethnography

Ethnographies, unlike policy studies, aim less for systematic representation and large-scale comparisons and more for holistic processes while giving insight into subjective dimensions and meaningful questions (van Maanen 2011). Ethnographies therefore have limitations in regard to policy recommendations. While I explored the Flamingo against the broader backdrop of Neuburg's red light geography, it remained one sauna club within one particular metropolitan region, in a nation where individual states and cities within them have considerable leeway on how to define their own regimes of prostitution. Neuburg did not have any sex worker rights organizations, as was common in a number of other cities. These conditions made it hard to aim for national representation. And yet I hope that by examining in depth this corner of German culture, this book and the exterior and interior landscapes of prostitution it unravels provide insight into Germany's culture of commercial sex, its relationship to sexuality, and its gendered cultural fabric more generally.

This study cannot provide nationwide representativeness for prostitution; it also cannot claim to provide a representative sample of women in the industry. Not all women were interested in talking to me or willing to do so—not at the Night Owl in the red light district, where I began this research, nor in the different apartment brothels and eros centers where my ability to communicate with them was limited. Neither is it representative of all the women at the Flamingo, where I conducted the bulk of my ethnographic work. Being aware that the women who were willing to be part of this study were a rather selective group, with many others not open to sharing their insights, I have resisted attempts to place them within broader categories and instead give weight to their individual experiences.

The same must be kept in mind for clients. There certainly were some who fit the stereotype of seeking no-strings-attached sex. However, the men who went to the club in search of sex with strings attached were a kind of men often overlooked by media and activists who consider prostitution an instrument for the oppression of women. Even if clients in search of sex with strings attached were concerned with representing themselves in a more humane, self-reflective manner than how they felt they were portrayed in the media, the forum posts and discussions revealed a community of sex clients subscribing to those values collectively. The danger of the love clown conjured up and warned against so fervently on the forum suggested this was not an isolated client experience but constituted a client culture where such behavior and ways of being resonated with a significant number of others. Documenting the existence of this under-recognized client population is important when discussing governance regimes that criminalize the purchase of sex and cast sex clients collectively as sexual exploiters, social misfits, and deviants.

Legalization: Stigma, Crime, and Labor Conditions

What does this research suggest about legalization? Did the law contribute to destigmatizing sex work, did it improve working conditions in the sex industry and emancipate sexual labor, and did it reduce the criminal underbelly the law intended to do away with?

Insofar as legalization is understood as a form of state-regulated prostitution (Weitzer 2017), the Prostitution Act of 2002 could be more properly understood as a form of decriminalization, as it eliminated state regulation by abolishing mandatory health checks; it decriminalized brothel owners, who were no longer subject to charges of procurement; and it abolished the concept of immoral labor, thus making sex workers, at least in theory, eligible for formal employment and thus for the same benefits as other employees.

But it was more complicated than that. On the one hand, prostitution was not criminalized per se before 2002, but neither was it consistently legal everywhere afterward, as shown in the discussion of Neuburg, where the red light district was entirely engulfed by the restricted zone and thus had become de facto a zone of maximum police control. Further, the Prostitution Law so fervently discussed in public provided little advantage to sex workers, for whom little or nothing had changed. The key objective of destigmatizing and emancipating sexual labor remained elusive for sex workers, as most remained self-employed freelancers rather than formal employees of brothel venues and thus were effectively barred from employment benefits.

One of the most sobering aspects of this research was the realization about the extraordinary fees sex workers were charged by brothel owners, particularly in the large-scale business models of eros centers and sauna club brothels. While such an arrangement gave sex workers relative independence, it came at a high if not punitive cost. The Prostitution Act of 2002 changed little in that regard except that it added another expense for sex workers in the form of a mandatory pretax.

Brothel owners, in particular sauna club owners, might have been the biggest beneficiaries of the Prostitution Act, as it gave them new legal freedom. However, depending on the labor of freelancers and with a limited power of directive, they faced the difficulty of labor enforcement and effective means to discipline their labor. Depending on the presence and visibility of a sizable number of sex workers to maintain their flow of clients, the

Flamingo officially relied on the soft power of madams to enforce a labor discipline they could not legally implement. Unofficially, however, the Flamingo seemed to rely on Zuhälter and the labor discipline they could enact. Without them, the Flamingo might well not have been able to present the number of sex workers on the brothel floor necessary for the business to run profitably and for guests to be satisfied. Functioning as labor disciplinarians and intermediaries, Zuhälter provided a vital service to management that served the club but was hardly conceived of as an advantage by sex workers in general. The fact that such a symbiotic system for the exploitation of sex workers could get entrenched in an upscale brothel raises serious doubts about this business model and its integrity.

If the labor conditions at the Flamingo thus did not conclusively eliminate control at the hand of repressive and exploitative Zuhälter, there were even more troubling and problematic aspects of the new labor regime in sauna club brothels. As the Flamingo not only marketed itself as an oasis of wellness for men but also offered clients more personalized sexual services and girlfriend sex, it demanded from sex workers more ongoing and open-ended interactions with clients. Different from the piecemeal service of old, which—clients complained—consisted of hasty sexual encounters plagued by perpetual haggling, the new kind of customary services offered included unprotected oral sex, French kissing, and working in the nude. While sauna clubs encouraged this new etiquette of sexual service delivery and clients seemed to demand it, it was not necessarily a blessing for sex workers. Instead of performing a service that was temporally and physically bounded, then, sex workers often spent a significant amount of unreimbursed time on client recruitment before the actual purchase, as they were trying to win over clients through verbal and physical flirtations. They also had to expend unreimbursed labor on socializing with clients in after-purchase customer care when they wanted to cultivate them as regulars. The club, meanwhile, reaped the benefits of this free labor. While these interactions were essential for the Flamingo, where clients expected extended socializing with sex workers before and after committing to purchase sexual services from them, this was essentially free labor the sex workers provided to the club. Without it, the club undoubtedly would have lost its appeal. Rather than constituting a form of *bounded authenticity*, girlfriend sex in this context meant open-ended interactions and the dismantling of physical and temporal boundaries. Instead of both parties exchanging an authentic sexual performance bound in time and obligation through a contract, many sex workers at the Flamingo engaged in a labor of *boundless intimacy*, as sexual labor did not begin or end with the purchase.

The new Prostitution Protection Law of 2017 was a step back into greater state regulation: it demanded mandatory counseling and registration of sex workers, mandatory condom use for any kind of sexual intercourse, and criminal background checks for brothel owners. The law passed despite the protest of sex worker rights organizations. While subjecting brothel owners to criminal background checks might be helpful in eliminating or curtailing the role of Zuhälter as labor disciplinarians, none of these new regulations addressed the issue of exorbitant fees or the labor regime of boundless intimacy as it has become entrenched in sauna clubs.

Sexual Enlightenment and the Sexual Imperative

One of the goals of this book was to probe how prostitution worked in a progressive social democracy with a liberal attitude toward sexuality. Beyond questions of labor and policy, I wanted to understand the relationships between different actors in the industry—how they understood their roles in it and the roles of others—and what the place of prostitution was in society overall. Was Germany an example of the brave new world of postindustrial societies and its commodified intimacy an expression of a new regime of recreational sexuality? Did the German example provide evidence for the predictions of sociologists that intimacy would be increasingly commodified and therefore liberated in late postindustrial societies?

That was my hope: to find a culture and a society that legalized prostitution, a culture with an enlightened understanding of sexuality, free from a double moral standard and embracing autonomous citizens making decisions about the purchase and sale of sexual services, without fear of legal or moral repercussions or criminal entanglements. My hope was that Neuburg, and Germany more generally, would provide a more emancipated, self-determined, and satisfying way to address sexuality and sexual needs and pleasure as well as an ability to tap into the potentially lucrative earnings for selling sexual services.

At the end of my research, however, Brigitte's ambivalence resonated with my own. While I found a society where sexuality was less censored, I also found a society bombarded with appeals to sexual gratification, or what I have called the *sexual imperative*. While I found women who were self-confident about their work in the industry and its earning possibilities, I also met those who saw it as a dead end and deeply disturbing. While I found a modern and luxurious workplace in the new sauna club mega brothels, it came with a labor regime of extended casual encounters that provided clients with a semblance of a girlfriend experience but also constituted a growing encroachment on sex workers' bodies and emotional labor. While I found a business model that emancipated brothel owners as legal entrepreneurs, it was a model that seemed to work only as long as Zuhälter acted as unofficial labor disciplinarians. While I found the brothel to be a workplace that fostered familiality and a sense of belonging among its employees, I also discovered that with the sense of family and apparent generosity from the boss came the expectation for unquestioning loyalty from below. And finally, while I found men to whom the brothel offered never-before-seen levels of sexual fulfillment and a sense of deep social connection with the women, the establishment, and, most of all, their peers, I also found a client culture wary of a spiral of dependency and desperation. Key to holding such contradictory outcomes in place was the gift economy operating in multiple aspects of the industry and creating and maintaining the web of shared vulnerabilities.

The macro perspective of the sex industry in the Neuburg region formed a backdrop and context for the micro perspective of the Flamingo FKK sauna club. Exploring the public image of commercial sex in one metropolitan region, including its visual landscape, its red light district, and a comparative analysis of three key venues in the first half of the book, I went on in the second part of the book to offer an intimate analysis of the Flamingo as a place of work and of leisure, a place of commerce and a stage for gift exchanges and the relationships and affective bonds that were created through these various bonds. What I found was that the Flamingo did not function only along the logic of the market but also along the logic of the gift. Gift exchanges and the open-ended relationships and affective component they made possible provided a cocoon of connective tissue that tied individual actors together. The plethora of emotional entanglements resulting from this gift economy engendered a sense of validation and connectedness, a sense of family and belonging. But it also created a web of dependency and obligations, of forced loyalty and coercion.

Enlightened Sexuality and Beyond

The girlfriend experience and bounded authenticity have been presented as a phenomenon of postindustrial societies and their new ethics of recreational sexuality: to represent the enjoyment of sex without the need for long-term commitment and ongoing obligations. By their nature as commodities, sexual labor and prostitution were to be a finite transaction without leaving outstanding obligations.

This study of the Flamingo throws a different light on sexual purchases in brothels. The stereotypical client in search of sexual pleasure without strings attached was juxtaposed with the client in search of care objects and attachment, for whom the club offered the opportunity to initiate intimate friendships with women. Instead of money serving as a means to sever future commitments, it provided some clients with an excuse to initiate gift exchanges. The intensity with which these relationships were carried out and the danger of a potentially one-sided gift exchange was evident in the specter of the love clown and made visible in the violent murder committed by a client.

If gifts exchanged between clients and sex workers meant for sex workers a delicate game of hedging to keep client expectations in manageable dimensions, the hosting ritual between clients and house illustrated how it facilitated a much more lucrative form of income for the Flamingo. Functioning similar to a potlatch for the house, clients engaged in a competitive performance of generosity with each other, trying to gain prestige through lavish consumption. The dark side of the gift economy, however, was illustrated in the kinds of relationships it created between owner and employee, where the owner's generosity instilled not only fierce loyalty and a sense of family obligations in his employees but also relations of indebtedness and extortion.

While these forms of gift exchange often undergirded the Flamingo's economic transactions and financial bottom line, another iteration of a gift exchange existed in the relations between clients and their sharing of erotic exploits and self-revelations. Through such intimate exchanges, clients cultivated a community with each other, not only as a group of consumers but also as a social and moral community with rules for ethical behavior of its own. For some, it displaced other social networks and their relationships outside the world of prostitution.

The men who went to brothels sought relationships and social connections independent of or in addition to whatever other companionate form of relationships they engaged in. Thus, this study also questions the notion of a new postindustrial society where intimacy is sought without commitment. Instead, the power of the Flamingo to attract men and function as a fulcrum for social connections challenged the widely held belief that men are genuinely less interested in emotional bonds and social connections, thus raising questions about male sexuality more generally.

Clients and the Pornosphere

The notion of the Flamingo as serving a need for belonging and social connections seems to run counter to the rampant sexualization and objectification of women in advertisement and what I have called the sexual imperative. Can both observations be true, and if so, how can they be reconciled? The final chapter on clients, their tribulations, and their sense of community links back to the sexual imaginaries that came into such sharp relief during the early stages of this project. Was Germany, with its liberal approach to advertisement and prostitution, merely a case of unfettered commercialism, where sexual commerce, now emancipated, competed with other advertisement for erotic attention and in the process continuously raised the bar for eroticism? Or was Germany indeed a more permissive and progressive society where citizens were freed from outdated moral standards, where the liberated pornosphere and the democratic processes it enabled produce a more just society for all? If that were so, why did a sizable number of men find themselves troubled by their involvement in this industry?

If, as Habermas (2004) argued, our exterior world is always a reflection of our interior world, then the advertisement and public slogans presented in the public landscape suggested a sexual imaginary both limiting and transgressive, both old-fashioned sexist as well as provocatively new and nonconforming—and, thus, a different iteration of what McNair (2013) described as a "liberated pornosphere." And yet there was a contingent of men who, rather than feeling empowered through the opportunities and freedom that legalized prostitution offered them, felt deeply troubled by their involvement in this industry. This suggests that the greater openness in the public discourse about sexuality and sexual gratification made prostitution both a more accessible endeavor and a more publicly debated topic. This kind of transparency, however, also meant one's personal involvement was harder to hide and more difficult to justify. The code of silence and acceptance about male patronage of prostitution, so common in sexually conservative societies, did not exist in Germany in the same way. In addition, the relative ease of pursuing sexual relationships outside of prostitution deemed those who sought recourse to this option a failure of masculinity. This raises the question of whether the outspoken, in-your-face sexual discourse in the public space was not in fact making sexual commerce a more questionable practice, something that could be much less hidden and therefore subject to greater social control.

Sex clients followed the sexual imperative so prominent in public spaces. Sexual curiosities could be satisfied, sexual pleasures enjoyed, insecurities overcome, and self-confidence acquired, all in the marketplace. Doing so, however, placed these men in the deficit ledger of masculine accomplishments. The thrill they might find and the brave new ersatz intimacy with other men they cultivated also entailed the risk of dependency and isolation. They moved in and out of the milieu more than any other actors in the industry. And yet, in a society that embraced sexual exploration, they seemed to have difficulty reconciling the image of a sexually enlightened man with that of a man who paid for sex, as so many clients felt compelled to hide their hobby from family and friends. This was an unexpected outcome in a society where wetting sexual appetites was a normalized feature of public space. The question, then, is whether legalization, even if it might have contributed to making prostitution more widespread, also made it more publicly debated and less socially acceptable.

GLOSSARY

Colloquial Expressions

Abnutzungserscheinungen: Wear and tear

Abzocke (noun): Rip-off; *abzocken* (verb): to rip off

Abzockhure (AZH): A trick; a sex worker who has managed to coax out of her client a large amount for her services. It has a decidedly more negative connotation than the comparable English term *trick*.

aufstellen: Zuhälter lingo for assigning street territory to a sex worker

Besorg's dir doch einfach: Just go and get it for yourself

Bordellkönig: Brothel king

die goldenen Jahre: The golden years

die Mädels: The girls

Falle schieben: Pretend sex

Gegen die Wand: *Head On* (film)

Geiz ist geil: Stinginess is sexy

Geltungssucht: A craving for prestige

Hol sie Dir aufs handy runter: Get her down on your cell phone

Sich einen runterholen: To jerk off

Solide: Respectable folks

spazieren gehen: Go for a walk (recruiting clients)

Wichsbrüder: Wankers

Wiederholungsfaktor: Repeat factor

Common Terms and Organizations

Altersprostitution: Old-age prostitution

Altluden: Former or senior Zuhälter (from *Lude* = Zuhälter)

Armutsprostitution: Poverty prostitution

Armutszeugnis: Sign of ineptness

Bebauungspläne: Zoning laws

Bundeskriminalamt: Federal Criminal Police Office

Bundestag: Parliament

die "Sitte": Police vice unit

eingeschränktes Weisungsrecht: Limited right to issue directives

evangelisch: Protestant

Feuchtgebiete: *Wetlands* (novel)

Glühwein: Sweet spiced wine

Halbwelt: Demiworld

Hartz IV: Long-term unemployment benefits

Hausdame: Madam

Hurenbock (sing.), Hurenböcke (pl.): Whoremonger

Kirchturmparagraph: Church tower ordinance

Laufhaus (sing.), Laufhäuser (pl.): Literally, a "walk-through house"—a dormitory style brothel where women rent individual rooms where they work and live

Liebeskasper: Love clown

Menschenhandel: Human trafficking

Milieudelikte: Crime related to the red light milieu

Opi: Grandpa

Prostitutionsschutzgesetz: Prostitute Protection Law

Reglementierung: A system in which the state regulates prostitution through close police control

Rotlichtmilieu: Red light milieu

schwerer Menschenhandel: Aggravated human trafficking

Sittenwidrigkeit: Immorality

Sperrbezirksverordnung: Restricted zone ordinance

Stiftung Warentest: Consumer Reports

Terminwohnungen: Apartment prostitution

Verrichtungsboxen: Sex boxes

Weltanschauung: Worldview

Wohnmobile: Trailers

Zickenkrieg: Bitch war

BIBLIOGRAPHY

"§ 3 ProstG—Einzelnorm." n.d. Accessed March 24, 2019. https://www.gesetze-im-internet
.de/prostg/__3.html.

Abu-Lughod, Lila. 2000. "Locating Ethnography." *Ethnography* 1 (2): 261–267.

Ackermann, Galia. 2014. *FEMEN*. Cambridge, UK: Polity.

Agustín, Laura María. 2007. *Sex at the Margins: Migration, Labour Markets and the Rescue
Industry*. London: Zed Books.

———. 2008. "Sex and the Limits of Enlightenment: The Irrationality of Legal Regimes to
Control Prostitution." *Sexuality Research and Social Policy* 5 (4): 73–86.

Allison, Anne. 1994. *Nightwork: Sexuality, Pleasure, and Corporate Masculinity in a Tokyo
Hostess Club*. Chicago: University of Chicago Press.

Amnesty International. 2015. "Q&A on the Policy to Protect Human Rights of Sex Workers."
Amnesty International USA. Last modified August 11, 2015. https://www.amnestyusa
.org/press-releases/qa-on-the-policy-to-protect-human-rights-of-sex-workers/.

Ashworth, G. J., P. E. White, and Hilary P. M. Winchester. 1988. "The Red-Light District in
the West European City: A Neglected Aspect of the Urban Landscape." *Geoforum* 19
(2): 201–212.

Attwood, Feona. 2006. "Sexed Up: Theorizing the Sexualization of Culture." *Sexualities* 9 (1):
77–94.

———. 2014. *Mainstreaming Sex: The Sexualization of Western Culture*. London: I. B. Tauris.

Badische Zeitung. 2009. "Sex-Flatrate im Bordell erregt Gemüter." July 10, 2009. https://www
.badische-zeitung.de/sex-flatrate-im-bordell-erregt-gemueter.

Barth, Ariane. 2011. *Im Rotlicht: Das explosive Leben des Stefan Hentschel*. München: Ullstein
eBooks.

Bauman, Zygmunt. 2014. *Liquid Love: On the Frailty of Human Bonds*. Cambridge, UK:
Polity.

Behar, Ruth. 1997. *The Vulnerable Observer: Anthropology That Breaks Your Heart*. Boston:
Beacon.

Berlin, Cora. 2012. *Sexarbeit in Germany! Arbeitsweisen, Sexpraktiken, Behörden, Steuern,
Ausstieg: Ein Ratgeber Und Aufklärer*. Norderstedt: Books on Demand.

Bernstein, Elizabeth. 2007. *Temporarily Yours: Intimacy, Authenticity, and the Commerce of
Sex*. Chicago: University of Chicago Press.

———. 2010. "Bounded Authenticity and the Commerce of Sex." In *Intimate Labors: Cultures,
Technologies, and the Politics of Care*, edited by Eileen Boris and Rhacel Salazar
Parreñas, 148–165. Stanford, CA: Stanford University Press.

———. 2014. "Introduction: Sexual Economies and New Regimes of Governance." *Social
Politics* 21 (3): 345–354.

———. 2018. *Brokered Subjects: Sex, Trafficking, and the Politics of Freedom*. Chicago:
University of Chicago Press.

Blair, Jessica Dawn, Jason Duane Stephenson, Kathy L. Hill, and John S. Green. 2006. "Ethics in Advertising: Sex Sells, but Should It?" *Journal of Legal, Ethical and Regulatory Issues* 9 (2): 109–118.

Blevins, Kristie R., and Thomas J. Holt. 2009. "Examining the Virtual Subculture of Johns." *Journal of Contemporary Ethnography* 38 (5): 619–648.

Böhm, Michael. 2017. "Bordellkönig bleibt hinter Gittern." *Augsburger Allgemeine*, April 4, 2017. Accessed May 18, 2021. https://www.augsburger-allgemeine.de/bayern /Bordellkoenig-bleibt-hinter-Gittern-id42569441.html.

Böhm, Roland. 2018. "Vermeintlich faire Prostitution: 'Bordellkönig' steht wegen Menschenhandels vor Gericht." Spiegel Online. March 23, 2018, sec. Panorama. http:// www.spiegel.de/panorama/justiz/stuttgart-bordell-koenig-und-paradise-gruender -juergen-rudloff-vor-gericht-a-1199698.html.

Bourdieu, Pierre. 1990. *The Logic of Practice*. Stanford, CA: Stanford University Press.

Bovenkerk, Frank, and Guido J. Pronk. 2007. "Fighting Loverboy Methods (English): Over de Bestrijding van Loverboymethoden (Dutch/Flemish)." *Justitiële Verkenningen* 33 (7): 82–95.

Bovenkerk, Frank, Dina Siegel, and Damián Zaitch. 2003. "Organized Crime and Ethnic Reputation Manipulation." *Crime, Law & Social Change* 39 (1): 23–38.

Bovenkerk, Frank, and Marion van San. 2011. "Loverboys in the Amsterdam Red Light District: A Realist Approach to the Study of a Moral Panic." *Crime, Media, Culture* 7 (2): 185–199.

Bradburd, Daniel. 1998. *Being There: The Necessity of Fieldwork*. Washington, DC: Smithsonian Institution.

Brennan, Denise. 2001. "Tourism in Transnational Places: Dominican Sex Workers and German Sex Tourists Imagine One Another." *Identities* 7 (4): 621–663.

———. 2003. "Selling Sex for Visas: Sex Tourism as a Stepping-Stone to International Migration." In *Global Woman: Nannies, Maids, and Sex Workers in the New Economy*, edited by Barbara Ehrenreich and Arlie Hochschildt, 154–161. New York: Metropolitan Books.

———. 2004. *What's Love Got to Do with It?: Transnational Desires and Sex Tourism in the Dominican Republic*. Durham, NC: Duke University Press.

———. 2014. *Life Interrupted: Trafficking into Forced Labor in the United States*. Durham, NC: Duke University Press.

Brents, Barbara, and Kathryn Hausbeck. 2001. "State-Sanctioned Sex: Negotiating Formal and Informal Regulatory Practices in Nevada Brothels." *Sociological Perspectives* 44 (3): 307–332.

———. 2007. "Marketing Sex: US Legal Brothels and Late Capitalist Consumption." *Sexualities* 10 (4): 425–439.

Brents, Barbara G., and Crystal A. Jackson. 2013. "Gender, Emotional Labour and Interactive Body Work: Negotiating Flesh and Fantasy in Sex Worker's Labour Practices." In *Body/ Sex/Work: Intimate, Embodied and Sexualized Labour*, edited by Carol Wolkowitz, Rachel Lara Cohen, Teela Sanders, and Kate Hardy, 77–92. New York: Palgrave Macmillan.

Brents, B. G., C. A. Jackson, and K. M. Hausbeck. 2010. *The State of Sex: Tourism, Sex, and Sin in the New American Heartland*. New York: Routledge.

Brents, B. G., and T. Sanders. 2010. "Mainstreaming the Sex Industry: Economic Inclusion and Social Ambivalence." *Journal of Law and Society* 37 (1): 40–60.

Bruckert, Chris, and Tuulia Law. 2013. *Beyond Pimps, Procurers and Parasites: Mapping Third Parties in the Incall/Outcall Sex Industry.* Ottawa: Rethinking Management in the Adult and Sex Industry Project.

Bruckert, Chris, and Colette Parent. 2018. *Getting Past "the Pimp": Management in the Sex Industry.* Toronto: University of Toronto Press.

Bundeskriminalamt (BKA). 2009. "Lagebilder—Bundeslagebild Menschenhandel 2009." Last modified May 21, 2010. https://www.bka.de/SharedDocs/Downloads/DE /Publikationen/JahresberichteUndLagebilder/Menschenhandel/menschenhandelBund eslagebild2009.html.

———. 2013. "Bundeslagebilder Menschenhandel—Bundeslagebild Menschenhandel 2013." Last modified September 26, 2014. https://www.bka.de/SharedDocs/Downloads/DE /Publikationen/JahresberichteUndLagebilder/Menschenhandel/menschenhandelBun deslagebild2013.html;jsessionid=93E2E15C29D372AE586D74319A0F0855.live0601?nn= 27956.

———. 2017. "Bundeslagebilder Menschenhandel—Bundeslagebild Menschenhandel Und Ausbeutung 2017." Last modified August 7, 2018. https://www.bka.de/SharedDocs /Downloads/DE/Publikationen/JahresberichteUndLagebilder/Menschenhandel/mensc henhandelBundeslagebild2017.html?nn=27956.

Bundesministerium for Familie, Senioren, Frauen, und Jugend (BMFSFJ). 2007. "Bundesfamilienministerin von der Leyen: 'Prostitution ist kein Beruf wie jeder andere—Ausstieg ist das Ziel.'" Press Release. Accessed July 28, 2019. https://www .bmfsfj.de/bmfsfj/aktuelles/presse/pressemitteilungen/bundesfamilienministerin -von-der-leyen---prostitution-ist-kein-beruf-wie-jeder-andere---ausstieg-ist-das-ziel -/102372?view=DEFAULT.

Butler, Judith. 2015. *Notes toward a Performative Theory of Assembly.* The Mary Flexner Lectures of Bryn Mawr College; Mary Flexner Lectures. Cambridge, MA: Harvard University Press.

Cahn, Claude. 2002. *Roma Rights: Race, Justice, and Strategies for Equality.* Sourcebook on Contemporary Controversies Series. Amsterdam: IDEA.

Carbonero, M. Antònia, and María Gómez Garrido. 2018. "Being Like Your Girlfriend: Authenticity and the Shifting Borders of Intimacy in Sex Work." *Sociology* 52 (2): 384–399.

Certeau, Michel de. 1984. *The Practice of Everyday Life.* Translated by Steven Rendall. Berkeley: University of California Press.

Cho, Seo-Young, Axel Dreher, and Eric Neumayer. 2013. "Does Legalized Prostitution Increase Human Trafficking?" *World Development* 41 (January): 67–82. https://doi.org /10.1016/j.worlddev.2012.05.023.

Connell, Raewyn. 2005. *Masculinities.* Second edition. Berkeley: University of California Press.

Crouthamel, Jason. 2014. "Before Porn Was Legal: The Erotic Empire of Beate Uhse." *Journal of the History of Sexuality* 23 (1): 127–129.

Cryer, Jon. 2015. "Jon Cryer Reveals the Inside, Insane Account of Charlie Sheen's Infamous Meltdown." *Hollywood Reporter,* March 18, 2015. https://www.hollywoodreporter.com /features/jon-cryer-reveals-inside-insane-782410.

Cunningham, Scott, and Todd D. Kendall. 2016. "Examining the Role of Client Reviews and Reputation within Online Prostitution." In *The Oxford Handbook of the Economics of*

Prostitution, edited by Scott Cunningham and Manisha Shah, 9–32. New York: Oxford University Press.

Cusick, Linda, Hilary Kinnell, Belinda Brooks-Gordon, and Rosie Campbell. 2009. "Wild Guesses and Conflated Meanings? Estimating the Size of the Sex Worker Population in Britain." *Critical Social Policy* 29 (4): 703–719.

Czarnecki, Dorothea, Henny Engels, Barbara Kavemann, Wiltrud Schenk, Elfriede Steffan, Dorothee Türnau, Consultant on Human Trafficking, and Naile Tanis. 2014. *Prostitution in Germany—A Comprehensive Analysis of Complex Challenges*. April 2014. https://www.spi-research.eu/wp-content/uploads/2014/11 /ProstitutioninGermanyEN_main.pdf.

Davies, James. 2010. "Disorientation, Dissonance and Altered Perception in the Field." In *Emotions in the Field: The Psychology and Anthropology of Fieldwork Experience*, edited by James Davies and Dimitrina Spencer, 79–97. Stanford, CA: Stanford University Press.

Deflem, Mathieu. 2003 "The Sociology of the Sociology of Money." *Journal of Classical Sociology* 3 (1): 67–96.

Der Spiegel. 2010. "AKW-Debatte: Roche offeriert Wulff Sex für Atom-Veto." November 14, 2010. https://www.spiegel.de/panorama/leute/akw-debatte-roche-offeriert-wulff-sex -fuer-atom-veto-a-729009.html.

———. 2012. "Menschenhandel—Betreiber von Flatrate-Bordellen müssen für Jahre ins Gefängnis." April 5, 2012. https://www.spiegel.de/panorama/justiz/lange-haftstrafen -fuer-menschenhandel-in-flatrate-bordellen-verhaengt-a-826016.html.

———. 2013. "Coverpage: Bordell Deutschland 22/2013." May 26, 2013. https://www.spiegel.de /spiegel/print/index-2013-22.html.

Deutsche Welle. 2007. "Hartz Sentenced, Fined in VW Sex-and-Bribery Trial." January 25, 2007. https://www.dw.com/en/hartz-sentenced-fined-in-vw-sex-and-bribery-trial/a -2327127.

Dewey, Susan. 2011. *Neon Wasteland: On Love, Motherhood, and Sex Work in a Rust Belt Town*. Berkeley: University of California Press.

Dewey, Susan, Isabel Crowhurst, and Chimaraoke Izugbara, eds. 2018. *Routledge International Handbook of Sex Industry Research*. New York: Routledge.

Dewey, Susan, and Tonia St. Germain. 2016. *Women of the Street: How the Criminal Justice-Social Services Alliance Fails Women in Prostitution*. New York: NYU Press.

Dewey, Susan, and Tiantian Zheng. 2013. *Ethical Research with Sex Workers: Anthropological Approaches*. Springer Briefs in Anthropology. Anthropology and Ethics. New York: Springer.

Dücker, Elisabeth Stüwe von. 2005. *Sexarbeit: Prostitution—Lebenswelten und Mythen*. Bremen: Ed. Temmen.

Elias, James. 1998. *Prostitution: On Whores, Hustlers, and Johns*. Amherst, NY: Prometheus.

Enloe, Cynthia. 1989. *Bananas, Beaches and Bases*. London: Pandora.

Eriksen, Thomas Hylland. 2016. *Globalization: The Key Concepts*. Second edition. Key Concepts Series. London: Bloomsbury Academic.

European Parliament. 2014. "Punish the Client, Not the Prostitute." Last modified February 26, 2014. http://www.europarl.europa.eu/news/en/press-room/20140221IPR36644 /punish-the-client-not-the-prostitute.

Evans, Adrienne, Sarah Riley, and Avi Shankar. 2010. "'Technologies of Sexiness: Theorizing Women's Engagement in the Sexualization of Culture." *Feminism & Psychology* 20 (1): 114–131.

Farley, M. 2004. "'Bad for the Body, Bad for the Heart': Prostitution Harms Women Even If Legalized or Decriminalized." *Violence Against Women* 10 (10): 1087–1125.

———. 2006. "Prostitution, Trafficking, and Cultural Amnesia: What We Must Not Know in Order to Keep the Business of Sexual Exploitation Running Smoothly." *Yale JL & Feminism* 18:109.

Farley, M., J. Bindel, and J. M. Golding. 2009. *Men Who Buy Sex: Who They Buy and What They Know*. Eaves, London: Prostitution Research & Education, San Francisco: December 2009. https://i1.cmsfiles.com/eaves/2012/04/MenWhoBuySex-89396b.pdf.

Farley, M., J. M. Golding, E. S. Matthews, N. M. Malamuth, and L. Jarrett. 2015. "Comparing Sex Buyers with Men Who Do Not Buy Sex: New Data on Prostitution and Trafficking." *Journal of Interpersonal Violence* 32 (23): 3601–3625. https://doi.org/10.1177/0886260515600874.

Feige, Marcel. 2003. *Das Lexikon der Prostitution: Das ganze ABC der Ware Lust—die käufliche Liebe in Kultur, Gesellschaft und Politik*. Berlin: Schwarzkopf und Schwarzkopf.

———. 2004. *Die Wa(h)Re Lust: Zuhälter, Prostituierte und Freier erzählen*. Berlin: Schwarzkopf & Schwarzkopf.

———. 2013. *LUDE! Ein Rotlicht-Leben: Die Geschichte eines Zuhälters*. Vol. 1. Munich: dotbooks.

Fetz, Steffi. 2013. "Femen-Aufschrei in der Herbertstraße." *Zeit*, January 26, 2013, sec. Gesellschaft. https://www.zeit.de/gesellschaft/zeitgeschehen/2013-01/femen-herbertstrasse-protest.

Frankfurter Allgemeine (FAZ). 2015. "Urteil im 'Loverboy'-Prozess: Alles nur Theater." August 28, 1915. http://www.faz.net/aktuell/gesellschaft/kriminalitaet/loverboy-wegen-schweren-menschenhandels-verurteilt-13773400.html.

Fraser, Nancy. 1990. "Rethinking the Public Sphere: A Contribution to the Critique of Actually Existing Democracy." *Social Text*, no. 25/26:56–80.

Gasser, Benno. 2010. "In Köln bewähren sich die Sexboxen." *Tages-Anzeiger*, September 16, 2010, sec. Zürich. https://www.tagesanzeiger.ch/zuerich/stadt/In-Koeln-bewaehren-sich-die-Sexboxen/story/11982755.

Gerheim, Udo. 2011. *Die Produktion des Freiers: Macht im Feld der Prostitution: Eine soziologische Studie*. Bielefeld: transcript.

Giddens, Anthony. 1992. *The Transformation of Intimacy: Sexuality, Love, and Eroticism in Modern Societies*. Stanford, CA: Stanford University Press.

Gill, Rosalind. 2012. "Media, Empowerment and the 'Sexualization of Culture' Debates." *Sex Roles* 66 (11–12): 736–745.

Goffman, Erving. 1959. "The Moral Career of the Mental Patient." *Psychiatry* 22 (2): 123–142.

———. 1963a. *Behavior in Public Places: Notes on the Social Organization of Gatherings*. New York: Free Press.

———. 1963b. *Stigma; Notes on the Management of Spoiled Identity*. Englewood Cliffs, NJ: Prentice-Hall.

———. 1972. *Relations in Public; Microstudies of the Public Order*. New York: Harper & Row.

———. 1979. *Gender Advertisements*. Vol. 1. New York: Harper & Row.

Gordon, Mel. 2006. *Voluptuous Panic: The Erotic World of Weimar Berlin*. New York: Feral House.

Gossage, Howard Luck. 1995. *The Book of Gossage: A Compilation, Which Includes "Is There Any Hope for Advertising?" Gossage, Howard Luck, 1917–1969; Is There Any Hope for Advertising?* Chicago: Copy Workshop.

Graeber, David. 2001. *Toward an Anthropological Theory of Value*. New York: Palgrave Macmillan.

———. 2011. *Debt: The First 5,000 Years*. First Edition. Brooklyn: Melville House.

———. 2014. "On the Moral Grounds of Economic Relations: A Maussian Approach." *Journal of Classical Sociology* 14 (1): 65–77.

Grenz, Sabine. 2005. "Intersections of Sex and Power in Research on Prostitution: A Female Researcher Interviewing Male Heterosexual Clients." *Signs: Journal of Women in Culture and Society* 30 (4): 2091–2113. https://doi.org/10.1086/428418.

———. 2007. *(Un)Heimliche Lust: Über den Konsum sexueller Dienstleistungen*. Vol. 2. Aufl. Wiesbaden: VS Verl. für Sozialwiss.

Habermas, Jürgen. 1996. *The Structural Transformation of the Public Sphere: An Inquiry into a Category of Bourgeois Society*. Translated by Thomas Burger. Cambridge, UK: Polity.

———. 2004. "Public Space and Political Public Sphere—the Biographical Roots of Two Motifs in My Thought." Commemorative Lecture, Kyoto, November 11, 2004. http://ikesharpless.pbworks.com/f/Kyoto_lecture_Nov_2004,%20Jurgen%20Habermas.pdf.

Handelszeitung. 2012. "Nobel-Champagner im Bordell: Nächster Manager-Sex-Skandal." HZ, September 11, 2012. https://www.handelszeitung.ch/management/nobel-champagner-im-bordell-naechster-manager-sex-skandal.

Hart, Keith, and Wendy James. 2014. "Marcel Mauss: A Living Inspiration." *Journal of Classical Sociology* 14 (1): 3–10. https://doi.org/10.1177/1468795X13494725.

Hebdige, Dick. 1991. *Subculture: The Meaning of Style*. London: Routledge.

Heberer, Eva-Maria. 2013. *Prostitution: An Economic Perspective on Its Past, Present, and Future*. Berlin: Springer.

Heineman, Elizabeth D. 2011. *Before Porn Was Legal: The Erotica Empire of Beate Uhse*. Chicago: University of Chicago Press.

Hellmann, Kai-Uwe, and Guido Zurstiege. 2008. *Räume des Konsums: Über den Funktionswandel von Räumlichkeit im Zeitalter des Konsumismus*. Wiesbaden: Springer.

Herz, Annette Louise. 2006. *Trafficking in Human Beings: An Empirical Study on Criminal Prosecution in Germany*. Vol. 1. Aufl. Forschung Aktuell; 33. Freiburg im Breisgau edition iuscrim: Max Planck Institute for Foreign and International Criminal Law.

Herz, Annette Louise, and Eric Minthe. 2006. *Straftatbestand Menschenhandel: Verfahrenszahlen und Determinanten der Strafverfolgung*. München: Luchterhand.

Heyl, Barbara Sherman. 1977. "The Madam as Teacher: The Training of House Prostitutes." *Social Problems* 24 (5): 545.

Hoang, Kimberly Kay. 2011. "'She's Not a Low-Class Dirty Girl!': Sex Work in Ho Chi Minh City, Vietnam." *Journal of Contemporary Ethnography* 40 (4): 367–396.

———. 2015. *Dealing in Desire: Asian Ascendancy, Western Decline, and the Hidden Currencies of Global Sex Work*. Berkeley: University of California Press.

Hochschild, Arlie. 1983. *The Managed Heart*. Berkeley: University of California Press.

Hoefinger, Heidi. 2011. "'Professional Girlfriends': An Ethnography of Sexuality, Solidarity and Subculture in Cambodia." *Cultural Studies* 25 (2): 244–266.

Höhn, Maria H. 2002. *GIs and Fräuleins: The German-American Encounter in 1950s West Germany*. Chapel Hill: University of North Carolina Press.

Holtz-Bacha, Christina. 2011. *Stereotype?: Frauen Und Männer in Der Werbung*. Vol. 2., aktualisierte und erw. Aufl. Wiesbaden: VS-Verl.

Horning, Amber. 2013. "Peeling the Onion: Domestically Trafficked Minors and Other Sex Work Involved Youth." *Dialectical Anthropology* 37 (2): 299–307.

Horning, Amber, and Anthony Marcus. 2017a. "Introduction: In Search of Pimps and Other Varieties." In *Third Party Sex Work and Pimps in the Age of Anti-Trafficking*, edited by Amber Horning and Anthony Marcus, 1–13. Cham, Switzerland: Springer.

———. 2017b. *Third Party Sex Work and Pimps in the Age of Anti-trafficking*. Cham, Switzerland: Springer.

Horswill, Abbe, and Ronald Weitzer. 2018. "Becoming a Client: The Socialization of Novice Buyers of Sexual Services." *Deviant Behavior* 39 (2): 148–158.

Hubbard, Phil, and Mary Whowell. 2008. "Revisiting the Red Light District: Still Neglected, Immoral and Marginal?" *Geoforum* 39 (5): 1743–1755.

Hughes, Donna M. 1999. *Pimps and Predators on the Internet: Globalizing the Sexual Exploitation of Women and Children*. Kingston, RI: Coalition Against Trafficking in Women.

———. 2000. "The 'Natasha' Trade: The Transnational Shadow Market of Trafficking in Women." *Journal of International Affairs* 53 (2): 625.

———. 2002. "The Demand: The Driving Force of Sex Trafficking." *The Human Rights Challenges of Globalisation: The Trafficking in Persons*. Honolulu: University of Hawaii.

Huisman, Wim, and Edward R. Kleemans. 2014. "The Challenges of Fighting Sex Trafficking in the Legalized Prostitution Market of the Netherlands." *Crime, Law and Social Change* 61 (2): 215–228.

Hunecke, Ina. 2011. *Das Prostitutionsgesetz und seine Umsetzung*. Criminologia, Band 19. Hamburg: Dr. Kovacs.

Hydra e.V. (Bündnis der Fachberatungsstellen für Sexarbeiterinnen und Sexarbeiter e.V. [bufaS e.V.]) 2015. "Stellungnahme zum Referentenentwurf des Bundesministeriums für Familie, Senioren, Frauen und Jugend eines Gesetzes zur Regulierung des Prostitutionsgewerbes sowie zum Schutz von in der Prostitution tätigen Personen (ProstSchG-RefE) [*Position about the Proposal for a Law to Regulate Prostitution Businesses and for the Protection of Those Working in Prostitution*.]" September 2015. https://www.bmfsfj.de/resource/blob /119038/dd71497753d283d9ff24ddffff9526298/bufas-data.pdf.

Illouz, Eva. 1997. *Consuming the Romantic Utopia: Love and the Cultural Contradictions of Capitalism*. Berkeley: University of California Press.

———. 2017. *Cold Intimacies: The Making of Emotional Capitalism*. Cambridge, UK: Polity.

Irigaray, Luce. 1997. "This Sex Which Is Not One." In *Feminisms: An Anthology of Literary Theory and Criticism*, edited by Robyn R. Warhol and Diane Price Herndl, 363–369. New Brunswick, NJ: Rutgers University Press.

Jacobs, Jane. 1992. *The Death and Life of Great American Cities*. New York: Vintage Books.

Jacobs, Katrien. 2007. *Netporn-DIY-Web-Culture-and-Sexual-Politics*. Lanham, MD: Rowman and Littlefield.

Jeffreys, Sheila. 2009. *The Industrial Vagina: The Political Economy of the Global Sex Trade.* RIPE Series in Global Political Economy. London: Routledge.

———. 2013. "The 'Agency' of Men: Male Buyers in the Global Sex Industry." In *Rethinking Transnational Men*, edited by Jeff Hearn, Marina Blagojevic, and Katherine Harrison, 75–91. New York: Routledge.

Jensen, Robert. 2007. *Getting Off: Pornography and the End of Masculinity.* Cambridge, MA: South End.

Jones, Zoey, and Stacey Hannem. 2018. "Escort Clients' Sexual Scripts and Constructions of Intimacy in Commodified Sexual Relationships." *Symbolic Interaction* 41 (4): 488–512.

Katona, Noemi. 2017. "Loved or Seduced? Intimate Relationships between Hungarian Sex Workers and Pimps in Berlin's Kurfürstenstrasse." In *Third Party Sex Work and Pimps in the Age of Anti-Trafficking*, edited by Amber Horning and Anthony Marcus, 49–69. Cham, Switzerland: Springer.

Kavemann, B., and H. Rabe. 2009. *Das Prostitutionsgesetz: Aktuelle Forschungsergebnisse, Umsetzung und Weiterentwicklung.* Budrich: Opladen.

Kavemann, Barbara. 2008. "Report by the Federal Government on the Impact of the Act Regulating the Legal Situation of Prostitution (ProstG)." BMFSFJ. Accessed July 17, 2020. https://www.bmfsfj.de/blob/93346/f81fb6d56073e3a0a80c442439b6495e/bericht -der-br-zum-prostg-englisch-data.pdf.

Kavemann, Barbara, Heike Rabe, Claudia Fischer, and Cornelia Helfferich. 2007. "Vertiefung spezifischer Fragestellungen zu den Auswirkungen des Prostitutionsgesetz: Ausstieg Aus Der Prostitution, Kriminalitätsbekämpfung und Prostitutionsgesetz." Sozialwissenschaftliches Frauenforschungsinstitut, Freiburg. BMFSFJ.

Kelly, Patty. 2008. *Lydia's Open Door: Inside Mexico's Most Modern Brothel.* Berkeley: University of California Press.

Kempadoo, Kamala, Jyoti Sanghera, and Bandana Pattanaik. 2012. *Trafficking and Prostitution Reconsidered: New Perspectives on Migration, Sex Work, and Human Rights.* Vol. 2. Boulder, CO: Paradigm.

Kennedy, M. Alexis, Carolin Klein, Jessica T. K. Bristowe, Barry S. Cooper, and John C. Yuille. 2007. "Routes of Recruitment: Pimps' Techniques and Other Circumstances That Lead to Street Prostitution." *Journal of Aggression, Maltreatment & Trauma* 15 (2): 1–19.

Kiewel, M., M. Kluckert, E. Stratmann, T. Winterstein, J. Meyer, and P. Rossberg. 2012. "Deutschland ist das Bordell Europas: Menschenhandel, Flatrate-Sex, Gewalt! Das miese Geschäft mit Zwangs-Prostituierten." *Bild*, December 18, 2012. https://www.bild .de/news/inland/zuhaelterei/deutschland-ist-das-bordell-europas-27703494.bild.html.

Kontos, Maria, and Kyoko Shinozaki. 2007. "Integration of New Female Migrants in the German Labor Market and Society and German State Policies on Integration: A State of the Art." Frankfurt am Main: Institut für Sozialforschung an der J.W. Goethe Universität Frankfurt.

Kontos, Silvia. 2009. *Öffnung der Sperrbezirke: Zum Wandel von Theorien und Politik der Prostitution.* Sulzbach am Taunus: Ulrike Helmert.

Kreuzer, Margot Domenika. 1989. *Prostitution.* Stuttgart: Schwer.

Kubitscheck, Judith. 2012. "'Pussy-Club'-Zuhälter muss acht Jahre hinter Gitter." *Die Welt*, April 5, 2012. https://www.welt.de/politik/deutschland/article106159670/Pussy-Club -Zuhaelter-muss-acht-Jahre-hinter-Gitter.html.

Lancaster, Roger. 2011. *Sex Panic and the Punitive State*. Berkeley: University of California Press.

Law to Regulate the Legal Relationships of Prostitutes—Prostitution Law (Prostitutionsgesetz—ProstG) 2001. 2002. *StGB*. Accessed June 15, 2020. https://www.gesetze-im-internet.de /prostg/__3.html.

Lemke, Jürgen, and Andreas Marquardt. 2011. *Härte: Mein Weg aus dem Teufelskreis der Gewalt*. Berlin: Ullstein eBooks.

Löw, Martina, and Renate Ruhne. 2009. "Domesticating Prostitution: Study of an Interactional Web of Space and Gender." *Space and Culture* 12 (2): 232–249.

———. 2011. *Prostitution: Herstellungsweisen einer anderen Welt*. Berlin: Suhrkamp.

Malarek, Victor. 2011. *The Johns: Sex for Sale and the Men Who Buy It*. New York: Arcade.

Marcus, Anthony, Amber Horning, Ric Curtis, Jo Sanson, and Efram Thompson. 2014. "Conflict and Agency among Sex Workers and Pimps: A Closer Look at Domestic Minor Sex Trafficking." *ANNALS of the American Academy of Political and Social Science* 653 (1): 225–246.

Mauss, Marcel. 1990. *The Gift: The Form and Reason for Exchange in Archaic Societies*. Translated by W. D. Halls. New York: W. W. Norton.

McClure, Laura. 2014. *Courtesans at Table: Gender and Greek Literary Culture in Athenaeus*. New York: Routledge.

McGinnis, Michael Vincent. 2005. *Bioregionalism*. London: Routledge.

McLuhan, Marshall. 1970. *Culture Is Our Business*. New York: McGraw-Hill.

McNair, Brian. 2013. *Porno? Chic!: How Pornography Changed the World and Made It a Better Place*. New York: Routledge.

Meshkovska, Biljana, Melissa Siegel, Sarah E. Stutterheim, and Arjan E. R. Bos. 2015. "Female Sex Trafficking: Conceptual Issues, Current Debates, and Future Directions." *Journal of Sex Research* 52 (4): 380–395.

Milrod, Christine, and Martin A. Monto. 2012. "The Hobbyist and the Girlfriend Experience: Behaviors and Preferences of Male Customers of Internet Sexual Service Providers." *Deviant Behavior* 33 (10): 792–810.

Milrod, Christine, and Ronald Weitzer. 2012. "The Intimacy Prism: Emotion Management among the Clients of Escorts." *Men and Masculinities*, 15(5): 447–467.

Mitchell, Gregory. 2015. *Tourist Attractions: Performing Race and Masculinity in Brazil's Sexual Economy*. Chicago: University of Chicago Press.

mk online. 2016. "Solwodi: 'Deutschland ist zum Bordell Europas geworden.'" Interview with Lea Ackermann, Gründerin von Solwodi. April 15, 2016. https://mk-online.de/meldung /solwodi-deutschland-ist-zum-bordell-europas-geworden.html.

Molland, Sverre. 2011. "'I Am Helping Them': 'Traffickers,' 'Anti-traffickers' and Economies of Bad Faith." *Australian Journal of Anthropology* 22 (2): 236–254.

Morris, David B. 1996. "About Suffering: Voice, Genre, and Moral Community." *Daedalus* 125 (1): 25–45.

Murphy, A. K., and S. A. Venkatesh. 2006. "Vice Careers: The Changing Contours of Sex Work in New York City." *Qualitative Sociology* 29 (2): 129–154.

Nagel, Mechthild. 2015. "Trafficking with Abolitionism: An Examination of Anti-Slavery Discourses." *Champ penal / Penal field* 12. https://doi.org/10.4000/champpenal.9141.

Neal, Mark. 2016. "Dirty Customers: Stigma and Identity among Sex Tourists." *Journal of Consumer Culture*, June 18 (1): 131–148.

Nencel, Lorraine. 2014. "Situating Reflexivity: Voices, Positionalities and Representations in Feminist Ethnographic Texts." *Women's Studies International Forum* 43:75–83.

——. 2017. "Epistemologically Privileging the Sex Worker." In *Prostitution Research in Context: Methodology, Representation and Power*, edited by Marlene Spanger and May-Len Skilbrei, 67–84. London: Routledge.

O'Connell Davidson, Julia. 2005. *Children in the Global Sex Trade.* Cambridge, UK: Polity.

Outshoorn, Joyce. 2012. "Policy Change in Prostitution in the Netherlands: From Legalization to Strict Control." *Sexuality Research and Social Policy* 9 (3): 233–243.

Paasonen, Susanna, Kaarina Nikunen, and Laura Saarenmaa. 2007. *Pornification: Sex and Sexuality in Media Culture.* Oxford: Berg.

Padilla, Mark. 2007. *Caribbean Pleasure Industry: Tourism, Sexuality, and AIDS in the Dominican Republic.* Chicago: University of Chicago Press.

Parreñas, Rhacel Salazar. 2011. *Illicit Flirtations: Labor, Migration, and Sex Trafficking in Tokyo.* Stanford, CA: Stanford University Press.

Pates, Rebecca. 2012. "Liberal Laws Juxtaposed with Rigid Control: An Analysis of the Logics of Governing Sex Work in Germany." *Sexuality Research and Social Policy* 9 (3): 212–222.

Prasad, Monica. 1999. "The Morality of Market Exchange: Love, Money, and Contractual Justice." *Sociological Perspectives* 42 (2): 181–213.

Radio Zwickau. 2011. "Mord an Chemnitzer Bordellkönig beschäftigt das Landgericht." November 11, 2011. https://www.radiozwickau.de/beitrag/mord-an-chemnitzer -bordellkoenig-beschaeftigt-das-landgericht-140940/.

Ray, Audacia. 2007. *Naked on the Internet: Hookups, Downloads, and Cashing in on Internet Sexploration.* Emeryville, CA: Seal.

Rechtslupe. 2016. "Steuerzahlungen im Bordell nach dem Düsseldorfer Verfahren—und die spätere Erstattung." June 30. https://www.rechtslupe.de/steuerrecht/steuerzahlungen -bordell-duesseldorfer-3111598.

Reinsch, Melanie. 2015. "Interview zum Prostituiertengesetz: 'Deutschland ist das Bordell Europas.'" *Berliner Zeitung*, November 9. https://www.berliner-zeitung.de/politik /interview-zum-prostituiertengesetz--deutschland-ist-das-bordell-europas--23059082.

Remiess, Alexander. 2009. *Gekaufte Illusionen.* First ed. Remscheid: Re Di Roma.

Renzikowski, Joachim. 2007. "Reglementierung von Prostitution: Ziele und Probleme—Eine kritische Betrachtung des Prostitutionsgesetzes." Berlin: Bundesministerium für Familie, Senioren, Frauen und Jugend (BMFSFJ). https://doi.org/10.15496/publikation-5655.

——. 2009. "Das Prostitutionsgesetz und strafrechtlicher Handlungsbedarf." In *Das Prostitutionsgesetz: Aktuelle Forschungsergebnisse, Umsetzung und Weiterentwicklung,* edited by Barbara Kavemann and Heike Rabe, 133–152. Opladen and Farmington Hills: Barbara Budrich.

——. 2012. "Plädoyer für eine gewerberechtliche Reglementierung der Prostitution." In *Regulierung von Prostitution und Prostitutionsstätten*, edited by Bundesministerium für Familien, Senioren, Frauen, und Jugend (BMFSFJ), 14–22. Rostock: German Government.

Roche, Charlotte. 2013. *Feuchtgebiete.* Berlin: Ullstein.

Roche, Charlotte, and Tim Mohr. 2009. *Wetlands.* 1st ed. New York: Grove.

Roos, Julia. 2002. "Backlash against Prostitutes' Rights: Origins and Dynamics of Nazi Prostitution Policies." *Journal of the History of Sexuality* 11 (1/2): 67–94.

———. 2017. *Weimar through the Lens of Gender: Prostitution Reform, Woman's Emancipation, and German Democracy, 1919–33.* Ann Arbor: University of Michigan Press.

Rosewarne, Lauren. 2005. "The Men's Gallery: Outdoor Advertising and Public Space: Gender, Fear, and Feminism." *Women's Studies International Forum* 28 (1): 67–78.

———. 2007. *Sex in Public: Women, Outdoor Advertising, and Public Policy.* Newcastle, UK: Cambridge Scholars.

Ruhne, Renate. 2005. "Räumliche Kontrollformen der Prostitution und die Ordnung der Geschlechter," *Sic! Forum für Feministische Gangarten,* March 2005, 12–15.

———. 2006. "Boulevard und Sperrbezirk: urbane Ideale, Prostitution und der Kampf um den öffentlichen Raum der Stadt." *Sozialwissenschaften und Berufspraxis* 29 (2): 192–207.

Sanders, T. 2008. *Paying for Pleasure: Men Who Buy Sex.* Cullompton, UK: Willan.

Sansi, Roger. 2014. "The Pleasure of Expense: Mauss and *The Gift* in Contemporary Art." *Journal of Classical Sociology* 14 (1): 91–99.

Scharff, Christina. 2017. *Digital Feminisms: Transnational Activism in German Protest Cultures.* New York: Routledge.

Schelm, Timo. 2013. *Ratgeber für Liebeskasper: Ein Thailand-Leitfaden.* Second ed. Norderstedt: Books on Demand.

Schrag, Wolfram. 2007. *Medienlandschaft Deutschland.* Bayerische Landeszentrale Für Politische Bildungsarbeit, UVK Verlagsgesellschaft.

Schubert, Stefan. 2012. *Wie die Hells Angels Deutschlands Unterwelt eroberten.* München: Riva.

———. 2014. *Gangland Deutschland: Wie kriminelle Banden unser Land bedrohen.* München: Riva.

Schulte, Maike. 2007. "Flasche Schampus für 18.000 Euro: Bordell im Luxusrausch." *Rheinische Post (RP) Online.* January 10, 2007, Düsseldorf. https://rp-online.de/nrw/staedte/duesseldorf/bordell-im-luxusrausch_aid-11415755.

Schuster, Ulrike. 2018. "Prostitution an der Grenze—Elendsstrich in Tschechien." *Süddeutsche Zeitung,* February 2, 2018. https://www.sueddeutsche.de/bayern/prostitution-im-grenzgebiet-bayern-tschechien-1.3851097.

Schwarzer, Alice. 2007. *Emma—die ersten 30 Jahre.* First ed. München: Collection Rolf Heyne.

———. 2008. "Statt Reform Grossbordelle." *Emma,* January/February 2008, 38–39. https://www.emma.de/lesesaal/48534.

Scoular, Jane. 2010. "What's Law Got to Do with It? How and Why Law Matters in the Regulation of Sex Work." *Journal of Law and Society* 37 (1): 12–39.

Sheftel, Anna, ed. 2013. *Oral History Off the Record—Toward an Ethnography of Practice.* New York: Palgrave Macmillan.

Siegel, Dina. 2014. "Women in Transnational Organized Crime." *Trends in Organized Crime,* 17 (1–2): 52–65.

Simmel, Georg. 1907. *Philosophie des Geldes.* Leipzig: Duncker & Humbolt.

Sobota, Heinz. 1978. *Der Minus-Mann: Ein Romanbericht.* Köln: Kiepenheuer & Witsch.

Soderbergh, Steven. 2009. *The Girlfriend Experience.* Magnolia.

Spiegel Online. 2009. "Poor Hygiene Standards: Germany Closes Two Flat-Rate Brothels." July 27, 2009, sec. International. https://www.spiegel.de/international/germany/poor-hygiene-standards-germany-closes-two-flat-rate-brothels-a-638594.html.

———. 2016. "Orgie in Budapest: Manager wegen Sexskandal bei Hamburg-Mannheimer vor Gericht." June 1, 2016, sec. Wirtschaft. http://www.spiegel.de/wirtschaft/unternehmen /hamburg-mannheimer-manager-wegen-sex-party-vor-gericht-a-1095193.html.

Staiger, Annegret. 2009. "The Economics of Sex Trafficking Since the Legalization of Prostitution in Germany in 2002." *The Protection Project Journal of Human Rights and Civil Society* 1 (2): 103–118.

———. 2017. "Perceptions about Pimps in an Upscale Mega Brothel in Germany." In *Third Party Sex Work and Pimps in the Age of Anti-Trafficking*, edited by Amber Horning and Anthony Marcus, 151–176. Cham, Switzerland: Springer.

Stalans, Loretta J., and Mary A. Finn. 2016. "Consulting Legal Experts in the Real and Virtual World: Pimps' and Johns' Cultural Schemas about Strategies to Avoid Arrest and Conviction." *Deviant Behavior* 37 (6): 644–664.

Steffan, Elfriede, Christine Körner, and Tzvetina Arsova Netzelmann. 2019. *Final Project Report: "Bestandsaufnahme der Angebote der Gesundheitsämter in Deutschland für Sexarbeiterinnen und Sexarbeiter."* Berlin: SPI.

Stern.de. 2005. "Prostitution: Mit dem Freier in die 'Verrichtungsbox.'" February 25, 2005. https://www.stern.de/panorama/prostitution-mit-dem-freier-in-die--verrichtungsbox --3551988.html.

———. 2009. "1,16 Euro pro Frau." July 27, 2009. https://www.stern.de/panorama/gesellschaft /flatrate-bordell-pussy-club-1-16-euro-pro-frau-3810308.html.

———. 2012. "Herr Kaiser hatte öfter Bock auf Lustreisen." August 30, 2012. http://www.stern .de/wirtschaft/news/sex-skandal-der-ergo-versicherung-herr-kaiser-hatte-oefter-bock -auf-lustreisen-1886704.html.

Takeyama, Akiko. 2016. *Staged Seduction: Selling Dreams in a Tokyo Host Club.* Stanford, CA: Stanford University Press.

TAMPEP. 2009a. "Sex Work in Europe. A Mapping of the Prostitution Scene in 25 European Countries." Accessed June 20, 2020. https://www.nswp.org/sites/nswp.org/files /TAMPEP%202009%20European%20Mapping%20Report.pdf.

———. 2009b. "Sex Work Migration Health: A Report on the Intersections of Legislations and Policies Regarding Sex Work, Migration and Health in Europe." Accessed June 20, 2020. https://tampep.eu/wp-content/uploads/2017/11/Sexworkmigrationhealth_final.pdf.

Telegraph. 2012. "Bild Newspaper Drops Page-One Nude Girl after 28 Years," *Telegraph*, March 9, 2012, sec. Finance. https://www.telegraph.co.uk/finance/newsbysector /mediatechnologyandtelecoms/media/9133767/Bild-newspaper-drops-page-one-nude -girl-after-28-years.html.

Tykwer, Tom, Hendrik Handloegten, Achim von Borries, et al., dir. 2020. *Babylon Berlin.* (Series 1 and 2). Sky and ARD.

Van Maanen, John. 2011. *Tales of the Field: On Writing Ethnography.* Second edition. Chicago: University of Chicago Press.

Wardlow, Holly. 2006. *Wayward Women: Sexuality and Agency in a Papua New Guinea Society.* Berkeley: University of California Press.

Weinkauf, Kathleen. 2010. "'Yeah, He's My Daddy': Linguistic Constructions of Fictive Kinships in a Street-Level Sex Work Community." *Wagadu: A Journal of Transnational Women's & Gender Studies* 8:14–32.

Weitzer, Ronald. 2000. "Prostitution: On Whores, Hustlers, and Johns." *Contemporary Sociology* 29 (2): 419.

————. 2006. "Moral Crusade against Prostitution." *Society* 43 (3): 33–38.

————. 2009. "Sociology of Sex Work." SSRN Scholarly Paper ID 1603416. Rochester, NY: Social Science Research Network.

————. 2012. *Legalizing Prostitution: From Illicit Vice to Lawful Business.* New York: NYU Press.

————. 2014. "The Social Ecology of Red-Light Districts: A Comparison of Antwerp and Brussels." *Urban Affairs Review* 50 (5): 702–730.

————. 2017. "Legal Prostitution: The German and Dutch Models." In *Dual Markets: Comparative Approaches to Regulation,* edited by Ernesto U. Savona, Mark A. R. Kleiman, and Francesco Calderoni, 365–385. Cham, Switzerland: Springer.

Wilbrand-Donzelli, Nicola. 2015. "Die Loverboy-Masche: Von der großen Liebe zur Prostitution gezwungen." *T-Online,* August 28, 2015. http://www.t-online.de/eltern /jugendliche/id_70453052/loverboys-die-unbekannte-gefahr-fuer-junge-maedchen .html.

Willis, Paul E. 1981. *Learning to Labor: How Working Class Kids Get Working Class Jobs.* Morningside ed. New York: Columbia University Press.

Wnendt, David. 2014. *Feuchtgebiete.* DVD. Twentieth Century Fox Home Entertainment.

Zelizer, Viviana A. Rotman. 2005. *The Purchase of Intimacy.* Princeton, NJ: Princeton University Press.

Zheng, Tiantian. 2009. *Red Lights: The Lives of Sex Workers in Postsocialist China.* Minneapolis: Minnesota University Press.

Zurstiege, Guido. 2008. "Der Konsum Dritter Orte." In *Räume des Konsums,* edited by Kai-Uwe Hellman and Guido Zurstiege, 121–141. Wiesbaden: Springer.

INDEX

abolitionism: legalized prostitution advocates in, 9–10; Nagel on, 167; patriarchal exploitation and, 219

Abzockhure (trick), 236, 243n16

Act Regulating the Legal Situation of Prostitutes (Prostitution Act) (2002), 1, 3; brothel owners advantages from, 14, 104, 247; critics of, 5; decriminalization form, 247; on employer limited directives, 118n10, 185; formal employment relations and labor protection, 12; health checkups abolishment, 12, 99; Kavemann studies of effects of, 15; on labor conditions, 5, 12; Merkel on reforms for, 16; on prostitution transparent market, 222; on sexual self-determination, 12–13, 118n7; on sex worker mandatory pretax, 247; sex workers' suit for clients' nonpayment, 12; state and local regulations conflict with, 15; supporters of, 4–5

affective ties, 8, 11, 26, 83, 201; at Flamingo, 9, 196; gifts and, 9

age of consent, US compared to Germany, 3

Allison, Anne, 197

Altluden, respectful name for retired Zuhälter, 62

anonymity: apartment brothel sex workers, 95; in sex clients' community forum, 219, 222–23, 238–39; lack of for sex workers in RLD, 95; sex workers' desire for, 21

Anti-Venereal Disease Law (1927), 73

apartment brothels, 25, 58, 118n4; client perspectives, 94, *117*; client professional services to, 94; forum online reports and, 242n7; girlfriend experiences in, 91; lack of visibility of, 76, 88; location of, 88–89, *117*; madams at, 20, 88–95; in Neuburg, 76; revenue and management of, 89–93, 113, 114, *117*; screening clients in, 92; sex workers' anonymity in, 95; sex

worker numbers in, 69, *117*; sex workers' perspectives on, 94–96, *117*; surveillance and, 89; websites of, 90

Ariana, at Flamingo: from Bulgaria, 151–53; on madams, 155–56; Protestant church experience, 154, 158–60; on Zuhälter, 171–72

Association for Erotic Trade Entrepreneurs (UED), on sexual services cost decline, 87

bachelor party hosting, 198–99

baseline communism, Graeber on, 202–3

Beate Uhse erotic shops, 3, 75

behavioral stigma, Goffman on, 238

Behavior in Public (Goffman), 38

Bernstein, Elizabeth: on bounded authenticity, 82, 114–16; on girlfriend experience, 82; on mainstreaming sexual commerce, 60; on market exchange, 82; on new sexual ethics, 7, 82; on recreational sexual ethic, 7, 82, 116, 241

best practice advice, 5, 14, 82

biker gang: Hells Angels club, 61, 169; Zuhälter and, 179–80

Bild: cover of, *43*; description of, 44; Flamingo advertisements in, 107; Page One Girl layout in, 41, 42, *42*, 44, 54n5; public space and, 43–44, *47*, 52–53; sex ads in, *41*, 42, 46, 107; on sex trafficking and low-cost brothels, 6; sexual commerce major advertising by, 46; slogan, *45*

Bild Plus online version, 44–45

Blevins, Kristie R., 229

bounded authenticity, 9, 26, 242; Bernstein on, 82, 114–16; girlfriend sex and, 248; market exchange emphasis from, 83; postindustrial sexual ethic and, 250–51

boundless intimacy, 9; client recruitment and, 115–16; in sauna club brothels, 26, 83, 116

ANNEGRET D. STAIGER is Professor of Anthropology at
Clarkson University. She is author of *Learning Difference: Race and
Schooling in the Multiracial Metropolis.*

www.ingramcontent.com/pod-product-compliance
Lightning Source LLC
Chambersburg PA
CBHW030644270326
41929CB00007B/192